TRADE, INQUISITION AND THE ENGLISH NATION IN PORTUGAL 1650-1690

ASPECTS OF PORTUGAL

Luis de Camoes
Selected Lyrics and Lusiads

Maurice Collis
The Grand Peregrination

Rose Macaulay
They Went to Portugal Too

L. M. E. Shaw
*Trade, Inquisition and the English
Nation in Portugal 1650–1690*

Michael Teague
In the Wake of the Portuguese Navigators

Trade, Inquisition and the English Nation in Portugal, 1650–1690

L. M. E. Shaw

OFERTA DA FUNDAÇÃO
CALOUSTE GULBENKIAN
LISBOA·PORTUGAL

CARCANET
in association with the
CALOUSTE GULBENKIAN FOUNDATION

First published in Great Britain in 1989 by
Carcanet Press Limited
208–212 Corn Exchange Buildings
Manchester M4 3BQ

This book is in the series *Aspects of Portugal*, published in Great Britain by
Carcanet Press in association with the Calouste Gulbenkian Foundation and with
collaboration from the Anglo-Portuguese Foundation.

SERIES EDITORS: Eugénio Lisboa, Michael Schmidt, Kim Taylor

British Library Cataloguing in Publication Data

Shaw, L.M.E.
  Trade, inquisition and the English nation
  in Portugal, 1650–1690 – (Aspects of Portugal)
  1. Portugal. Foreign trade with England, history
  2. England. Foreign trade with Portugal, history
  I. Title   II. Series
  382'.09469'042

  ISBN 0-85635-851-7

Typeset in 10/11 Plantin by Paragon Photoset, Aylesbury
Printed and bound in England by Short Run Press Ltd, Aylesbury

Contents

List of Illustrations

Acknowledgements

Having had access to the previously private archives of the Condes da Ponte has been of the utmost importance in clarifying both Anglo-Portuguese relations and Maynard's work during the Protectorate and early Restoration periods. I wish to record my gratitude to Senhora T. M. Schedel de Castello Branco for allowing me access to those records, and for her kindness, help and advice on matters in Lisbon.

I should also like to thank Mr Graham Gibbs, for his helpful guidance; the librarian at Ushaw College, Co. Durham, who allowed me to examine the then uncollated papers of the English College; the late Professor S. George West OBE, who gave me much help and advice and many useful introductions before he retired, and the Librarian of the Royal Commonwealth Society, who assisted me in my initial research into the early years of the English chaplaincies in Lisbon and Oporto.

Finally, I should like to record my gratitude to my husband for his constant help, support and encouragement.

Notes

Dates

During the period covered by this book, the Gregorian Calendar was in use in Portugal whilst the Julian Calendar was in use in England. Where documents only bear one date, when they emanate from Portugal it has been assumed that they have been dated in accordance with the Gregorian Calendar (New Style or N.S.); when they emanate from England, it has been assumed that they have been dated in accordance with the Julian Calendar (Old Style or O.S.). The only exception to this is that Francisco de Melo's letters addressed to Queen Luisa are assumed to have been dated in accordance with the Gregorian Calendar. The decision to make this assumption was taken after discussing the matter with Senhora Schedel de Castello Branco. Letters from Melo to the Council of State or other addressees in England are assumed to have been dated in accordance with the Julian Calendar.

Portuguese Spelling

The spelling of Portuguese names and words has been modernized in accordance with the Ortografia Moderna, excepting:

a) in quotations;

b) the names of people living today who have deliberately kept the old spelling of their names from choice;

c) titles and authors of books.

Exchange Rates and Monetary Values

There are many factors which make it impossible to give any exact exchange rates between English and Portuguese coins during the second half of the seventeenth century. Exchange rates varied from day to day then as they do now. Between 1664 and 1690 there are known to have been many devaluations of the Portuguese currency, but because Portuguese government records were destroyed in the 1755 earthquake, the dates of those devaluations are unknown. There were also silver and gold crowns or *crusados* as well as copper coins, whose values were not only affected by the exchange rates, but also by the extent to which they had been chipped and scraped. Coins were not always worth their face value. Further, a meaningful comparison between seventeenth century and twentieth century currency values cannot be made because, with the introduction of bank notes, exchange control, balance of payments management by Central Banks, speculative capital movements and different fiscal and inflation policies, there is no basis for expressing the historic exchange rate in today's values. The nearest approximation would be to compare wages in the seventeenth and twentieth centuries, but even then, because of the increase in what are now considered to be material necessities, we cannot properly appreciate what seventeenth century earnings meant in value to their earners.

PART I:
THE INQUISITION & THE TREATY ERA

1
Rivalries in Europe and Overseas

There were four principal questions at issue in seventeenth-century Europe which gave rise to the alignments of various states and the wars in which they were involved. The first question concerned the extent of the Ottoman (Turkish) Empire and the religious zeal shown by the Muslims in continually enlarging its boundaries. With its capital at Constantinople, the Ottoman Empire stretched from the Mediterranean Sea to the Caspian Sea; down the western shores of the Persian Gulf and the eastern shores of the Red Sea; across north Africa from Egypt to Tunis; it included the eastern Mediterranean islands and all south-eastern Europe, as well as Hungary. In 1683 the city of Vienna, seat of the Holy Roman Emperor, was besieged by the Ottomans. Dealing with that threat involved Austria, Venice, Poland and Russia, whose lands adjoined those of the Ottoman Empire, as well as maritime powers wishing to trade in the Mediterranean. In 1684 Pope Innocent XI formed a Holy League in an effort to expel the Turks from Europe, but by 1699, after the Treaty of Karlowitz, the Ottoman Empire had not been very greatly diminished. It had ceded Kaminiec, Podolia and Western Ukraine to Poland; Transylvania and Hungary to Austria, and Dalmatia and the whole of the Peloponnese except Corinth and the Aegean Islands to Venice. Russia obtained Azov.

Throughout the century, the southern and eastern waters of the Mediterranean and the seas off southern Portugal were dangerous areas for Christian shipping. Turkish and Moorish vessels preyed on those of Christian nations, enslaving their passengers and crews and holding them to ransom. None the less, English merchants and those of other nations had become established as traders in Aleppo and other parts of the Ottoman Empire. Indeed, the Treaty of Karlowitz was mediated by the Levant Company's agent, Paget.[1] The Dutch, British, French, Genoese and Venetians frequently sent fleets into those areas in an effort to control the ravages of Muslim vessels and, when possible, to pay the ransom for the release of captives. In England, customs commissioners collected one half of one per cent on goods passing through the customs for the purpose of ransoming such captives.[2] Treaties were also made, for example, with Algiers on 23 April, 17 July and 10 November 1662. Another was made with Tunis on 5 October 1662.[3]

These treaties were obtained by payment of large sums of money and they sought to ensure that if English vessels encountered Moorish ships there would be no fighting, and that if the Moors were satisfied after boarding that they were indeed English vessels, then the passengers and goods should be allowed to proceed safely on their journey.

The country which had the longest boundary with the Ottoman Empire was Poland. In size, population, commerce and industry, agriculture and forestry, Poland surpassed all her neighbours. An elective monarchy at that time, it included present-day Lithuania, Latvia, Byelorussia, the Ukraine, East Prussia and the free city of Danzig. The Duchies of Prussia, Courland and Livonia were fiefs of the Polish crown under their own rulers, with their own constitutions; they remained Protestant when Poland had become Catholic as a result of the Counter-Reformation in the sixteenth century. These duchies on the Baltic coast, together with Danzig, comprised virtually the whole seaboard and every port of importance in the kingdom.[4] Although Russia bordered Poland in the east, its territory did not extend to the shores of either the Baltic or Black Sea. This was to be changed in the early eighteenth century by Peter the Great.

Poland's neighbour to the north, Sweden, was another centre of trouble throughout the century. The kingdom of Sweden had long felt encircled by the United Kingdoms of Denmark and Norway. The only open frontier on the Baltic which Sweden possessed was along the west coast of Finland, which had been conquered and Christianized by the Swedish kings in the twelfth and thirteenth centuries. The desire to free Sweden from Danish pressure and thereby obtain safe access to the German and Polish shores of the Baltic, as well as free passage out of the Baltic into the North Sea, had therefore been the natural aim of the Vasa kings ever since Gustavus I (1523–60) had freed Sweden from Danish political rule.[5] Denmark controlled the narrow strait at the entrance to the Baltic from the North Sea, known as the Sound. The struggle for control of the Baltic was due only to political and economic considerations. Religion played no part in it, as both Sweden and Denmark had adopted the Lutheran Reformation.

A company of merchants known as the Hansards had had the monopoly of trade in the Baltic since the thirteenth century, but during the sixteenth century English and Dutch shipping began to enter the Baltic in search of cargoes of Norwegian cod, Swedish copper and iron, Russian hemp, tar and honey and Polish and East German grain and timber. These were the materials on which the livelihood of the industrialized areas of western Europe depended. To take timber as an example: by the seventeenth century, English forests had been denuded of suitable timber for ship-building and a ship built of foreign materials would call for the transport services of two or three ships of its own size to bring those materials to England.[6] Trade brought customs revenues, so control of the ports and customs from Reval to Kiel, and control of the estuaries of the rivers from the Narva to the Schlei were the principal issues in the struggle for what was known in the diplomatic language of the time as *dominium maris Baltici*.[7] The Baltic struggle directly influenced the internal history of Sweden, Denmark, Russia, Poland and Prussia. Although Sweden had gained control of the Baltic from Denmark by the mid-seventeenth century, by the eighteenth century that control had been gradually lost and partitioned between Russia and Prussia, whilst Brandenburg had taken the place of Poland on the Prussian coast.

The Baltic ports not in Polish or Danish territory were in the German section of the medieval organization known as the Holy Roman Empire, composed of a multitude of independent states and cities ruled by kings and lay and clerical princes. Many of those states and cities were Protestant, although the Emperor, of course, was Catholic. In name, the Emperor was supreme lord at the head of a feudal pyramid. In fact, his power depended on the resources derived from his patrimonial possessions and the qualified support of the mass of imperial knights, counts and abbots and temporary alliances with some prince or group of princes. What tangible authority the Emperor exercised was based on the fact that the imperial dignity had, since 1438, become hereditary by prescription in the House of Hapsburg. That family had accumulated most of the territory of southern Germany, with the Austrian possessions as the heartland and Vienna as the capital.[8] Their connection with the Spanish monarchs formed a Madrid-Vienna axis which greatly strengthened the emperor's hand, because during the first half of the seventeenth century, Spain was considered to be the greatest power in the Christian world.

The Hapsburg connection with Spain went back to the marriage of Juana, daughter of Ferdinand and Isabella of Spain, to Philip the Fair of Burgundy. Their son, Charles V, inherited the kingdom of Spain in 1516, together with its vast possessions overseas in south and central America, in the Far East, and outposts on the African coast. In 1519, Charles V had also inherited Burgundy and the Austrian dominions of his grandfather Maximilian I, and in the same year he was elected Holy Roman Emperor. Charles abdicated in 1556 and divided his realm, leaving Spain and her dependencies, to which the Netherlands had been assigned some years earlier, to his son Philip II, and the Austrian lands, together with Bohemia and Hungary, to his brother Ferdinand. By the Treaty of Cambrésis (1559), Philip II acquired Sardinia, Sicily, Naples and Milan, giving him virtual control of the Italian peninsula. Between that date and until the Treaty of Utrecht (1713–15), only Genoa, Savoy, Venice and the Papal states had an independent history in Italy. This therefore gave Spain great diplomatic control over the papacy, which was of inestimable value. Further, through his Portuguese mother, Philip II inherited the crown of Portugal in 1580, as a result of the death of King Sebastian on 4 August 1578 when the Portuguese army was utterly routed at the Battle of El Qsar-el Kebir, followed by the death in January 1580 of Sebastian's uncle and heir, Cardinal-King Henry. All Portugal's overseas possessions in Brazil, east and west Africa, India and the Far East were added to Spain's overseas dominions. Spanish overlordship in Portugal was greatly disliked by most of the population, however, and Philip had had to annex Portugal partly by force and partly by bribery. As he himself said at the time, 'Yo lo heredé, yo lo compré e yo lo conquisté' (I inherited it, I bought it and I conquered it').

At the beginning of the seventeenth century it seemed to contemporaries that Spain was the greatest power of the age. Like the British empire in a later age, Spain's empire was one on which the sun never set. The vast territorial possessions brought influence and political power; the Spanish treasure fleet replenished the exchequer annually with silver from Mexico, gold from Peru and spices from the Indies, and the Spanish army was considered to be one of the most efficient and powerful military machines of the age. With the death of Philip II, his three successors, Philip III (1598–1621), Philip IV (1621–65) and Charles II (1665–1700) revealed in increasing degree the steady degeneration of the Spanish Hapsburgs. They lacked the ruling instinct and left affairs in the hands of favourites, such as the Duke of Lerma, the Count of Olivarez and the German Jesuit Nithard. The austerity and simplicity of Philip II's court gave way to spectacular profligacy, and bribery throughout the administration was scarcely concealed. The economy of the country was drained by the cost of continual warfare and Spanish agriculture and industry suffered greatly by the expulsion in 1609–10 of the Moriscos, christian descendants of baptised moors. Trade was largely in the hands of foreign merchants who took their gains out of the country. This did not seem to be of importance until the bullion imports began to decline because the mines were being worked out.

It was the concentration of power in the hands of Spain that caused another great issue of the time. France felt surrounded politically and economically by Spain. Little could be done about this during the sixteenth century, because France itself was torn by civil wars, kindled by dynastic ambition, and by opposing political, social and economic objectives and religious antagonism. One party or another in France was always willing to appease Spain in order to defeat its domestic adversaries.[9] Not until the Peace of Vervins in 1598 was there relative peace within France and Henry IV and, later, Cardinals Richelieu and

Mazarin, set themselves the task of redressing the balance. France was one of the main protagonists during the Thirty Years' War (1618–48), which was a series of campaigns and shifting alliances revolving round the Baltic question and France's wish for expansion. France was allied to Sweden and the United Provinces, but also to any of the German states with an axe to grind against the emperor. France fought Spain in the Low Countries, in Italy and anywhere where their borders joined. France sent money and troops to aid the Catalans when they revolted against Spain (1640–52), and did the same to assist Portugal in its war of independence against Spain (1640–68). The Peace of Westphalia (1648), which ended the Thirty Years' War, did not end the war between France and Spain. That was only finally ended in 1659 after the Peace of the Pyrenees, when Louis XIV married Maria Theresa, daughter of Philip IV. The treaty was so drafted by the French Agent Lionne, that therein Maria Theresa renounced for herself, and therefore by implication for her husband, all claims to the paternal succession *provided that* a dowry of 500,000 crowns was paid within 18 months. As the dowry was never paid, as early as 1662 Louis could claim that his wife's renunciation was void.[10] After his father-in-law's death in 1665, Louis used this as an excuse to attack the Spanish Low Countries and Franche-Comté (known as the Burgundian circle), which barred France's desired expansion eastwards. Throughout the rest of the century, by means of diplomacy and continuous war; development of the army and navy; the encouragement and planning of industry and commerce; the encouragement of colonialization in North America and the West Indies, and by the encouragement of the arts, Louis worked not only to defeat Spanish and Hapsburg pretensions but to enhance France politically, economically and culturally. After the death of Charles II of Spain in 1700, Louis's own grandson became king of Spain as Philip V.

Mention was made above of the fact that English and Dutch shipping in the sixteenth century had begun to pass through the Sound in search of trade in the Baltic. It was the quest for trade by these two seafaring peoples that constituted the fourth great question at issue during the seventeenth century, for they replaced Spain and Portugal as the chief trading nations of the world. How England came to take over the greater part of Portugal's trade forms the subject of this book, but it is relevant here to explain the Portuguese and Spanish attitude and policy towards their dominions.

Portugal had been the first of the two countries to embark on overseas expansion, under the guidance and encouragement of Henry the Navigator. The history of the discovery and settlement of the islands of Madeira, the Azores and Cape Verde, and the discovery of the sea route to India in the fifteenth century together with the discovery and settlement of Brazil in the sixteenth century are well known. Also famous are Columbus's discovery of the West Indies for Spain in 1492, and Spain's settlement and acquisition of large tracts of land in south and central America in the early sixteenth century. What is not well known today is that Portugal and Spain did not just lay claim to the lands thay had actually discovered, but they divided the undiscovered world outside Europe between themselves, with papal sanction. At the Treaty of Tordesillas in 1494, two papal bulls, *Inter Caetera* and *Dudum siquidem*, were accepted by the monarchs of Spain and Portugal. A boundary line 270 leagues west of the Azores was to divide the interests of the two countries.[11] At that time it was thought that Columbus had found a westward route to India. When it was discovered, after Magellan's voyage round Tierra del Fuego into the Pacific, that there was another ocean and another continent between Europe and India to the west, the matter was solved at the Treaty of Zaragoza in 1529, when Charles V sold his rights in the Moluccas to Portugal for 350,000 ducats and an arbitrary line of demarcation was fixed seventeen degrees east of those islands, enabling Spain to hold the Philippines.[12] Spain and Portugal were able to do this because at that time it was generally accepted by the Christian world that the pope had the right to allocate lands and islands in the world to anyone he pleased, a right based on a document known as the Donation of Constantine. Although the Donation has long been known to have been forged in eighth century Rome, it was still enrolled in Decrees of Canon Law in the eighteenth century.[13] This allocation of lands outside Europe to Spain and Portugal lent an aura of sinfulness in Iberian eyes to those who broke the rules and went to discover and trade overseas for themselves. Whereas the invasion of other territories in Europe was viewed impassively, the planting of colonies and trading forays by others were not.

Two other factors led to the resentment of interlopers in the case of Portugal. First, there was the crusading zeal for the Catholic faith when the two chief interlopers were Protestant nations and, secondly, there was the sense of the tremendous cost in men and effort which such a small country had put into its discoveries, so ably recorded for posterity by Camões in the *Lusiadas*. For both Spain and Portugal during the sixteenth century repelling interlopers was necessary in order to defend a supposed right. By the seventeenth century, however, both their economies had become completely dependent on the products of their overseas possessions and they had to try to enforce those rights to survive. In insisting on sole control of their colonial trades Spain and Portugal set a fashion, and later colonial powers insisted on the same policy.

One of the first monarchs to break the rules was Henry VII of England. In 1496 he gave a licence to a Venetian settled in Bristol, John

Cabot, to search for a north-west passage to India. Cabot made two voyages. His first expedition found land in Newfoundland and Nova Scotia, and on the second he went south from Nova Scotia as far as New England. His was the first sighting of North America in modern times. He did not find India or gold, but he did find large shoals of fish. The geographical results appeared on the de la Cosa map. Portugal sent two brothers (the Corte Reals from the Azores), who claimed much of the land for Portugal, but after Vasco da Gama reached India, Portugal lost interest in Newfoundland.[14] It became a fishery centre in the sixteenth century, with English and Portuguese fishermen catching and drying cod for European consumption. By the mid-seventeenth century, however, the trade was in English hands.

During the reign of Elizabeth I (1558–1603), England had found a new spirit of independence, confidence and daring. The Spanish Armada was defeated in 1588 because English ships, gunnery and seamanship were superior to those of Spain and Portugal.[15] Drake sailed round the world in the *Golden Hind* (1577–80), English sea-dogs challenged and intercepted Spanish treasure ships returning from America, and interfered in the Guinea trade.

After the death of Elizabeth I, England and Scotland became a dual monarchy when James VI of Scotland became James I of Great Britain. He made peace with Spain in 1604, and the English challenge to Iberian colonial rights was more circumspect thereafter. The Stuarts of Scotland did not prove to be in tune with the spirit of the nation, for they hankered after the ideas of absolutism which were growing and developing on the continent. The struggle between Parliament and the monarchy begun in Elizabeth's reign culminated in the outbreak of the Civil War in 1642. In 1649 James I's son, Charles I, was beheaded by Parliament. The monarchy was restored in 1660 in the person of Charles II, but although England remained a monarchy, the powers of Parliament were increased after the revolution of 1688, when James II, Charles II's brother, was forced to abdicate because his ideas on religion and absolutism were disliked by the vast majority of the country.

None the less, throughout this period of constitutional development there was a growing realization of the importance of trade for the country. The development of shipping remained the first priority and wars were avoided unless considered essential to further trade. England did not take part in the Thirty Years War, but did fight three wars at sea against the United Provinces, in 1652–4, 1665–7 and 1672–3. It was inevitable that these two trading and seafaring nations should clash, but it was also perhaps fitting, in that both the United Provinces and Britain were trading countries with democratic forms of government, that Dutch William III should have been crowned king of England in 1688 jointly with his wife, Mary, daughter of James II. Under William's influence England became embroiled in continental wars again at the end of the seventeenth century.

The United Provinces only came into being as an independent state in the sixteenth century. In 1566 the seven northernmost Dutch-speaking states of the Spanish Netherlands revolted against Spanish overlordship, formally renouncing their allegiance in 1581. The war they fought for their independence was to last until 1648, when Dutch independence was formally recognized in international law by Spain by the Treaty of Münster. Throughout the rest of the century the Dutch suffered attacks from France, formerly their ally. It was the United Provinces which became the motivating force in the coalitions formed to withstand the pretensions of Louis XIV. In spite of this drain on their resources, the Dutch grew rich and powerful, especially at sea. Their wealth made them influential in world affairs and they were led by gifted men of the House of Orange. Nominally the Prince of Orange was only the first magistrate or 'Stadholder', but William I (assassinated in 1584) and his sons, Maurice (Stadholder 1584–1625) and Frederick Henry (Stadholder 1625–47), and William II (Stadholder 1647–50) occupied a quasi-monarchical position by force of personality. All political and economic power, in fact, was vested in the hands of the small oligarchy of 'regents', whose leader was known as the 'advocate' and, later, the 'grand pensionary'.

Being a relatively small nation and having land frontiers, the Dutch hired their army, but they built and manned their own ships, which, by the mid-seventeenth century, fetched and carried the greater part of the world's trade. The United Provinces became the entrepôt of world trade, and Amsterdam became the banking centre of Europe. The Netherlands had long been one of the chief centres for European trade, so trading expertise was there to be drawn upon, as were the rivers Scheldt and Rhine to transport merchandise throughout central Europe. Religious toleration was a feature of the country and Jewish exiles from Portugal and Spain, together with Huguenots from France, were equally welcomed. They brought their trading, manufacturing and financial expertise with them.

In their war with Spain after the formation in 1602 of the Dutch East India Company, the Dutch began a policy of concentrating their attacks on Portuguese territories overseas, as Portugal was the weaker partner in the Dual Monarchy. They gained control of the cloves, mace and nutmegs of the Moluccas, of the cinnamon of coastal Ceylon and the pepper of Malabar. In 1639 they secured the monopoly of European trade with Japan, and by 1663 the Dutch had also displaced the Portuguese in securing the lion's share of the carrying trade in Asian waters between Japan and Arabia. They attacked Portuguese settlements in east and west Africa and founded their own settlement at the

Cape of Good Hope in 1652. The rapid progress made by the Dutch in the East alarmed the English as much as it did the Portuguese, leading to the making of an Anglo-Portuguese Truce at Goa in 1635. A Dutch West India Company was formed and first attacked Brazil in 1624. In 1630 Pernambuco was invaded. Fifteen years later, the Dutch controlled the greatest and richest part of the sugar-producing north-eastern coastal districts of that country, almost halving the sugar production at the disposal of Portugal.[16]

The belief of the Portuguese that the union of their crown with that of Castile was the sole reason why their overseas dominions were attacked by the Dutch, and to a lesser extent by the English, was one of the chief factors in persuading the Portuguese to revolt against Spain in 1640. They did not consider that their own dominions were receiving a fair share of colonial protection.

Since 1621 Spanish affairs had been in the hands of Gaspar de Gusmán, Conde Duque de Olivares (1587–1645), favourite of Philip IV, whose aim it was to achieve the complete unification of the Iberian Peninsula by denationalizing the Portuguese nobility, calling it to serve in Madrid and then encouraging intermarriage with Castilian nobility.[17] When the Catalans revolted in the late spring of 1640, and Olivares ordered the Portuguese nobility to turn out and join the troops being sent to Catalonia, most of the Portuguese nobles decided to ignore this call to arms and to try instead to regain their independence from Spain. They probably had the connivance of Cardinal Richelieu in the plans they laid during the autumn of 1640.[18]

The revolution occurred on 1 December 1640, and was carried out with ease and expedition. John, Duke of Braganza, the nearest collateral of the House of Aviz, being the grandson of John III's niece Catherine and the leading aristocrat and biggest landowner in Portugal, was sworn in publicly as King John IV by the nobles on 15 December. Apart from dismissing a few Spanish officials and taking over the forts defending the Tagus and at Setúbal and Viana, where the garrisons surrendered, John IV made almost no changes in government personnel. In Portugal and in the colonies the same officials carried on in the same jobs. Only Ceuta, an enclave in North Africa opposite Gibraltar, refused to adhere to the new regime. John IV nevertheless faced many problems. For instance, the frontier fortifications on the Spanish border had long been neglected; wheat, formerly obtained from Spain, had to be imported from elsewhere to feed the population; the national studs had been discontinued after 1580; many Portuguese were already serving in the Spanish forces elsewhere in Europe and the ships used for convoy and patrol duties off the coast of Portugal were only half manned and could not be supplied, victualled, made seaworthy and fully manned in under two to three months.[19] Because it was winter,

John IV could reasonably assume that he had five to six months in which to buy the arms he needed to defend his frontiers with Spain, and to procure and prepare sufficient ships to defend Portugal's coasts. His first priority, therefore, was to obtain recognition from other European countries and from the pope of Portugal's independent status and of his own right to the crown. John IV set about his task with remarkable speed, for it is clear that action in this regard had been taken by 22 December 1640.[20]

It was not difficult to assemble the staff for the embassies, because the revolution had not entailed changes in government personnel. The problem for Portugal was what to offer as a bargaining counter at negotiations. John IV decided to reverse the country's former policy of never allowing foreigners to trade with the Portuguese dominions. He deliberately began what has been called a 'politique de traité de commerce'.[21] Thus on 8 February 1641, three English ships left Lisbon carrying ambassadors to France, England and the United Provinces. In March and April, ambassadors left for Denmark and Rome.[22] A treaty of peace and alliance was signed with France on 1 June 1641. France had refused to enter a league with Portugal, but under that treaty Portugal obtained the despatch to Lisbon of a squadron of twenty French ships, each to be of at least three hundred tons, and permission to buy arms and munitions and any other goods needed in France. In return, France received increased trade and commercial privileges in Portugal.

The embassy to Denmark was unsuccessful, but the Portuguese Ambassador to that country proceeded to Sweden where, on 29 July 1641, a treaty of peace and friendship was signed. The treaty was worded in such a way as to make it possible for the Swedes to go to Portuguese colonies. In return for materials for building ships, and arms and munitions transported to Portugal by Sweden, the latter was permitted to carry back spices, salt and other goods in exchange, or to take the balance of payment out in the form of currency or bullion. The latter was an unheard-of privilege, forbidden to other foreigners, and to the Portuguese themselves, on pain of death.[23]

Portugal only sought a truce with the United Provinces in order to avoid the necessity of recognizing the Dutch seizure of northern Brazil.[24] A ten-year truce was signed on 12 June 1641. It was a truce which was officially to begin forthwith in Europe, but was only ratified a year later and was not implemented in Asia until 1644. The Dutch soon made it clear that they were going to observe the truce in Europe because they needed Setúbal salt for their herring trade (a staple of the Dutch economy), but that war with Portugal would continue elsewhere in the world.[25] The Portuguese ambassador sent to The Hague returned to Portugal with two regiments of cavalry, and arms and munitions to the value of 250,000 florins.[26] Payment for these was to be made in salt. In addition, the Dutch obtained freedom of maritime trade in the Far East and free trade in Portugal, and Portugal promised to hire only Dutch shipping in the Brazil trade, should the Portuguese need extra shipping. Article 26 of the truce was unprecedented. By this the Dutch were given permission to practise the Protestant religion in their houses and on their ships.[27]

John IV knew that he could not expect to receive military or naval assistance from England, because England maintained amicable relations with Spain. The embassy he sent to England therefore asked Charles I for recognition of John's title to the crown and neutrality in his war with Spain. In return for these things, John IV was prepared to grant to English merchants in Portugal greater privileges than they had enjoyed in the past. He also wished to obtain confirmation of the truce in India, which had been made in 1635 by the Portuguese Viceroy and the President of the East India Company.[28] Charles I consulted with a representative committee of the Portugal merchants in England before instructing commissioners to negotiate with the Portuguese ambassador.[29] This was accepted procedure in such cases. It was the influence of the Portugal merchants which delayed the conclusion of this commercial treaty until 29 January/8 February 1642.[30] It appears that as soon as they knew of the final terms of the Dutch truce signed in June 1641, the merchants persuaded the commissioners negotiating on their behalf with the Portuguese delegation to press for equal concessions for English merchants in Portugal. They particularly wanted to obtain the same concessions regarding shipping in the Brazil trade, and religious toleration. The Portuguese could not promise to give the English first preference when hiring ships for the Brazil trade, however, without breaking their agreement with the Dutch, so it was finally agreed that in the Anglo-Portuguese treaty the question of employment of English ships should be referred to two commissioners to settle. Relations between Portugal and the United Provinces deteriorated rapidly, because of the continued Dutch attacks on Portuguese colonies and shipping, and the Portuguese then turned to the English merchants for the shipping they needed. John IV maintained that it was not in his power to concede religious toleration to Protestants, and referred the English demands to the Archbishop of Lisbon and a commission of ecclesiastics for consideration. They ruled that liberty of conscience could not be expressly conceded.[31]

Civil War broke out in England in 1642 and Charles I left London shortly after the signing of the treaty. The Portuguese delegation had to apply to Parliament in order to depart. The secretary of the delegation, António de Sousa de Macedo, remained in England as resident.[32] He allowed Royalists to send their mail in the Portuguese diplomatic pouches which went between London and Paris, thus enabling Charles I to communicate with Queen Henrietta Maria and his agents on the continent. When this was discovered, Parliament was led to view Portugal with great suspicion.[33] It was not an auspicious beginning to Anglo-Portuguese relations in the second half of the century.

2

The Commercial and Social Background
to Anglo-Portuguese Relations

i   Early Commercial Relations

When John IV introduced a commercial element into the treaty with
England in 1642, it was not new to Anglo-Portuguese relations, for up
to the sixteenth century commerce had played a large part in those
relations. Indeed, commercial relations antedated the first political
alliance between the two countries: the Phoenicians travelled to southern Britain for tin via the Straits of Gibraltar and the land that is now
Portugal, whilst the Roman British were familiar with the ports of
Felicitas Julia, and traded metal, furs and wolf dogs for fruit, oil and
wine.[1] Trade relations between England and Portugal are known to
have existed at the very beginning of the thirteenth century, for the
patent roll of the fourth year of King John I of England's reign contains
a safe-conduct for Portuguese merchants travelling to England with
their merchandise.[2] In following years there are records of numbers of
Portuguese merchants receiving safe-conducts to bring their goods to
England and by 1293 the commerce of Portugal had become so important that King Dinis (1279–1325) established a *bolsa do comercio*, or
stock exchange, in Flanders.[3] There is little evidence of English traders
residing in Portugal at that time, or even going there in English ships.
Some may have gone as supercargoes or factors, but it seems probable
that the Portuguese had restrictive legislation in favour of their own
vessels. A privilege of 1383 allowing two Englishmen to take out their
goods in any ship, not merely in those of the king of Portugal, not
withstanding laws to the contrary, would indicate that this was the
case.[4] Another factor encouraging trade was that after the conquest of
Seville in 1248, the Straits of Gibraltar had been opened to the Italian
merchants, and they began to use the sea route via Lisbon and Southampton to trade at the Bruges fairs, instead of travelling overland as
they had formerly been forced to do.[5]

By the middle of the fourteenth century, Lisbon was famous for the
number of foreign merchants who lived and traded there. In the
introduction to his *Chronica Fernando*, Fernão Lopes says that as many
as 450 foreign and native merchant ships anchored in the mouth of the
Tagus, giving every facility for the profitable exchange of goods.[6] Like

all other kings, the kings of Portugal found it to their advantage to encourage foreign merchants to trade in their lands, and to smooth out any difficulties. Taxes on imports and exports, and the revenues obtained from the selling of licences and safe-conducts issued to foreign merchants, formed a considerable portion of a king's income. It became customary, therefore, to grant privileges to foreign merchants of all nationalities, aimed at speeding trading negotiations and protecting the merchants themselves. The first known recorded privileges given by a Portuguese king were granted to two Florentines of the Bardi Company in 1339. The Florentines were allowed to govern themselves and settle their disputes, as well as given freedom to come and go, to import goods into Portugal and to export Portuguese wares. In the same reign, these privileges were also granted to other European trading peoples, the Genoese, Milanese, Piacentines and Cahorsins.[7]

During the middle of the fourteenth century, trade with England must have been considered valuable by the Portuguese cities of Lisbon and Oporto, for they jointly sought and made a fifty-year treaty of commerce with Edward III (1327–79) in 1359.[8] Although called a treaty, this agreement was basically a general safe-conduct, following medieval usage. It could be negotiated by Portuguese towns because of the charters or *forais* which those towns had obtained from their kings.[9] Following on this treaty, the number of itinerant English factors in Portugal increased sufficiently for them to make themselves felt as a 'nation'. They sought the right to have a consul, a privilege only of value to them if they were resident in the country. Their chief need was for swift justice, given the nature of medieval trade. An English merchant trading in Portugal would have either accompanied his goods, or sent them with a factor. Those goods were obtained on credit in England, and would only be paid for on his return to England. It was normal to carry on trade on a credit basis because coins were scarce. Although payment of interest was against the strict laws of usury, this was circumvented by the inclusion of an interest element in the agreed price.[10]

In Portugal, he would sell his goods either for cash, or in exchange for other goods to be taken back to England and sold there in order to pay his original suppliers. Thus if he became involved, as frequently happened, in long-drawn-out court cases whilst abroad, or met with other difficulties which caused him to be delayed, his funds would all be dissipated and he would lose his credit with his suppliers and go out of business.[11] To meet this need for swift justice, King Fernando (1367–83), on 29 October 1367, designated the judge of the customs house, or *juiz dos feitos da alfândega*, as the sole authority to take cognisance of and settle all disputes in which Englishmen were concerned.[12] When it was granted, the right to have a particular judge to hear commercial cases was probably not a notable innovation, yet in the course of time it was to become the foundation stone of a whole system of trade. By the seventeenth century, the special magistrate had become the judge conservator of the English nation, paid by them, and entitled on account of his seniority to take precedence over all the judges of other nations, so that all suits in which the English were involved with other foreigners could be brought to the English judge's court. The Portuguese preferred the institution to that of consul, for they regarded consulates as an infringement on the rights of national judges.[13]

All these commercial developments took place before the first political alliance was made in 1373, between King Fernando and Edward III at St Paul's on 16 June.[14] As a result of that treaty, English ships were sent to aid Portugal on Easter Sunday, 1384 and they broke through the Castilian siege of Lisbon, and the English archers went on to play an important part in the great battle of Aljubarrota, which was fought on 14 August 1385, and assured John I the throne. The Treaty of Windsor followed on 9 May 1386, and it was that political alliance which was to be ratified by each new sovereign of both countries until the end of the fifteenth century, the last ratification being in 1499.[15] In this treaty it was specified:

that there shall be between the two kings (Richard II and John I) their heirs and successors and between the subjects of both king-doms, an inviolable, eternal, solid, perpetual and true league of friendship, alliance and union, not only between each other, their heirs and successors, but also between and in favour of their king-doms, lands, dominions and subjects, vassals, allies and friends, wherever they may be, so that each of them shall have the obligation to assist and give aid to the other against all people now born or who shall come to be born and who shall seek to violate the peace of others or in any way make bold to offend their states . . .

In 1387, John I married Philippa of Lancaster, daughter of John of Gaunt and cousin of Richard II (1377–99). Two years later, the English in Lisbon were awarded all the privileges hitherto enjoyed by the Genoese and other Italians, including freedom from supervision in the loading of ships, which had been granted by King Pedro I (1357–67), and exemption from certain taxes.[16]

When making petitions for privileges, or when making commercial treaties, it was customary for the nations to use a privilege granted to another nation as a precedent. This is clearly seen in the next group of privileges granted to the English merchants in Portugal during the mid-fifteenth century, following the presentation of a group of petitions and complaints to Afonso V (1438–81) in 1454 and 1458.[17] The complaints illustrate the kind of day-to-day problems faced by English merchants in Portugal at that time. Although Afonso V did what he could to remedy the complaints, it will be seen that they were very similar to those made in the seventeenth century. Among the complaints made by fifteenth-century merchants were that the customs officers were dishonest and showed favouritism; that Portuguese merchants who purchased their goods delayed overlong in paying for them; that cloth was lost and stolen after being placed in the customs house, and that customs men stole goods when searching ships on their first arrival in port. Portuguese men of rank, it seems, would go into the customs house and insist on buying good cloth at cheap rates there and then, which made it impossible for merchants to sell their cheaper lines at the usual price later. Merchants were delayed by judgements and appeals from the customs house, and sometimes such cases prevented their return to England for two or three years, making them 'quite undone'. This was in spite of having the privilege of the services of a special judge. It was impossible to stop robbery of goods piled on the quayside when merchants were not allowed to carry arms and had to obey the curfew. Finally, the behaviour of the porters at the customs house was greatly resented. They sometimes stole the cloth and would often slam doors in the faces of merchants and belabour them with sticks when they took prospective customers to see their cloth. It was the remedies ordained by Afonso V for these complaints that became known as 'The Charter of the English'.[18]

During the fifteenth century, trade between the two countries came to be increasingly in the hands of English merchants, who were by then shipping their goods in English ships. The Bristol Customs Accounts for the eight months from Michaelmas 1465-May 1466 show that the entire cargoes of all the English ships employed in the Portugal trade, together with the greatest part of the Portuguese ships in that trade, are entered as belonging to English merchants. Roughly nine-tenths of Portuguese merchandise – wine, fruit, oil, wax and other goods – brought to Bristol in that period were imported by English merchants.[19] A possible reason for this was that the Portuguese merchants were increasingly directing their efforts towards the rapidly developing colonial trade. Portugal had been accustomed to obtaining cloth from England, so it was natural that English merchants should take over the trade.

We do not know with any certainty when the English merchants began to take up permanent residence in Portugal, nor when they first became organized in a factory (a name derived from the Portuguese word 'feitoria', meaning a trading depot). We do know, however, that an English brotherhood or guild existed at least from the time of King Duarte (1433–38), for he ordered solemn vespers and sung mass on every feast of St George and gave 550 reais brancos for the purpose, to be sung in the guild's chapel of St George in the cathedral of São Domingos. According to Frei Luís de Sousa, writing in the seventeenth century, the chapel was established by the kings of England who wished their subjects resident in Portugal to have a chapel of their own. The chapel was sustained by a levy on merchandise passing through the customs house, at the rate of ten reis for every piece of cloth. The chapel became very wealthy.[20] Naturally, after England became a Protestant nation in the sixteenth century, merchants resented being taxed for the upkeep of a Catholic chapel.

During the sixteenth century, Portugal became increasingly absorbed into the orbit of Spanish foreign policy, not only by a series of royal marriages, but because the two colonial powers resented the intrusion of English seamen in African and American waters in which they claimed a monopoly.[21] The Reformation, too, separated the allies, for the Portuguese had a horror of Protestantism, which to them was simply heresy.

Trade between England and Portugal still continued, both directly and through Antwerp, where the king of Portugal's factor resided, though the latter was withdrawn in 1549 owing to the Portuguese Crown's financial difficulties.[22] The English merchants in Portugal did not join those of Andalusia in 1531 when they petitioned Henry VIII and obtained a charter from him, in order to assist them in the difficulties they were experiencing as a result of the strained diplomatic relations between England and Spain.[23] Portugal placed an embargo on trade with England (officially operative from 1568–76) as a result of the seizure of William Winter's ship off Guinea.[24] When Queen Elizabeth I seized the Duke of Alva's pay ships, Spanish ports, too, were closed to English traders.[25] However, clandestine trade continued to both Portugal and Spain.[26] By 1569, legitimate traders between England and Portugal were estimated to number 120 in London, Bristol and Southampton.[27] This number was increasing; when an application was made to the queen for a charter to be granted to an exclusive company of merchants trading to Spain and Portugal in 1577, which was to include only those merchants so trading in 1568, several merchants, led by Alderman Pullyson, protested against the exclusiveness. They maintained that if the company were limited to merchants trading before that date, then many who had taken up the trade since would be ruined. Alderman Pullyson and his friends had been trading to Spain and Portugal by exporting their goods from Flanders, Hamburg and Emden, in the course of their trading as Merchant Adventurers. They argued that if they were not allowed to trade to Portugal indirectly, the Flemings, Spaniards and Frenchmen would replace them in the trade 'without bringing any of the same into this realm, to the great hindrance of the navigation . . . and the great diminishing of her majesty's cus-tom'.[28] The charter finally granted to the Spanish Company on 8 July 1577 allowed Alderman Pullyson and his friends to become members.[29] After 1605–6 the Spanish Company disintegrated rapidly,[30] but English merchants continued to live and trade in both Spain and Portugal.

Philip II of Spain (and after the dual union of 1580, Philip I of Portugal) must have considered that the trade brought by English merchants was necessary to Portugal, for in 1586 he appointed John Taylor to be the first consul to govern the English in that country. He and his successors were instructed to make and keep a collection of the privileges which had been granted to the English in Portugal.[31] By then, there were many Englishmen and their families residing there, as is evidenced by a petition signed by merchants in London and the great western ports, which states that they had factors and correspondents living in Portugal, enjoying various privileges and immunities.[32] It is certain that given the diplomatic climate between Spain and England, which was far from friendly, the merchants themselves were not in a position to push for privileges. That they continued to receive them underlines the importance of the English trade to Portugal.

Portugal was important to England, too, for Portugal bought more Suffolk and Kent cloths than did Spain, and much of the cloth which Spain did take was 'ventyd' in Portugal, i.e., English cloth was exported to Spain through Portugal. In 1569, it was estimated that the Portuguese annually took English cloth to the value of 2,050,000 ducats.[33] At the time of the negotiations for the 1642 treaty between England and Portugal, the Portugal merchants in England prepared a remonstrance setting out the value of their trade. According to that document, the trade from London alone, to Portugal and the Azores, amounted to at least £120,000 annually, employing 7,000 tons of ship-ping. Newfoundland sent 70,000 quintals of dried fish to Portugal every year, which was usually sold there for £70,000. That trade employed 4,000 tons of shipping and 1,300 fishermen and mariners. Ports such as Bristol, Exeter, Dartmouth and Plymouth, as well as Colchester, Ipswich, Hull and Yarmouth, enjoyed a flourishing trade with Portugal. It was stressed that the return trade brought to England great quantities of silver, salt, oils, fruit, spice and sugars. The English merchants liked trading with Portugal because aliens paid the same customs duties there as natives.[34] The latter privilege was one of the principal methods used to attract foreigners to trade in Portugal, for it enabled them to sell their goods at competitive prices.

ii *Merchant Privileges*

The granting of privileges to the merchants of all nations trading in Portugal was in no way singular. Any country wishing to encourage trade was obliged to do the same. For instance, merchants of all nationalities at Antwerp in its heyday (1500–50) received many privileges, because Charles V had wanted to attract trade by giving merchants what they needed to facilitate their operations.[35] The business of negotiating for privileges was done by the merchants themselves. Merchants of all nationalities, over the centuries, had evolved methods to deal with their problems and supply their needs in foreign lands in the course of trading. Those with the same interests had bound themselves into guilds, companies and leagues. The merchants of northern Germany, for instance, had come together in the Hanseatic League, which became a very powerful organization. To obtain the privileges they needed to facilitate trading, the groups of merchants had to make the most of diplomatic alignments and even send embassies abroad at their own expense. The Russia Company financed its embassies to the Tsar, though nominally the embassies were from the English sovereign, and the Levant Company maintained a permanent ambassador at Constantinople in the name of the English sovereign.[36]

From the Middle Ages onwards, merchants trading overseas had found that to prosper they needed liberty to come and go and to trade without hindrance; they needed quick justice in the shape of special judges or courts; a headquarters where their nation could meet and organize its trade, and customs concessions to enable them to compete with native merchants. After the coming of Protestantism, Protestant merchants also wanted liberty to practise their own religion in Catholic countries, and Catholics wanted liberty to practise theirs in Protestant lands. The Treaty of Utrecht of 1474 is an example of what great privileges merchants could obtain. In that treaty, in return for supplying Edward IV with a fleet to take him back to England from France in 1471, the Hansards were given a headquarters in Dowgate (the Steelyard), which became their own free property. Tax payable by them on exports and imports was to be less than that payable by Englishmen. They were to enjoy full liberty of trade and had the right to come and go throughout the land. They also received the right of judgement by special judges.[37] W. E. Lingelbach, who made a study of the English Merchant Adventurers in Hamburg at the end of the sixteenth century, has enumerated the privileges which the Merchant Adventurers negotiated, and received, in that city.[38] These included: freedom of trade; a building to be used as a base; freedom of religious worship; their own courts and right to judgement by the Senate in cases involving citizens of Hamburg, and they could testate according to English law.

The granting of privileges, however, did not guarantee that merchants would get them in practice. In earlier times, law and order was very much at the will of the monarch or prince and/or his nobles. Only if it suited them would they ensure that a decree was actually carried out, and that foreign merchants in their domains received the protection and facilities which had been negotiated. Those privileges naturally caused jealousy and animosity among native merchants, who customarily farmed the customs and could make difficulties if they wished.[39] In Portugal, John III was obliged to reissue the privileges previously given to the English nation on 6 March 1536 and then he had to confirm his own instructions on 27 March 1537.[40] Three years after the signing of the 1642 treaty with England, Thomas Bostock had to petition John IV to confirm all privileges which had been previously given to the English.[41]

A career as an overseas merchant was very uncertain, and physically and economically dangerous. Even in time of peace, merchants had to buy their safety in foreign lands, in the form of safe-conducts and licences. The Papacy was accustomed to making money in this way, for no Protestant merchant would travel to, or in, a Catholic country without buying a papal licence.[42] When taking goods overseas, merchants risked the possibility of shipwreck, piracy and damage to their goods by seawater. Their own prince could not protect them when they were far from home, even when he might have wished to do so. They were at the mercy of the authorities in whose lands they were, and they met with antagonism from local merchants. Because of the credit system of trade, the death of a debtor could involve them in expensive court cases and even more expensive delays. In time of war, of course, the merchants often had their property sequestered, and were themselves frequently imprisoned.

To be successful, therefore, merchants had to be tough, hardy and intelligent, besides being dedicated to their calling. Like their present day descendants, seventeenth century merchants wanted:

> To buy at the first or best hand or there,
>   where they may have the commodities cheapest.
> To fetch commodities from the immediate places
>   of production or growth.
> To sell commodities to the utmost market at
>   the highest price.[43]

In addition, of course, it was essential for them to have contacts and influence in the right places. Contacts and influence were certainly evident in the administrative levels of the Commonwealth. Wealthy, active merchants were influential in government, in parliament and throughout society.[44] English merchants did not have political matters in their own hands to the extent enjoyed by the Dutch, (who were ruled by a merchant oligarchy), but the existence of the Board of Trade gave them an official avenue through which to voice their interests, even if those were not always homogeneous. (For instance, the Spanish trade lobby was at odds with the French trade lobby when France and Spain were at war with each other.) Apart from these general advantages shared by the mercantile interest as a whole in England at the time, merchants interested in the Portugal trade enjoyed particular advantages, in that trade with Portugal always showed a balance in England's favour,[45] and that this satisfied the current economic orthodoxy propounded by Thomas Mun in *England's Treasure by Forraign Trade*, to the effect that the sole means of accumulating a surplus of treasure for the nation was to ensure the maintenance of a greater value of exports over imports.[46]

iii   *Society and the Economy in England and Portugal*

In the seventeenth century England and Portugal were alike in that they were both relatively small and their economies depended on trade. They were both geographically well placed to be trading nations, with good ports and harbours. Nevertheless, they were dissimilar in their social structures and religious beliefs and these greatly affected their approaches to the organization of commerce.

From early medieval times, England's economy had been largely geared to the export first of wool and, later, of woollen cloth, mainly directed through the Low Countries to central and northern Europe. After the decline of Antwerp in the sixteenth century, merchants had been forced to seek new markets. Manufacturers diversified their products to meet the needs of those markets by developing the 'new draperies'.[47] Fresh ventures were undertaken either as private expeditions or by the formation of charter companies and joint stock companies, to find markets in Africa, Asia, southern Europe and America. Even the colonies planted in America at the turn of the century were not state enterprises, so if they made losses, the losses were borne only by those venturing their capital and not by the state. Undoubtedly, the chief stimulus to increased exports was the nature of the cloth industry itself. It was all-pervasive, for a large proportion of the population had an interest in it: merchants, clothiers, spinners, dyers, fullers and also landlords, farmers and labourers, not to mention the seamen of the merchant navy involved in its export. As late as 1640, woollen cloth comprised between eighty and ninety per cent of exports from London.[48] England exported other goods such as leather gloves, shoes, wax, pewter, wrought iron, brass and hoops for barrels. Even agricultural products were exported, except in years of dearth.[49] The most essential imports were timber, pitch and hemp, which were obtained from the Baltic countries. A considerable portion of the sovereign's income came from customs duties, so it can be said that most people, from king to shepherd, had a vested interest in commerce.

It was because the importance of commerce was accepted by the nation as a whole that the merchant community in England was able to exert considerable influence at a national level. There had been an increasing tendency for monarchs to depend on their merchants since Sir Thomas Gresham had taught Queen Elizabeth I to use her own merchants rather than foreign bankers when she needed capital.[50] Merchants had become the chief tax farmers and bankers of the crown. Thus a Merchant Adventurer, Lionel Cranfield (1575–1645), rose to be Earl of Middlesex and the country's Treasurer.[51] Baronets, knights and esquires commonly put their sons into trade.[52] Merchants themselves combined business with land ownership. Merchants' sons became country gentlemen and their daughters were married into county families.[53]

Acceptance of the importance of the merchant community to the nation was shown when, in 1625, a Committee of Trade was set up as a subcommittee of the Privy Council. It was made permanent in 1630, and all matters of trade coming before the Privy Council were referred to it. As the king was generally present, the committee played an executive as well as an advisory role. The civil war gave even greater formal government acknowledgement of the importance to England of trade and commerce, when a Board of Trade was created in August 1650.[54]

Although both lawyers and practising merchants were heavily outnumbered in the House of Commons by rural landlords, their parliamentary energy and shared interests allowed the two groups to exert an influence disproportionate to their numerical strength. When Parliament wanted a loan, it turned to the City of London to obtain it. A committee of City merchants and army officers was closely consulted about the reorganization of the fleet, and measures were taken to reform the administration of the customs and to improve the source of naval finance.[55] It is fair to conclude, therefore, that the merchant community in England was in a position to influence government policy greatly in the mid-seventeenth century, and, in fact, did so.

In Portugal, conditions were very different. Portuguese society was still medieval and feudal in structure.[56] Whereas in England the system of primogeniture encouraged the gentry to apprentice their sons in trades because there was no legal barrier to their so doing, in Portugal

Roman Law prevailed, as it did elsewhere in Europe, and trade was proscribed to *fidalgos*, on the grounds that the consequent competition would be unfair to the plebeians and that *fidalgos* might be corrupted by too much money. Whereas in England gentility conferred no exemptions from taxation,[57] in Portugal it did. Unless *fidalgos* served the crown, their only avenue of employment was the church, but the Portuguese Crown had a feudal structure based on privilege that allowed the nobility and the church to syphon off a good share of the profits of overseas expansion for themselves. These profits they preferred to spend on land and buildings (churches, monasteries, palaces), and luxuries.[58] Thus the gains from over a hundred years of expansion had not, by the mid-seventeenth century, been used to encourage and increase trade. Further, after the first flush of expansion, the prices received for spices gradually dropped as supply began to satisfy demand and, by the mid-sixteenth century, Portugal had become a debtor nation. There were deficits of over 3,000,000 cruzados, and the king's factor in Antwerp reported that the rate of interest being charged on loans there was twenty-five per cent.[59]

As in Spain, the commerce of Portugal and its empire was controlled by the crown through the *Casa da India*, and commerce was all funnelled through Portugal. Portugal proper exported chiefly fruit, olive oil and salt. The country's great weakness was that it had long ceased to be self-sufficient in cereals. This may have been because the lure of court life and possible profits to be had from overseas possessions discouraged agricultural development. Furthermore, even though Portugal has a long coastline, seamen were so scarce in the sixteenth and seventeenth centuries that dried cod was caught and shipped by Englishmen to feed Portugal and its empire.[60]

Portugal's dependence on imports for basic foodstuffs was a disadvantage not suffered by England. The problem was exacerbated in Portugal because the Portuguese generally shunned trade and commerce, considering it ungenteel. By the mid-seventeenth century, Portugal's trade and commerce had come to be entirely in the hands of 'New Christians', descended from the Jews who had been forcibly baptized in 1497. The New Christians were despised by the rest of the strongly Catholic population, who generally aided and abetted the attacks made upon them by the Inquisition. Profits from trade were sent abroad instead of being reinvested in Portugal, in order to avoid their confiscation by the Inquisition. In spite of its vast empire, there were factors in Portugal's economy and society which inhibited commercial growth, and which encouraged the Portuguese to depend more and more on foreign merchants to supply their needs.

3

The Religious Factor in Anglo-Portuguese Relations

Religious differences were a constant source of friction between England and Portugal after the Portuguese Restoration in 1640. It is therefore important to understand the position of English Protestants who were living in Portugal, as well as that of the Portuguese themselves.

i Difficulties for Protestant Englishmen in Portugal

Portugal was arguably the most intensely religious country in Europe during the seventeenth century. If an interest in commerce and trade permeated England's society, Portugal's society was woven round the Roman Catholic church. A contemporary merchant estimated that a third of the population or more was in holy orders.[1] Professor Boxer put it more colourfully when he said that from the mid-sixteenth century to mid-eighteenth century, Portugal was probably the most priest-ridden country in Christendom, only exceeded elsewhere in this respect by Tibet.[2] The church in Portugal was said by the same contemporary merchant to have owned a third of the land,[3] whilst much of the East India trade was in the hands of the Jesuits, who also owned many sugar mills in Brazil.[4] This serves to underline the medieval nature of Portuguese society. Members of the church were to be found in all charitable institutions and schools; working as civil servants, lawyers and clerks; acting as advisors to the king and nobility as well as carrying out parochial duties.

Contemporary descriptions of the extent to which the church in Portugal permeated everyday life help in comprehending why Protestant merchants in seventeenth-century Portugal felt so strongly the need for religious privileges. Each parish priest had four or five coadjutors and a curate, who wore a red ribbon with the key of the tabernacle of the sacrament round his neck.[5] On the first day of Lent, every house was visited by one of the parish clergy and a note was taken of everyone living there over the age of seven. This was in order to ensure that everyone went to confession and mass. When people went to confession, they were given a certificate which they handed to the priest when they communicated, and the latter then struck their names off the list. Everyone was obliged to confess at least eleven times a year and to attend their parish church a minimum of eleven times.[6] There were between 5,000 and 6,000 begging friars in Lisbon, who begged in a loud singing tone, carrying a linen bag on their backs. They would not accept scraps, and they gave away what they did not eat. The poor kissed their sleeves and robes. Lay persons of both sexes who were oblates, aspiring to a monastic life, often wore the cords of some religious order and had to go to mass more often than other laymen, who only attended on Sundays and holy days. Many men took the habit of some order, but did not take final vows or live in the monastery until their elder brothers were married and had fathered children. Little girls were often dressed as nuns, even when toddlers, and many were forced to enter nunneries, otherwise their families would have turned them out of their homes.[7]

Every priest said a mass a day for which he was paid a testoon, but despite the numbers of priests they could not keep pace with the orders for masses, paid for by the bequests of the dying. The pope supplied many indulgences for the souls of those in purgatory, which were simply affixed to what were known as 'privileged' altars. They were expensive to obtain but helped to keep pace with the demand for masses. Ribbons were wrapped round images in churches. When old, they were changed; the old ones being sold for their 'virtue'. Some men begged with a saint's relic in a glass box. They would not always expect a gift of money, but would expect to have the relic kissed. Each evening a bell in every church was rung. Everyone in the streets had to stand still and say ave marias. Coaches stopped and even comedians in their farces did the same. At 9 p.m., the bells were rung again and everyone said prayers for the souls in purgatory.[8]

A picture of Catholic zeal comes from another contemporary description by Edward Hinde, the English chaplain in Oporto between 1685–6, who wrote a series of letters to the Reverend Dr Francis Turner, Bishop of Ely.[9] According to Hinde, the owner of a ship lost on the bar to the entrance of Oporto fancied that the bar and sea together might be under an excommunication. It was common for an excommunication to be put on an inanimate object. To counteract the supposed curse at Oporto, an image of Christ was set up in a painted boat which, with the bishop, priests and nobles on board, followed by smaller ships, sailed down the river in an exorcism ceremony, firing small guns. Meanwhile, Hinde said, all the people lining the banks fell on their knees and thumped their chests as they did when receiving the sacrament.[10] In the church of São Domingos in Oporto, there was a huge cross with an image of the Saviour. As the Jesuit in the pulpit preached, he gradually withdrew the nails from the image to suit his discourse, and the congregation sighed, shed tears, lamented and wrung their hands, beating their breasts.[11] In Lent, it was customary to have processions with people doing penance by crawling on their bare hands and knees around the city, some lashing themselves on their backs with an instrument, the ends of which were set full of sharp pricks, about the length of rowels of a spur, until their backs were 'as raw as a piece of beef and as bloody as butchers'.[12]

The Portuguese regarded themselves as soldiers of Christ and were prepared to do battle against all those whose faith was not their own. For them, to condone heresy was one of the greatest sins. In the vanguard against heresy was the Inquisition. Originally established in 1229 after the Albigensian Crusade, the Inquisition had become of little importance by the end of the fourteenth century, but it was revived by Ferdinand and Isabella of Spain in 1478, to ensure the conformity of the New Christians, as the converted Jews were disparagingly called. From Spain the revived Inquisition spread to Rome and northern Italy, but it was not established in Portugal until the mid-sixteenth century.[13]

In 1606, following the Anglo-Spanish treaty of 1604, the theologians, canons and professors of the universities of Coimbra and Evora, met to give their opinions on how Protestants should be treated in Portugal.[14] By 1607, the consensus of opinion was that a heretic could not be punished by the church till proved to be pertinacious and impenitent. The ordinary English heretic who went to Portugal had never had instruction in the true faith, so was not pertinacious and impenitent. He had too little knowledge of religious truths. However, if the Inquisition captured an English heretic who was learned (i.e. was educated and, particularly, understood Latin),[15] they could turn him over to the secular arm and have him put to death. If they took an ignorant man, they would instruct him, but if after that he would not recant, then he could be put to death. The canons of Coimbra also believed that any heretic who ridiculed the church could be punished, whether or not that person was invincibly ignorant.[16] The doctors of theology and canonists at Evora, which was the seat of the most active Inquisition, maintained that the Inquisition had jurisdiction to proceed, in a broad sense, against any and all heretics, because ordinarily they had sufficient instruction to be adjudged as formal pertinacious heretics. Boys and rustics could not be so treated.[17]

These pronouncements made the Inquisition a permanent threat to all Protestants going to Portugal. In every port there was an official visitor of foreign ships, appointed by the Inquisition, who was always the first person on board when a ship arrived in port. He searched the vessel and all the passengers and crew, with a staff of scribes, guards and interpreters, who made careful note of the name and nationality of the ship; the name of its master; the number of passengers and crew, and their religion. A record was also kept of the books and images found on board, for the Inquisition controlled censorship and all books had to be approved before they were printed or allowed into the country. No bibles were allowed ashore.[18] On first going ashore Protestants must have been amazed at the number of ecclesiastics in the streets. What was a Protestant to do when church bells were rung and aves were said? Unless he took his hat off and did likewise, he would be accused of ridiculing the church and thus be punished, whether ignorant or not. At best he would be accused of scandalous behaviour. The Host was frequently carried in procession along the streets, when all Catholics knelt and uncovered their heads. A Protestant would have considered that as bowing to false images.

In daily life there were pressures from all sides to persuade Protestants to conform. Always, in the background, was the known threat of the Inquisition, with its methods of torture, mental and physical. When a person was taken by the Inquisition, no one would dare to ask about or seek to help the prisoner. If they did, they too would be liable to be accused and taken, for inquiry was considered to be a form of criticism, and, according to the *Regimento*, that was a sin.[19] Before 1656, there was no Protestant consul to look after English nationals in Portugal. The consul in 1640 had been called Richard Chandler, but both he and his wife were recalled to England in 1642 for 'seducing the king's subjects from their religion'.[20] A certain John Ryder was appointed under a Portuguese patent in 1644, and in 1650, John IV appointed (at the request of Charles II in exile) a Father John Robinson, who was a priest at the English College in Lisbon.[21] There was no one who could or would speak at the highest level for English Protestants where religious matters were concerned.

It would seem from later documentation that Protestants living on their own would have been in danger of forced conversion if they became ill and had no one to fend off a priest. In 1705, Elizabeth Vasconcellos (née Chester) was given the sacrament by a Catholic priest when she was unconscious. On recovering, she could not remember it and denied having become a Catholic, so she was taken by the Inquisition.[22] Protestants were not allowed burial in cemeteries, and in Lisbon, bodies had to be disposed of in unconsecrated ground on the south bank of the Tagus at night. To make doubly sure that scandal was avoided, they had to be boxed into sugar chests and transported there on an English ship.[23] In Oporto, all English Protestants had to be buried secretly at low tide on the river bank: no service was allowed and no records were kept.[24] A similar position pertained in Spain. When the ambassador's secretary died at Santander in 1622, he could not be buried at all. He was laid to rest at sea, but fishermen, fearing for their catch while the coffin of a heretic was in the water, threw it back on land. There is no record that bodies buried on the sea-shore and river banks of Portugal were treated as they were in Malaga. There, they had to be buried at night on the shore in an upright position in the sand, until washed out to sea or torn up by dogs. The corpses were still further insulted by the dumping of refuse and ordure in the vicinity.[25]

It is clear from contemporary references that many merchants and factors were married and had their families with them in Portugal. All children over seven years of age were considered to have reached the age of reason by the Catholic church. It was frequent practice to persuade young girls and boys to leave their parents, or to abduct them from their homes, and to place them in households of Portuguese gentry. There they were instructed in the Catholic faith and were frequently forced to enter holy orders. Certainly they were lost to their parents. The practice was also current in the eighteenth century, and the only abducted child ever known to have been returned was that of Consul Milner in 1710.[26]

It was difficult for merchants to avoid becoming involved in court cases, in spite of having the services of a judge conservator. In cases of litigation, it had long been customary for Catholics to maintain that the evidence of heretics was inadmissible because their oaths could not be trusted. The idea was current in Spain in the mid-fifteenth century,[27] and was resurrected at intervals in Portugal.[28]

Difficulties were also created for English Protestants by the presence of large numbers of English Catholic exiles and priests. It is not surprising that many merchants became Catholics whilst living in Portugal and Spain. Many simply lived as Catholics whilst away from England. Richard Hakluyt reported that the merchant who went devoutly to communion in England sent his son in Spain to hear mass, and that this was kept secret for the sake of the trade.[29] In 1648, the priest in charge of the church of Santa Maria la Mayor in Seville, reported that Englishmen often received the sacrament, ate fish on fast days and gave generously to the parish church.[30]

In contrast, foreign Catholic merchants in London were not molested for their faith and were able to attend the chapels of their government representatives. Embassies in all countries had the right to use their chapels for their own staff and their own nationals, but embassies of Catholic countries in London had substantial numbers of priests, some acting as clerks and secretaries, who provided services for their co-religionists at large.[31] The Venetian embassy housed more than twenty priests, who held six masses daily and ten on festivals, which were attended not only by foreign Catholics, but also by English Catholics resident in London.[32] When the Spanish embassy had to close in 1655, twenty religious begged shelter in the Venetian embassy, i.e. the twenty priests were additional to the staff in the embassy, who would have received exit permits.[33] It was the attendance of *English* Catholics in embassy chapels to which the English government objected. The abuse of privilege by ambassadors led to periodic attempts to control attendance, but the government's chief interest was in seeing that the embassies were not providing English, Scottish and Irish priests to preach to them in English.[34] The Portuguese embassy frequently housed English priests who had been trained in the seminary of St Peter and St Paul in Lisbon expressly to return to England as missionaries. This was known to the government. On 4 December 1649, an order was issued to search the Portuguese embassy for English priests. On 4 November 1652, an order was issued to present information about Catholics known to be going to the embassy.[35] By the outbreak of the Civil War, Catholics were not subjected to indignities at the time of burial. Normally, they were given parish burial by agreement, though the burial service seems to have been said by the priest before the departure of the corpse, and burial at night was still usual until about 1700.[36] There was certainly nothing to stop foreign Catholics from worshipping privately in their homes and on their ships, and they were not searched for bibles or missals before coming ashore. Thus when the English merchants wanted Portugal to grant them the same privileges which had been granted to the Dutch in 1641, they were not asking for more than what was allowed to Portuguese residents in England.

Their religion was important to many English merchants. When a possible treaty was being discussed with Spain in 1652/3, a list of thirty-five articles was drawn up by Parliament and presented to ambassador Cárdenas. Amongst them was a request that the English Protestants in Spain be allowed to practise their religion in their houses and ships and to use bibles and religious books. This request was rejected by the Inquisition in a *Consulta* of the Council of the Inquisition of 31 March 1653.[37] Portugal, however, was not in such a strong position as Spain, and was in greater need of a treaty with England. This placed the English merchants trading with Portugal in a stronger position than their fellow merchants trading with Spain.

ii   *The Inquisition and the Portuguese Monarchy*

Though John IV was the sovereign of Portugal, he delayed the ratification of the 1654 treaty for two years, maintaining that he could not override the rulings of the Inquisition. In order to understand his position *vis-à-vis* the Inquisition, it is necessary to outline the structure of the organization of the Inquisition and the king's place within that structure.

The papal bull of 1 November 1478 which gave approval for the establishment of the Inquisition in Spain, allowed the Spanish monarchs to remove or replace inquisitors at will.[38] By the third decade of the sixteenth century, when Portugal applied to the pope for an Inquisition to be established on the same terms as the Spanish, Rome was not so amenable. The Castilian Inquisition was not popular in Rome, and papal advisers were convinced that John III only wanted to obtain the wealth and property of those arrested by the Inquisition. So the papal decree promulgating the tribunal in Portugal (5 May 1536) only permitted the king to select one inquisitor, whilst the pope selected three.

By the mid-seventeenth century, the structure and method of proceeding of the Inquisition had been laid down in *regimentos* or standing orders in 1552, 1613 and 1640.[39] The position in 1640 was that the king chose the inquisitor general, but his choice had to be approved by the pope. Once he was in office, the inquisitor general owed his first duty to the pope and dealt directly with him, without reference to the king. In his hands from then on were the powers of death and excommunication, even of the king himself, because as a spiritual power the Inquisition claimed supremacy over civil agents. This was in spite of the fact that the Inquisition was theoretically a royal tribunal. The inquisitor general also appointed the inquisitors of the *mesas* or tribunals. In the seventeenth century there were four of these: Evora, Coimbra, Lisbon and Goa.[40] Each tribunal had three inquisitors and a large staff of deputy inquisitors, judges, notaries, procurators, ushers, advocates and familiars or bailiffs. Each also had its own prison with alcaide, guards, dispensers, barbers, chaplains, cooks, surgeons and physicians.[41] The Inquisition also controlled censorship.[42]

With the establishment of the Inquisition, John III had doubtless hoped to reinforce his own influence with the church, and to have more patronage at his disposal in the shape of ecclesiastical livings for younger sons of the nobility. In practice, however, it was the Inquisition which grew more and more powerful, and the nobility came to rely greatly on the Inquisition for preferment, as well as looking to the king. Not only did the Inquisition increase the number of livings for priests, but it also employed nobles and members of the gentry as familiars, or bailiffs. These latter enjoyed great privileges and protection, and were numerous. There were a hundred familiars in Lisbon, forty in Oporto, fifty in Coimbra and the same in Evora, but even a small town such as Pinhel, which came under the Coimbra tribunal, had six.[43] The pope granted to all familiars the same plenary indulgence as was granted by the Lateran Council to those who succoured the Holy Land.[44] To hold certain posts under the crown it was necessary to prove that there was no Jewish blood in one's veins, as it was to become a familiar. A certificate of *puresa de sangue*, therefore, enabled a man to serve not only his king but also his church. The certificate was issued, and the enquiry was made, by the Inquisition.[45] Once nominated, a familiar was paid for each day of work: in 1694, the rate was five hundred reis per day. Being a familiar was a part-time occupation, for a familiar could be, and frequently was, employed in the service of the crown or state. He was granted the privilege of being judged by papal courts, except for certain specified grave crimes.[46] Familiars were only obliged to serve in the army if the king himself were present on the field, and they were excused taxes and other duties of citizenship.[47]

In practice, the Inquisition soon acquired judicial sovereignty in Portugal. All its servants had the privilege of being judged in its own courts. All churchmen were, of course, judged in episcopal courts, but the Inquisition had power over them also. By claiming an interest on a question of faith, cases could be transferred from episcopal to inquisitorial courts. The Holy Office had power to imprison and punish churchmen, whether they were seculars or belonged to one of the orders. The church could not shed blood, so sentences of death were passed to the lay courts for execution. The latter merely carried out the recommendations made by the inquisitorial courts. Even bishops were not immune and the Inquisition had power to proceed against emperors and kings. By means of the *edital* or edict, which had to be obeyed on pain of excommunication, it could override any civil law of which it disapproved. In 1642, when the Chamber of Commerce at Evora complained to the Inquisition that too many merchants were being taken prisoner, the Inquisition issued a directive to the effect that it was a crime under pain of excommunication to suggest that the Inquisition was taking too much power into its own hands. In fact, the Inquisition had become the determiner of its own legal position, as well as of its place with regard to religious matters.[48] The Inquisition had become not just a state within a state, but above the state.

John IV was unfortunate, because although the pope had never recognized Portugal's independence from Spain or his own right to rule, he could issue instructions to the Inquisition in Portugal which had to be obeyed by everyone, including the king, on pain of excommunication. Spanish power in the Italian peninsula was such that it kept successive popes from recognizing the independence of Portugal until 1670, two years after the end of the Portuguese war of independence from Spain. Furthermore, the inquisitor general during the first thirteen years of John IV's reign was D. Francisco de Castro (1574–1653), who had not approved the restoration and remained actively pro-Spanish. In July 1641 he led an unsuccessful conspiracy against the king. His co-insurgents, including the Marquês de Vila Real, the Duque de Caminha and the Conde de Armamar, were executed. The inquisitor general was imprisoned, but the king did not have the power to take away his office whilst he was in prison, so he continued to function as the inquisitor general. He was eventually set at liberty on 5 February 1643. By right, too, the inquisitor general had a seat on the Council of State.[49]

In theory, the king should have had financial control of the Inquisition, because all the confiscations made by that tribunal when prisoners were apprehended were paid in the first instance into the office of the Crown Fiscal (*fisco*), half the value being passed from there to the coffers of the Inquisition. In practice, far from obtaining a profit from confiscations, the crown had had to finance the cost of tribunals at its own expense in the beginning, and then, with the approval of the pope, in conjunction with the dioceses. Pope Gregory XIII (1572–85) abandoned two-thirds of the fruits of the first canonries to become vacant in Lisbon, Evora and Coimbra, and half of future ones to help finance the Portuguese Inquisition.[50] Philip II of Spain gave an annuity from the monopoly of the sale of playing cards to the Portuguese Inquisition.[51] By the mid-seventeenth century, it is doubtful whether the crown received any of the money from confiscations made by the Holy Office, because by then the *juiz do fisco* or judge of the Crown Fiscal, had come to owe his appointment to the inquisitor general, who only obtained the assent of the crown to the man of his choice; he had become a servant of the Inquisition.[52] When Philip IV of Spain looked into the question of the accounts of the *juiz do fisco*, in 1627, he was told by Inquisitor General D. Fernão de Mascarenhas, that the assets of the Holy Office belonged to things spiritual, so it was not lawful for the king to meddle with something which had nothing to do with him. In any case, the crown was loath to claim its share, because if the Inquisition had not maintained itself from confiscations, it would have had to be maintained at the cost of the crown.[53] That would have been an impossibility in the circumstances not only of post-Restoration Portugal, but even of Spanish Portugal of the earlier seventeenth century.

Thus, besides being above the state from the legal and judicial points of view, the Inquisition had also become a social necessity. It was a source of patronage, providing work for men of all classes in society. Without the confiscations to pay their salaries, thousands would have been out of work. Too many people owed their daily bread to a vested interest, whose head not only opposed the king, but could, if necessary, excommunicate him. The king did not even obtain any financial benefit from the Inquisition. He therefore cannot be said to have been sovereign in his own domains. At best, he shared the sovereignty with the Inquisition, and it was to become an increasingly bitter marriage of power.

Nothing illustrates this more clearly than the way the Inquisition was eventually able to overrule John IV regarding the steps he took to protect the economy by forming the Brazil Company (A Companhia do Comercio do Brasil). Trade and commerce in Portugal were almost exclusively in the hands of New Christians, and John IV, aided and abetted by the Jesuit Padre António Vieira, wanted to obtain New Christian capital for the formation of the Brazil Company, which, in 1648/49, was vital to Portugal's existence as a nation.[54] In order to persuade New Christians to invest their capital in such a company, he had to guarantee that money so invested would not be subject to confiscation by the Inquisition. Before taking action, John IV consulted the inquisitors, as well as other churchmen. With the support of the Jesuits and the Augustinians, he published an *alvará* or decree on 6 February 1649, exempting the capital of those contributing to the Brazil Company from confiscation in the event that the New Christians themselves were accused and taken by the Inquisition. This was because property was always sequestered on arrest by the Inquisition and not on sentence. After several years of torture and questioning in prison, prisoners came out and were handed over to the secular arm to carry out the judgements passed on them; whatever the judgement passed, they were never able to recover their property. The *alvará* stated that the king did not intend to remit punishment of confiscation for heresy, or interfere in the jurisdiction of the Inquisition; possessions confiscated would continue to go to the *fisco*, but John IV agreed to restore them himself to the owners or their heirs. The Inquisitor General reported all this to Rome, and obtained from the pope a brief declaring the *alvará* to be void.[55] John IV was gradually forced to recognize the papal brief, although he insisted that money actually invested in the Brazil Company itself should remain immune from confiscation, save in very special circumstances and on certain conditions agreed with the Company's representatives.[56] In 1653, all three estates of the Cortes begged that the *alvará* be rescinded, because it was prejudicial to the faith, a scandal to the country and so detested by all Portuguese that no tribunal in the country had yet been brought to accept it.[57] The request of the Cortes was a clear indication of the general anti-Jewish feeling pervading Portugal and the support enjoyed by the Inquisition. It is ironic that in 1654 the Spanish government came to an agreement with the Spanish Inquisition, whereby the latter confiscated only the personal property of financiers and left undisturbed those assets that involved state finance.[58]

There is no doubt that the Inquisition was aware of the support it enjoyed and understood the extent of its power. Between 1650 and 1656 when John IV died, it staged an increasing number of *autos da fé*.

An *auto* was held in Lisbon on 1 December 1652 (the twelfth anniversary of the Restoration), at which the king was forced to witness the degradation of Duarte da Silva, a New Christian whose efforts and capital had been largely responsible for the creation of the Armada Real do Mar Oceánio, which sailed for Brazil from Lisbon on 18 October 1647 and raised the Dutch blockade of Bahia.[59] Duarte da Silva had been taken by the Inquisition in December 1647, fourteen months before the *alvará* was published, when the king was not receiving his share of the confiscations in the *fisco*,[60] so it should not be inferred that the king was ungrateful to the New Christians who helped him, or that he was unduly greedy.[61] At the same *auto*, the king witnessed the death of Manuel Fernandes Villa Real, who had been taken by the Inquisition when John IV was about to send him on a mission to obtain warships for use against Spain.[62]

In October 1654 the General Council of the Inquisition called at the palace with a written declaration saying that either the Inquisitorial tribunals would have to be closed, or they would have to proceed against the judges of the *fisco* until all confiscations had been passed to them. To meet the cost of the *auto da fé* celebrated a few days previously, the inquisitor general had been forced to obtain money by issuing *juros*, or bonds, giving as security the sequestrations not yet released by the crown. For the provision of food for the poor prisoners, the Holy Office had been obliged to accept a gift of one thousand *reis* from the Brazil Company, a humiliation for the Inquisition.[63]

John IV was a stubborn man and despite the papal voidance of his 1649 *alvará*, on 26 October 1655 he published a further *alvará*, taking from the Inquisition their gradually acquired authority over the *fisco* The *alvará* ordered that the administration of the *fisco* should be passed to the *Conselho da Fazenda*, or Treasury, and be administered by the functionaries of the latter. No longer was the *juiz do fisco* to be nominated by the Inquisitor General, nor was the Inquisition to meddle in affairs of finance, because it was a distraction from their principal duty which was of a spiritual and religious nature.[64]

John IV died on 6 November 1656. It is perhaps as well that he did so, for not only was an edict published by the inquisitor general on 18 January 1657, declaring the *alvará* of 6 February 1649 to be void, but the Inquisition also published a papal bull of excommunication on all those who in any way had assisted in the promulgation of that *alvará*. No names were mentioned, but everyone knew that John IV would have been top of the list.[65] It is perfectly clear from a *consulta* of the Council of State of 23 November 1656, that the majority of the members of that council genuinely believed that any remission of confiscations of New Christian property was laxness in the fight against heresy and that that would displease God. The Consulta begged the Queen

Regent, Luìsa, the widow of John IV, to rescind the *alvará*. They also stated that King Sebastião had been routed at El Qsar-El Kebir in 1578 because a similar deal had been made with New Christians in order to obtain money for his expedition.[66]

Another aspect of John IV's struggle with the Inquisition concerned the appointment of bishops. When bishops died, their replacement became a problem, because John IV had not been recognized by the pope. The Inquisition opposed the election of acting bishops by the chapters, arguing that the pope, as supreme head of the church, had all the royal monarchic power as well as being the fount of all spiritual jurisdiction, which could only be transferred to ecclesiastics with his express permission. None the less, bishops were essential to ordain priests, so acting bishops were appointed by chapters and the rents which should have gone to Rome were used to fight the war with Spain.[67] The stand taken by the Inquisition, however, gave an excuse to scrupulous priests to go to Rome to lay complaints against the king and, as time went by and properly ordained bishops died, to go to Spain for ordination. John IV forbade priests to leave the country without his permission, but there are constant references in his letters to the fact that priests continued to go.[68]

The struggle which John IV waged with the Inquisition is very relevant to the events which will be related in succeeding chapters. The king knew that the Inquisition was supported by the nobility, and feared and revered by the people. At the same time, he knew that Portugal could not exist without trade and commerce, if the war against Spain was to be continued. That meant that the interests of the economy were in direct opposition to those of the Inquisition. None the less, John IV was a sincere Catholic, and his attitude to Protestantism was highly conventional. Thus, when the Dutch were allowed to have Protestant worship on their ships and in their homes under article 26 of the Truce signed with Portugal on 12 June 1641, the concession was made largely because the truce was essential to Portugal's existence as an independent nation. It may be that the Inquisition allowed article 26 to be ratified because inquisitor general, D. Francisco de Castro, was too busy preparing the coup against John IV, which took place on 28 July 1641, to deal with particulars of a truce which might soon lose validity. The truce was only for ten years. When the English merchants demanded the same concession in the treaty being negotiated by Portugal with Charles I, John IV asked the Archbishop of Lisbon D. Roderigo da Cunha, to call together a commission to examine the suggested religious articles in the treaty. The commission, composed of representatives from the Holy Office, Jesuits, Franciscans, Dominicans, Augustinians and secular clergy, produced a report dated 24 October 1641. It maintained that a Catholic king could not say to

Protestant merchants 'we give you the right to hold private services of worship', but he could say 'we shall not disturb you if you hold private services of worship'. What they were emphasizing was that the king had no final authority in matters of religion.[69] The findings of that commission are included in the wording of Article 17 of the treaty between Great Britain and Portugal of 29 January/8 February 1642:

> And forasmuch as the benefits of commerce and peace would be rendered fruitless, if the subjects of the most renowned King of Great Britain were molested on the account of their consciences, so long as they go to the kingdoms and states of the most renowned King of Portugal for commerce or business; therefore, that their commerce may be safe and secure, as well by sea as by land, the most renowned King of Portugal shall take care, and give orders that they be not molested or troubled on the said score of conscience, provided they give no scandal to others. And although the most renowned King of Portugal acknowledges he has no power to determine or dispose of faith and religion, nevertheless, from a motive of amity and great affection, which he has for the most renowned King of Great Britain and the English nation, he will take care that the English, and the other subjects of the said King, have and enjoy as great liberty in the practice and exercise of their religion, in all the kingdoms, states, and territories of the King of Portugal, as shall be allowed to the subjects of any other Prince or Commonwealth whatsoever.

In specifying that the English would only be given as much liberty in the practice of their religion '*as shall be*' given to the subjects of other princes in Portugal, it was made clear that they were not to enjoy the privileges given to the Dutch at an earlier date. The Dutch truce was free of any 'no scandal' clause, popular with the Portuguese because it was capable of wide interpretation.

The English and Dutch were not the only Protestants to desire religious concessions to be spelt out in a treaty. The Swedes also asked for the concessions given to the Dutch when negotiating their treaty with Portugal. This was refused, but they were told that private worship in their houses was possible in Portugal for all Protestants, provided that they gave no scandal. In Article 23 of the treaty concluded between Portugal and Sweden on 29 July 1641, the Swedes obtained the right to a cemetery, the first Protestant nation to obtain such a concession in a treaty.[71]

iii   *The Proceedings of the Inquisition*

The Inquisition was originally devised in the thirteenth century to ensure unity and conformity of Catholic worship and the upholding of morals. Its badge was a cross set between an olive branch and a sword, with the words 'justitia' and 'misericordia' (justice and compassion). In accordance with Roman Catholic belief at that time, the trials and troubles of this life were inflicted by God to fit men for life hereafter, therefore repentance and physical suffering on earth helped to ensure a speedier passage through purgatory to heaven. The self-flagellation described by Edward Hinde in the first section of this chapter is an example of this idea.

The popular demand for the establishment of an Inquisition in Portugal in the sixteenth century was due to the situation which arose after thousands of Jews there had been forcibly converted to Christianity at the end of the fifteenth century. There had always been large numbers of Jews in Portugal, living in *judiarias* or ghettos. They had their own synagogues and they had their own minister directly under the king (the *Arrabi-mor*), being governed by their own law. They did not have to appear in courts of law on a Saturday; divorce was sanctioned and they were not forbidden to lend money at interest. For these privileges they paid high taxes, but they contributed greatly to the economic life of Portugal, for they practically had the monopoly of finance and the customs administration. Besides being treasurers and bankers to kings, they were also the intellectuals of medieval Portugal, its doctors, chemists, geographers and astronomers. In addition, they formed the bulk of artisans of all kinds.[72]

In 1492 Spain exiled all Jews and some sixty thousand were allowed to purchase the right to settle in Portugal. Others were allowed to enter provided that they paid a tax of eight *cruzados* per adult and agreed not to stay longer than eight months. King John II (1481–95) bound himself to find shipping to transport them abroad, but this was provided tardily and there were insufficient ships. Those who went on board were disembarked at the nearest point in Africa; seven hundred children were sent to São Tomé Island in the Gulf of Guinea and the remainder were sold as slaves.[73] John II was succeeded by his cousin Manuel I (1495–1521), who married Isabel, the eldest daughter of the Spanish monarchs. A condition of the marriage was that all Jews and Muslims should be expelled from Portugal. Manuel had no intention of parting with a large and valuable community, and in order to keep them in Portugal attempted to enforce the education of Jewish and Muslim children as Christians at the expense of the crown. Some Jews were forcibly converted, but the threat against the Muslims was dropped for fear of reprisals against Christians in Muslim territory. In 1497, before the marriage was celebrated, it was announced that unbaptised Jews must be shipped from Lisbon. Some of the wealthier Jews left independently, but when the rest arrived as ordered, they were herded together and forcibly baptised, after which they were granted twenty years' grace during which no inquiry was to be made into their beliefs. They were not allowed to leave the country without permission.[74]

No one really believed that those who had been forcibly converted had really accepted Christianity, but because they were baptised Christians, they were able to intermarry with Christians. This they did, and because they were wealthy, they married into some of the oldest and best families. Many of the former Jews continued to observe Jewish practices in secret, but others must have become good Catholics with the passing of time. None the less, there were strong grounds for believing that there was much heresy in Portugal, which was just what the Inquisition had been devised to control.

During the sixteenth century there was a conjunction of factors which persuaded the Catholic population that it would be advisable to apply to the pope for permission to establish an Inquisition in Portugal. As usual in Europe, Jews were disliked because they were financiers, usurers and tax-gatherers, and they were blamed when there was economic scarcity; pogroms occurred in Portugal as elsewhere. In particular, the belief that New Christians were secretly practising their Jewish religion was anathema to Catholics, who welcomed the Inquisition as a means of preventing such deviation. Cortes made this clear in 1525.[75] King Manuel's twenty-year period of grace for inquiry into the New Christians' private beliefs had passed, so John III did not feel constrained on that account. He also wanted to ease his economic difficulties, and have more patronage at his disposal to sweeten the nobility. Finally, the Church was delighted at the prospect of greater opportunities to control heresy, with the promise of promotion for so many ecclesiastics, not to mention the increased source of revenue accruing from the confiscation of prisoners' property.

After the pope gave permission to set up the Inquisition, various tribunals were established in the principal towns. Proclamations went out in August 1536 inviting accusations to be made by all citizens against anyone suspected of being a heretic or morally perverted.[76] The main thrust of the Inquisition was indubitably aimed at punishing people of Jewish descent suspected of not being good Catholics, because signs of heresy were listed as including wearing white or dressing gaily on a Saturday; working on a Sunday; cleaning or sweeping the house on a Friday; testing the sharpness of a knife on the thumb, and not eating pork, fish in its skin or rabbit.[77] The invitation to accusers was accompanied by a warning to the effect that if anyone were later found to have known of a deviation and not to have reported it, that person would surely be taken and punished also.

The Inquisition was a meticulously run institution. Every one of its proceedings was regulated by the *Regimentos*, and each case or process was carefully documented. The records of the Lisbon and Coimbra Inquisitions are still virtually intact, and are today available for examination. When the Inquisition was in operation, however, everything was secret. Anyone disclosing the methods and proceedings of the Inquisition was severely punished by it. People were forced to become informers on pain of excommunication or of being accused of favouring heretics and themselves being imprisoned. The accused never knew who had made the accusation against them, or even of what they were accused. They did know that their families would be helpless and homeless as a result of the confiscation of their property. When more than one member of a family was arrested, the arrests were made separately, so that the accused did not know. It was essential that the mind of the prisoner should be broken by a sense of utter loneliness. When being examined the accused were never allowed to get sight of fellow prisoners.

Inquisition prisons varied in size of cells, usually they were very small and dark, with no furniture except a hard quilt and a 'useful pot'. Warders walked up and down to ensure complete silence, and not even coughing was allowed. The first cough led to a warning, but the second earned a severe beating. When warders thought the psychological moment had come, the accused were taken for questioning and asked to confess their errors, but as they had not been told of what they were accused, this presented difficulties. When their replies were unsatisfactory, they would be taken to the torture chamber and tortured on the rack or the pulley. The latter involved having hands tied behind the back; being suspended from a pulley attached to the ceiling and jerked up and down with heavy weights tied to the feet. Both forms of torture disjointed arms and legs, so doctors visited the cells to put them in place. Whilst the prisoners were still in a weak state, they were visited by a priest who exhorted them and gave kindly warnings, half-veiled promises and insidious advice. No one was released before a full, signed confession had been obtained and he or she had also incriminated someone else. A constant supply of prisoners was essential to maintain the Inquisition. Imprisonment usually lasted from three to seven years.[78]

Prisoners came out at *autos da fé*, which were great festive occasions attended by royalty. Two stages were erected in a public place, one for the Inquisitors and other authorities and the second for the prisoners. In between the stages was a temporary altar draped in black. Early in the morning a procession would form. It was led by Dominican friars, carrying the Inquisition standard, followed by the penitents, some wearing *sambenitos* (long yellow robes with a large black cross on them) and some without, depending on their crimes. All wore black coats without sleeves, went barefoot and carried a wax candle. They were followed by penitents who had narrowly escaped burning, whose *sambenitos* had upside-down flames painted on them. Behind them came the negative or relapsed prisoners, to be burnt; they had ascending flames painted on their *sambenitos*. Lastly came those professing doctrines against the faith of the Roman Church, who also had pictures of dogs, serpents and devils with open mouths on their *sambenitos*. All wore tall mitres, and all were accompanied by familiars. Those going to be burned also had a Jesuit on either side, continually preaching to them. The prisoners were followed by more familiars on horseback, the inquisitors and other Inquisition officers on mules and, finally, the inquisitor general on a white horse riding with nobles not employed by the Inquisition.

The church was not allowed to shed blood, so the prisoners were 'relaxed' or handed over to the secular arm of the law to be punished in accordance with the decrees of the Inquisition. Punishments varied from fasting each Friday for six months to scourging, and parading through the town stripped to the waist, bearing the insignia of the offence, whilst the town crier went before proclaiming the sentence. Other punishments included being sent to the galleys and exile. The practice of burning in severer cases was derived from the Gospel according to St John 15:6: 'If a man abide not in me, he is cast forth as a branch and is withered and men gather them and cast them into the fire, and they are burned.' Those who died confessing the Catholic faith were garotted before being burned. Those who did not, were burned alive.[79] In Lisbon the burning took place on the Ribeira (now the Praça do Municipio). Prisoners were chained to stakes four yards in height, and fixed to a small ledge half a yard from the top. Jesuits continually exorted them until the fires were lit by an important personage, as a great honour. The people shouted 'let the dogs' beards be burned' and burning furze would be held to their faces to further shouts of joy. The flames seldom reached higher than the ledge supporting the prisoners, so that if there was no wind it might take them one and a half to two hours to die, for they were roasted, not burned. The populace who watched this with transports of joy would tenderly lament the deaths of public malefactors.[80]

For those who were not condemned to die, punishment was not the end of a case. Often the *sambenito* had to be worn in public, especially on Sundays and festivals after release. It was finally hung up in the parish church with an inscription, to be a lasting humiliation. Punishment was visited on children and grandchildren of prisoners, in that they had to forfeit their right to public offices and educational and scientific posts. Those who died in prison by suicide were adjudged guilty. Those who died of natural causes or maltreatment had their processes carried on as if they were alive. If relatives and friends would not give evidence, then the accused were declared guilty and their families suffered the subsequent ignominy. Bodies in effigy were burned at *autos*. The Inquisition could convict for a fault committed forty years beforehand and take bones from graves and burn them.[81]

It has been said that the Inquisition was no harsher than the secular arm of the law at the time. A readiness to resort to execution was certainly a general feature of the law, and popular enjoyment of executions was not confined to those for religious causes. Still, the Inquisition itself recognized that its methods infringed safeguards for the accused accepted during that period. In his *Regimento* of 1774, the inquisitor general, Cardinal Cunha, referred to the 1640 *Regimento* and said that the latter contained 'errors' against natural rights and the legal customs of the time. Those 'errors' were enumerated as being:

a) Hiding from the accused names of his/her accusers and anything by which they could be identified. It was against the Ordenações Filipinas then in practice as the code of law in Portugal.

b) The condemning of an accused because of a single testimony unsubstantiated by three legal statements referring to the crime, the place, the time, then considered to be essential rights.

c) Use of torture which was not authorised by the Ordenações and had been abolished by unwritten law.

d) The disgrace imposed on all people who had been through the Holy Office, even when absolved, which was against both holy and human law.

e)The accused could not seek redress of the crown.[82]

The Inquisition was able to operate in a manner not in accordance with contemporary legal custom simply because there were no possible external constraints on its power in Portugal. The threat of excommunication it wielded, and the horror of its prisons, ensured everyone's obedience to its dictates.

4

The War of 1650 and the Six Articles

In spite of the ancient alliance, in 1650 a state of war existed between England and Portugal. In common with most of Europe, the Portuguese had been horrified at the execution of Charles I in January 1649, but John IV had extended *de facto* recognition to the Commonwealth by continuing to trade with England. However, he found it impossible to remain neutral in the English civil war after the arrival in Lisbon of a fleet of Royalist ships under the command of Prince Rupert, Charles II's cousin, which was followed in March 1650 by the arrival of a Commonwealth fleet under the command of General-at-sea, Robert Blake.[1] John IV's policy towards the Commonwealth was overborne in the Council of State by those who considered that to break with the Stuarts would be to attack royalty itself and repudiate legitimacy and order.[2]

Accordingly, although Rupert behaved like a pirate and attacked Commonwealth shipping off the coast of Portugal, he was welcomed and given every assistance.[3] His proceedings finally brought protests from Pedro Vieira da Silva, the Portuguese secretary of state, who told him that whilst John IV did not wish to prejudice the king of Great Britain, he did not want to prejudice his own kingdom either. Trade with the Commonwealth was essential for Portugal, as disruption of trade meant no money from the customs. There were many Englishmen in Portugal, and Portugal needed English ships because of the war with Spain.[4] The problem was that Rupert attacked English ships using the excuse that they did not acknowledge the royal standard flown on his own ships, but had they so acknowledged Rupert's ships, they would have been liable to confiscation in English ports where their cargoes were obtained or conveyed.[5]

Blake brought out with him Charles Vane of the Committee of the Admiralty and the Navy, who was to be the Agent for the Commonwealth in Portugal. The latter appointment had been made at the suggestion of the Portugal merchants in London.[6] He was put ashore in Cascais, but when Blake's fleet endeavoured to enter the mouth of the Tagus, the forts were ordered to fire on his ships. He succeeded in entering, and anchored in the Bay of Oeiras, blocking the exit of the river. From then on, although the Portuguese continued to negotiate with Vane, Blake was carefully denied supplies, victuals and water.[7]

Rupert's men seized three of Blake's crew and imprisoned them on their own ships.[8] On 10/20 April, an attempt was made to plant a bomb on the *Leopard*, the vice-admiral's ship, and Blake's men were attacked ashore.[9] Blake allowed the Portuguese squadron bound for India to sail on 21 April,[10] but because it was apparent that John IV was forming a Portuguese armada up river with Rupert's ships, when the Brazil fleet sailed on 21/31 May 1650, Blake picked off nine merchantmen as they cleared the Tagus, and added them to his fleet. These were English ships, freighted by the Portuguese; Blake removed their captains and reshuffled the crews, putting his own men on every one of them.[11] It was Blake's duty to do this because armed conflict seemed near, and under his instructions he had the right to dispose of English shipping as he thought fit. However the Portuguese were enraged. On 26 May/5 June, Blake was reinforced by the arrival at Cascais of General-at-sea Edward Popham, with nine vessels.[12]

During these events, Blake and Vane had continued to have discussions and negotiations with Portuguese government representatives,[13] but whilst holding the talks, John IV had issued orders to the governors of Madeira, Azores, Aveiro, Viana and Porto to detain all English ships found in their areas on any pretext; to keep an eye on the English merchants and to make inventories of all English property.[14] Vane was dismayed when he saw Popham on board the *Resolution* and read the latter's instructions, i.e., to demand the delivery of Rupert's ships and to attack if the Portuguese refused. Vane never returned to shore but sailed back to England.[15] On Sunday, 2/12 June 1650, at 10 a.m., all English ships and property in Portugal and the dominions were finally confiscated and the merchants and seamen imprisoned.[16] The confiscations contravened the spirit of the 18th article of the 1642 treaty, which stipulated that if anything should arise between Portugal and England which might occasion the interruption of commerce and correspondence between their subjects, public advice thereof should be given to the subjects of both sides, allowing two years to transport their merchandize and goods.[17] Doubtless this treaty proviso did not disturb John IV because he would always be able to maintain that the treaty had been made between himself and Charles I, and not between himself and the government in England.

There were perhaps sixty English merchantmen in Portuguese metropolitan ports at that time, and nine or more ships were with the Brazil fleet in Bahia. English merchants had property on Portuguese ships, as well as ashore.[18] In Lisbon itself, all but seven merchants, who had shown themselves to be violently Royalist in sympathy, were arrested.[19] The Commonwealth government retaliated (thereby also contravening Article 18), by arresting all Portuguese merchants in London, New Christians, practising Jews and refugees from the

Inquisition, confiscating their property and putting them in the Marshalsea prison. This involved only fifteen persons, however, whose property was negligible by comparison.[20] On Monday, 3/13 June, Blake seized thirteen fishing vessels.[21]

John IV had obviously appreciated that the result of his order to confiscate English property would lead to a blockade of Lisbon and other Portuguese ports, and he had taken what counter-measures he could, as is shown in letters he wrote to the governors of Setúbal, Madeira, S. Miguel and the Islands, the Algarve, Terceira, Brazil and Viana.[22] None the less, hostilities with England, as well as war with Spain and renewed Dutch attacks on Portuguese shipping, could not be supported by Portugal at that time. Between 1647 and 1648 alone, Portugal had lost 249 ships because of Dutch attacks.[23] While Blake's fleet patrolled the coast of Portugal, food supplies in Lisbon dwindled and prices soared.[24] No ships were freighted for Brazil.[25] John IV had sent orders to Brazil to the effect that the returning sugar fleet should delay sailing and not arrive before January 1651, but twenty sugar ships from Rio did sail, convoyed by three men-of-war.[26] Only eleven ships escaped from the attacks made on the convoy by Blake, Popham and the Zeeland privateers.[27] On board the seven prizes taken by Blake were four thousand chests of sugar and four hundred men. Most of the sugar belonged to English merchants, and had just been confiscated by the Portuguese.[28]

As soon as Prince Rupert and his fleet had sailed from Lisbon on 12/22 October 1650,[29] John IV decided to send an envoy to London because he wanted to remedy the ill-feeling between England and Portugal. He chose Dr João de Guimarães, an advocate of the High Court of Appeal, who had been Portuguese resident in Sweden from 1643–49.[30] Guimarães was to be accompanied by a priest named Manuel Pinto, who was being sent to England to give support to English Catholics, and 'even convert some who are not Catholics, if God allows it'.[31] On 22 November and 5 December, instructions were sent to the governors of Madeira and Terceira, to free their English prisoners, provided that they posted bond and made no attempt to leave the kingdom. Their property was, however, not returned to them.[32]

Guimarães' instructions have not been preserved, but his letters of credence gave him power to negotiate with Parliament regarding all matters concerning the arrival of the Royalist fleet in Portugal, and also, if necessary, to confirm the treaty of amity and commerce between the two nations. The envoy was not given a specific rank, because it was thought that if he were unsuccessful in his mission, the effect would be less serious for Portuguese prestige than it would be if he were an ambassador.[33] John IV clearly did not wish to admit that a state of war existed between England and Portugal, because by so doing, he would have recognized the legitimacy of the regime in England. Further, by releasing the prisoners and acting as if war did not exist, John IV hoped that he could persuade England that peace was already in being and only needed to be confirmed. The rulers of the Commonwealth were not impressed by John IV's tactics. They were just as anxious for full recognition as rulers as John IV was to be acknowledged as king of Portugal. The exact date of Guimarães' arrival in Southampton is not known, but on 15/25 December he wrote to Parliament announcing that he had come to treat for the preservation and confirmation of the ancient peace between England and Portugal, and to remove the obstacles which by defect of ministers, rather than by the consent of the king or Parliament, had lately happened.[34] Even before he wrote that letter, however, on 13/23 December, the Council of State had sent orders to the governors of Portsmouth and Southampton asking that he be put under guard. 'There is a person come from Portugal, pretending to be sent as a public person from the king there to Parliament here'.[35] In Parliament's letter to Guimarães, he was asked to advise whether he came as an ambassador or agent and to send a copy of his credentials. Then Parliament came straight to the point and said:

> Not seeing any mention of power to treat touching satisfaction for past injuries and damage done whereof this Commonwealth has just cause to complain, we therefore desire to know whether you have power in that behalf upon signification whereof we shall proceed to give you further answer.[36]

On 24 December/3 January 1650/1, the Council of State informed Blake of Guimarães' arrival, but ordered him to ignore it and prosecute his former instructions to seize Portuguese prizes at sea.[37] The Council realized that there would be no hope of obtaining any compensation unless the threat to Portugal were maintained. Captain William Penn's squadron, therefore, sailed from Falmouth on 20/30 December 1650, to attack the Portuguese at sea. It took thirty-six prizes in the Atlantic.[38]

At the Council of State meeting on 10/20 February 1650/1, Guimarães was presented with six preliminary articles to which the Council wanted an affirmative answer before they would even begin negotiations:

1. All Englishmen in prison should be released.
2. All ships and goods which had been seized should be restored and reparations made for losses and damages to the owners.
3. Those responsible for killing English seamen in Portugal and who had tried to blow up the ship *Leopard* should be brought to justice.

4. Portugal should pay the cost of the fleets sent to pursue Rupert, estimated at £214,000 (later reduced to £180,000 by Parliament who agreed to take into account the value of Blake's prizes).
5. Portugal should make restitution for goods seized by Prince Rupert.
6. Portugal should pay compensation for English ships sold by Rupert in Portugal.[39]

During subsequent negotiations, Guimarães assumed that the six articles were the basis of a peace, and that once he had accepted them peace would exist. If the English wished to insist on a treaty with commercial clauses, he would accept the 1642 treaty immediately, with one or two additional articles if so desired.[40] This was unacceptable and rejected by Parliament, which considered measures to help the prisoners and to capture more Portuguese prizes.[41] Guimarães' mission failed, and he returned to Portugal in June 1651.[42] How far the two countries were from understanding each other is seen from a letter sent to Guimarães by John IV, in which he states that the losses of merchants were not matters that ought to enter into the accord between the two countries.[43] None the less, the imprisonments and confiscations in Portugal affected all English ships and crews and all merchants and their stocks, regardless of whether they were known to be Commonwealth men or not. The Commonwealth's actions are understandable when the extent of the confiscations and damage done to merchants and seamen is appreciated.

Treatment meted out to the imprisoned merchants was unacceptably hard even by seventeenth century practices. For instance, Richard Beare or Beere was put into solitary confinement in Santarem, fifty miles from Lisbon, and George Lane was for five months in the castle of the Knights of the Order of Christ at Tomar, ninety miles away from his home in Lisbon.[44] So imprisoned, they could not do business through merchants of other nationalities, which in cases of imprisonment was then the custom. It is likely that their wives and families would have been left without support, for there were only two avenues of charity for Englishmen in Portugal at that time. One was the 'poor box', or 'contribution fund', run by the Englishmen themselves, the funds for which were obtained by payments of a percentage of their trade and controlled by the Treasurer of the factory.[45] The other was the Catholic church. The first had ceased to operate after the confiscations and imprisonments, and the second was not available to those who wished to remain Protestants. Credit at interest could only have been obtained against collateral, and all the merchants' trading stocks and household goods had been impounded. It is not known whether compensation was claimed specifically for this aspect of the affair as records of what transpired during negotiations are not detailed enough. Theoretically, the merchants' assets were only confiscated, and bonds for their release could have been taken from those assets, but how were poor seamen, whose pay was always in arrears, to manage? There is evidence that even established merchants needed help, because the bonds for the release of John Bushell and Richard Beare were given by John Mules, an Englishman born, who was a subject of the king of Portugal, having lived there for thirty years and who was married to a Portuguese woman. He was a Catholic and was always kind and courteous to Parliament's friends in prison.[46]

The Portuguese also confiscated ships in Oporto, the Azores, Madeira and elsewhere in their dominions, and John IV's instructions regarding the confiscations were followed minutely. Inventories of ships and equipment were drawn up and included even the cooking utensils in the galleys. The heaviest losses in the Bahia sequestration were suffered by the Bushell brothers, who lost at least the recorded 216 chests of sugar but probably lost more unrecorded chests, as masters are known to have hidden cargo books.[47] The Bushells were men of importance to the Commonwealth government, for when Blake sailed for Lisbon in 1650, he had, among other funds, letters of credit worth £10,000, partly arranged through Edward Bushell.[48]

The merchants of Bristol all together reported £5,630 in direct losses.[49] The total claim of London merchants for losses of all kinds was £140,839. 10. 6d.[50] As the items confiscated were carefully recorded and ordered to be kept safely, the imprisoned men should have had all their goods returned to them on their release in November/December 1650, but it was not until 8 January 1652 (N.S.) that the Treasury Council advised John IV to begin returning the properties to their owners, and even then, it was not until 22 June 1652 that the king wrote to the governor of Oporto to restore all goods to their rightful owners.[51] Naturally, in the meantime, impounded goods disappeared, deteriorated and dwindled. It was hard, if not impossible, to control authorities in the islands and other towns in Portugal. The governor of Madeira helped himself to English property,[52] and John IV was not averse to using the sequestrated English money to send two ships to Angola to fight the Dutch. It would be replaced, he said, but he countermanded the order three weeks later,[53] when the Commonwealth government was demanding the return of the goods before negotiating a peace.

England had not sought the war with Portugal, but the Portuguese support for Rupert and the nature and manner of the confiscations, made war inevitable. In Portugal it was openly admitted that the confiscations were carried out for economic as well as political reasons.[54] It is unlikely that Portugal ever seriously intended to return well-gunned English ships, for instance. Merchants were always well informed, and they must have been aware of the advice being given to John IV, which would have been communicated to the Portugal merchants in London and to the Commonwealth government. It is therefore not surprising that Guimarães met with such a chilly reception.

England's stature among the nations was growing. On 3 September 1650 (O.S.), Cromwell had won the Battle of Dunbar. On 3 September 1651 (O.S.), Charles I was defeated at the Battle of Worcester, and the royalist cause was seen by everyone to have failed. Furthermore, it was obvious that England's sea power was increasing rapidly.[55] These facts no doubt played their part in persuading John IV to sign a decree on 10 January 1652 (N.S.), authorising the return of sequestered properties.[56]

Relations between Englishmen and Portuguese in Portugal gradually improved, though claims for damages continued to reach the Council of State in England. In the summer of 1652, John IV decided to send his chamberlain (*Camareiro Mór*), Dom João de Sá e Menezes, Conde de Penaguião, to England with the style of ambassador extraordinary. The Conde left Lisbon prepared to sign articles regarding compensation prior to negotiating a treaty of peace.[57] He reached Plymouth on 11/21 August 1652, and on 17/27 August, Parliament issued an order welcoming him to England.[58] Penaguião was received by Parliament on 30 September/10 October at 11 a.m. and delivered his speech in Portuguese,[59] handing an English copy to the Speaker. From that speech, it was clear that the Portuguese attitude to preceding events had in fact changed very little. The Conde said that Portugal was not to blame as far as her intentions were concerned, and errors of commanders on both sides were the cause of complaints and offences. The plundering of the Portuguese fleet had so enraged the people that they could not have been restrained by either reason or force without the compensation that was demanded, so that what appeared to be a wrong was really a remedy: the imprisonment of the merchants and the sequestrations of their goods had, in fact, prevented the murder of the one and the robbing of the other. Satisfaction had been made for their losses and injuries, and the English in Portugal now enjoyed their liberty, freedom from taxation, their privileges and their property, and their ships and goods had been restored to them.

It was true that the order for the return of the confiscated goods had been promulgated in June 1652, but there is no evidence that the English merchants had feared attacks by the populace in May/June 1650. No satisfaction had been made for losses and injuries done to Englishmen, and though they had their liberty, they had not received all their property back and their ships had certainly not been returned to them. The English government was still being petitioned for unsettled claims in 1680. In any event, it became clear that Portugal was looking for room to negotiate regarding the six articles, and even John IV was prepared to accept them if necessary as the price of peace with England. Penaguião finally signed the articles on 5/15 January 1653.[60]

There was no change in the terms of any of the articles, except Article 4. Under that article, a lesser figure of £50,000 was to be paid in instalments. The sum of £20,000, or its equivalent in Portuguese money, was to be paid in Lisbon on 1 March, or within one month after the presentation in Lisbon of the ambassador's bill obligatory, whichever was the earlier; £15,000 was to be paid in English currency on 31 July 1653 (O.S.), and £15,000 was to be paid in English currency on 1 November 1653 (O.S.) in London.[61]

The signing of the Six Articles was a diplomatic victory for the Commonwealth, but the Conde de Penaguião had carried out a difficult mission with skill and diplomacy. Not only had he had to deal with a resentful Commonwealth government, he had also had to counteract the deliberate efforts of the Spanish ambassador, Cárdenas, to prevent any agreement being reached. Whether or not Sir Henry Vane was a pensioner of Spain, as was reported by the Genoese representative in London,[62] other parliamentarians were said to have been recipients of gifts by Cárdenas. Between October 1650 and March 1651, his secret accounts indicate that he distributed gifts worth £945 in Parliament, with the help of the Master of Ceremonies, Sir Oliver Fleming. Many gifts of wine were also distributed.[63]

Although Portugal released all the prisoners as required under Article 1, the released prisoners' goods were not all restored to them, nor were reparations made in accordance with the provisions of Article 2. There is no known record that those responsible for the killing of English seamen in Portugal and who tried to blow up the *Leopard* were brought to justice (Article 3). The restitutions to be made by Portugal regarding the goods seized by Rupert and the compensation payable for English ships sold by Rupert in Portugal (Articles 5 and 6) were never finalized. Portugal never made any payment under Article 4 until forced to do so at gun-point in 1656. However, the signing of the Six Preliminary Articles put an end to the hostilities at sea, and enabled negotiations for a treaty of peace and commerce to proceed.

5

The Making and Ratification
of the 1654 Treaty

i The Negotiations

After the signing of the Six Preliminary Articles on 5/15 January 1653, negotiations began for a new treaty between England and Portugal. Because the balance of trade was in England's favour; because the Portugal trade gave England access to Portuguese colonies in America, Africa and Asia, and because it encouraged the development of English shipping, the Portugal merchants found themselves in such a strong position that only the Spanish trade lobby opposed the making of a treaty with Portugal. Portugal's political and economic position was fully understood by the Portugal merchants: the country was economically dependent on colonial products needing transport to Portugal; and because of the patterns of trade built up over the centuries, Portugal was largely dependent on England for textiles, wheat and dried cod from Newfoundland. By the time the negotiations began, Portugal had also come to rely on freighting English vessels for use in the Brazil trade.[1] Portugal badly needed an ally strong at sea and able to protect her economic lifelines and long coastline. The principal sea powers in Europe at that time were the Dutch, French, Spanish and English. The Dutch, who were doing their utmost to sink Portuguese ships outside European waters, and the Spanish were Portugal's enemies, whilst France was proving unwilling to enter a firm alliance with Portugal: until Mazarin achieved peace with Spain, France found it necessary not to offend her Dutch allies. Thus an alliance with England was a necessity. Besides, England in 1653 was at war with the Dutch and her seamen could always be relied upon to stand and fight them in encounters at sea. That was one of the chief reasons why the Portuguese preferred to freight English ships.[2]

The Conde de Penaguião was therefore presented with a list of thirty-eight articles for consideration and negotiation.[3] The articles are too detailed to have been drawn up by anyone not entirely familiar with the Portugal trade. The list of suggestions included privileges which the English had long enjoyed by royal grant and *foral*, but which, as has been seen, where frequently withheld. These were the privileges known as the 'Charter of the English', and which were also enjoyed by other nations in Portugal. Doubtless, in view of Portugal's political and economic difficulties, it was considered the right time to press for the inclusion of previously granted privileges in a treaty, so that in future they might be better observed. The occasion was taken to press for new privileges also.

The first article on the list, in fact, had been asked for in 1641 and had been refused. It requested that Englishmen be allowed to exercise their religion freely in all the ports and places where they resided in Portugal and its dominions, and that in those places a convenient piece of land should be appointed for the burial of their dead. It also requested that Englishmen be free from molestation for their English bibles and for religious books by the Inquisition or any person or tribunal whatsoever. Another article asked that they be freed of all the powers of the Inquisition, and if their debtors were seized by the Inquisition, those debts should be paid within two months of arrest. If English merchants had previously sold goods to Portuguese merchants later taken by the Inquisition, the Portuguese merchants' debts (owing to the credit system of trading) could not be recouped by the English merchants, unless the *fisco* could be persuaded to settle the English merchants' accounts. It was seen in Chapter 3 that even the king was unable to obtain his share of the confiscations from the *fisco*, so it is not surprising that the English merchants were always unsuccessful.[4] Provision to cover this contingency had been made in Article 6 of the 1642 treaty, but the time allowed had been one year.[5] The merchants also wished to be freed from the necessity of contributing to the old guild chapel of St George, in the church of São Domingos, because as Protestants they no longer wished to contribute to a Catholic chapel.

The merchants wanted a number of personal freedoms which they had enjoyed by right of royal decree and *foral* for a long time. These included: no arrest or imprisonment without the consent of the judge conservator; ability to buy and sell and possess houses, warehouses and other property without hindrance; the bearing of arms; owning and riding of horses; freedom to disregard provisions of local sumptuary laws and to decline service under the Portuguese king.

With reference to commerce, the merchants wanted special safeguards regarding the payment of customs duties, taxes, harbour and wharfage fees, etc., and they wished harbour fees to be graded according to the size of the ship. They wanted provision to be made so that English vessels should not be compulsorily loaded or unloaded or freighted without the consent of their owners, and requested that Portugal should be obliged to freight English ships and only English ships. If a third party happened to take Portuguese prizes to England or English prizes to Portugal, they wanted them to be returned to their owners. They wished to have free and unrestricted trade in all parts of Portugal and the Portuguese empire, without the necessity of obtaining special licences which were normally demanded to allow ships to sail to Brazil and other colonies. They also wanted to be able to return from the Portuguese colonies to England direct, without having to call at Portugal first.

A request was made that the English should be assessed for duty at the same rate as Portuguese merchants, that is 23%, and that they should not be charged the same duty twice if their vessels visited more than one port. This request was not surprising, as Portuguese taxes were extremely high. A merchant shipping goods to Lisbon paid 23% duty on them on arrival. Then he had to purchase a licence to go to Brazil. On re-exporting the goods to Brazil, where they would be sold to purchase the sugar or other return cargo, a re-export tax of 3% had to be paid. A tax of 10% was payable in Bahia or Rio. On arrival back in Lisbon, a further 23% duty had to be paid, together with an additional 3% re-export tax before being able to carry the goods to England, where further duties were payable.[6]

On being presented with these requests, the ambassador protested, on 7 February 1653 (O.S.), that he must again emphasize that he was not in England to construct a completely new treaty, but only to ratify the peace.[7] He maintained that free trade in the Portuguese dominions could only be conceded by Cortes, (an institution comprising the three estates of clergy, nobles and people, which theoretically had to consent to the revocation of laws, although the power to make new laws lay with the Crown). Trade with Brazil was regulated by the Brazil Company and a treaty could not abrogate its rights and privileges.[8] He argued that there had been no war between England and Portugal in India, so that the Goa Convention of 20 January 1635 still applied. Regarding Africa and the Islands, no more rights than those enjoyed already under the 1642 treaty could be given. He denied that Portuguese harbour charges were excessive and averred that as Portuguese merchants in England paid 10% more than English merchants in customs duties in England, the English merchants in Portugal should be satisfied at being taxed at the same rate as other nations.[9] He maintained that the request that only English ships should be freighted was impossible, as it was contrary to the request that none be freighted without the consent of their owners. There would be insufficient English ships unless they were freighted forcibly. Regarding the request for religious freedoms, he said these could not be increased without the consent of the pope and the church. The king of Portugal had no authority in such matters and was bound by canon law. Restrictions on Protestant worship were for the protection of Protestants because the populace was quick to take offence in religious matters. He considered that merchants should wait for at least a year for payment of debts owed to Englishmen by Portuguese taken by the Inquisition.[10] In other words, the ambassador argued for the status quo. Portugal's position had not changed with regard to the proposed treaty since the departure of Guimarães in June 1651. Portugal was clearly standing out against requests for religious privileges, and did not want previously granted privileges (other than those incorporated in the 1642 treaty), to be given treaty status.

Continuing pressure from the English negotiators made the ambassador advise the Council of State that the treaty was ready to sign and that he would be returning soon to Portugal.[11] Presumably this was a way of intimating that Portugal was not prepared to cede anything further. Then he asked for assistance in securing a ship to facilitate his departure.[12] On 6/16 June 1653, the Council of State had a full discussion on the Portugal question. All counsellors who could attend did so, and it was decided to hold firm, because it was believed that the ambassador was bluffing.[13] This was a wise decision. On 10/20 June 1653, orders were given for a frigate to be prepared,[14] and the *Nonesuch* was ready by 13/23 July.[15] Then the ambassador began to give ground, saying that the question of the 23% tax would have to be referred to the king and, if included in the treaty, would have to be in a secret article.[16]

Something of the importance which the Portuguese treaty had for the Council of State can be gauged from the fact that their meeting on 6/16 June took place in the midst of the Battle of Gabbard Sands, which was fought from 2/12–12/22 June, when Blake, Monk, Deane, Penn and Lawson utterly defeated De Ruyter.[17] The Dutch representative in London wrote to their High and Mighty Lordships in The Hague on 24 June/4 July, saying that the Portuguese ambassador had excelled in lighting fireworks to celebrate the English victory.[18] Although unyielding over the treaty, the Council was conciliatory to the ambassador himself and to his brother. The latter, D. Pantaleão de Sá e Menezes, was allowed to send 250 horses to Portugal. As a favour, because wheat was an item of strategic importance, permission was given for the export of 1,000 quarters of wheat, provided that the price in England was not more than 3s. a bushel.[19] Even more remarkable was the fact that the ambassador was allowed to import, between 10/20 August and 9/19 December 1653, free of all customs, seventy-one chests of sugar, together with three boxes of fruits and sweetmeats, seven boxes of bacon and sweetmeats, twelve boxes of oranges, three cases of bottled sweet water, three boxes of perfume and two pipes of wine.[20] Seventy-one chests of sugar would have been over 45,000 lbs in weight. It is not known what type of sugar was imported, but the average retail price of sugar in London at that time was one shilling per pound,[21] so the sugar would have been worth £2,250 and perhaps more. This concession may have been made because no remittances were sent by Portugal to the ambassador. His difficulties over debts later became the subject of an enquiry in the Council of State.[22]

Meanwhile, the method of examining claims of merchants and seamen under the provisions of the Six Articles was also being discussed. The Council of State wanted the claims determined in London by a board consisting of an equal number of Portuguese and Englishmen. The ambassador appointed Jerónimo da Silva de Azevedo (Secretary to the legation), Francisco Fereira Rebelo (Portuguese Agent) and Vitalem de Souza, a lawyer,[23] to the board, but he wanted the claims determined in Lisbon, for he thought that although seeming and feigned proofs which might serve some particular purpose could be produced in England, legal proof could only be found in Portugal.[24] This was assuredly to cast doubts on the veracity of the claimants. It is not clear what he meant by 'legal', but it is presumed that he inferred that claims could only be certified correct in Portugal. The claimants also had a right to be suspicious of a Portuguese certification, for who in Portugal would have been sufficiently detached to act as a fairer mediator than could be found in England? In any case, the merchants always kept careful records; their books were forwarded to London and were always accepted as evidence in Chancery Proceedings. The official inventories were in Lisbon, but copies were forwarded to London, thus both sides were able to present their case with adequate evidence. Had the claims been determined in Portugal, it is doubtful whether more than a small number of claimants could have afforded the costs involved in travelling to and staying in Portugal whilst their claims were adjudged.

It was at this stage of the negotiations that two serious connected incidents occurred (on 21 November/1 December and 22 November/2 December 1653) at the New Exchange in the Strand, involving the ambassador's brother, Dom Panteleão de Sá e Menezes. In the first incident Pantaleão and his friends severely wounded two men, and in the second they killed another. Pantaleão was beheaded in the Tower on 10/20 July 1654 for his part in the affrays. The affair was a *cause célébre* at the time, and is well documented.[25] In the context of the treaty negotiations between England and Portugal, however, all that needs to be said is that the concern of the Portuguese king to secure the release of Pantaleão and the other Portuguese arrested with him, took second place to the conclusion of a treaty with England. A costly peace treaty with a friendly England was better for Portugal than a more costly war with a hostile England, particularly since the signing of the Anglo-Dutch treaty of 5/15 April 1654 opened up the prospect of greater Dutch depredations on Portuguese shipping. The Portuguese realized that a treaty with England would preclude an Anglo-Spanish alliance. Moreover, although the Pantaleão affair may have moved the Portugal merchants to petition for his release,[26] there is no evidence of a concerted effort on their part either to influence the course of justice, or to ingratiate themselves with the Portuguese by moderating their demands. In the event, they seem to have taken the correct measure of Portugal's need for a treaty of alliance with England, and there is no evidence that English merchants in Portugal suffered any difficulties as a result of the trial and execution of Pantaleão.

The treaty was signed at 8 a.m. on 10/20 July, a few hours before Pantaleão's execution, to enable Penaguião to leave London before sentence was carried out. He went to Gravesend to await a vessel for his return to Portugal.[27] On 18/28 July, Cromwell instructed the commander of the frigate conveying him home to treat him with all courtesy and to give him the best conveniences and accommodation on his ship, also every honour and respect due to 'a person of so great quality as he is'.[28] Cromwell's concern and sympathy for Penaguião doubtless stemmed from the fact that he was privy to the knowledge that before his death Pantaleão had written to Cárdenas, the Spanish Ambassador, saying that he considered himself to be a Spaniard (*soy Hispano*). Thus he was a traitor to Portugal.[29]

ii *The Ratification*

For Cromwell, the treaty signed with Portugal was part of a wider scheme. Its signature marked the end of England's non-alignment policy. Because Article 1 forbade either party from adhering to any war, counsel or treaty to the damage of the other, England could no longer enter into the sort of treaty being sought by Spain, as Spain was at war with Portugal.[30] On the other hand, England had become aligned with French interests because France, too, was already at war with Spain. This was deliberate on Cromwell's part. The feasibility of using the large numbers of English ships and soldiers available in what came to be called the Western Design, had been under discussion for some time.[31] The plan was opposed by General Lambert in the Council of State and by the Spanish merchants.[32] For decades, Spain had been linked by treaty with England, and yet had carried on active warfare against English trade and shipping in American and West Indian waters.[33] Cromwell now proposed to do the same; to fight a war against Spain in the West Indies, without declaring war in Europe. The risk of losing trade was not so great, even if open warfare did ensue, as in fact it did in the autumn of 1655. Alastair McFadyan has shown that Cromwell and the Council were well aware that trade could be continued in war time, albeit with difficulty and with some injury to the English merchants in Spain.[34] The use of Portuguese ports was essential for the implementation of such a policy, because only Lisbon and Cadiz in the south of Europe on the Atlantic littoral had facilities for servicing fleets all the year round. They both had safe anchorage for many vessels, facilities for careening, graving, tallowing and repairing, and supplies of rigging, cordage, sail-cloth, timber, pitch and masts. Most importantly, each had a colony of English merchants to change sterling into local currency and advance large sums of credit to an English fleet when necessary. As Cromwell proposed to attack Spanish America, it was vital that Lisbon should be available to the Protectorate fleet.

Article 28 of the treaty allowed six months for its ratification. It soon became clear, however, that John IV had no intention of ratifying the treaty as it stood. Furthermore, no progress was being made regarding the compensation payable under the terms of Article 25, to cover the losses incurred by the confiscations of English property by Portugal during 1650. On 20 January 1655 (N.S.), John IV published a decree to the effect that half the customs paid by the English in the customs at Lisbon was to be deposited in the hands of two English merchants (to be named by the English), who were to give receipts to the customs for money so received. The money was not to be paid out until the publication of the peace treaty. The merchants objected. Why was the half-custom limited to Lisbon? What about the other ports? What about the tax for the large trade in cod fish, which was paid *in specie* and did not pass through the customs? Specific mention of English merchants absolved Scots and Irish from paying, but they were members of the Commonwealth. The beneficiaries under Article 25 wished repayment to begin from the date of the decree and not from the date of the publication of the treaty. Ship owners complained that under the king's decree, it would take more than twenty years to settle the debts.[35]

It was at this juncture that Thomas Maynard, who was to figure prominently in Anglo-Portuguese relations for the next thirty-four years, is first known to have been officially employed on government business. According to Captain Henry Hatsell, the naval shore captain at Plymouth, Maynard was sent to Portugal as Cromwell's agent in July 1655, with a letter to John IV urging him to ratify the treaty.[36] Cromwell had doubtless sent him out to Portugal because, instead of ratifying the treaty as signed by Penaguião, John IV had sent back to England what Cromwell later called 'a pretended ratification of a treaty, so different from what was agreed by his ambassador, that it was quite another thing'. Unfortunately it is not known how John IV changed the treaty.[37] Maynard returned to England on 11 September, with a reply from John IV which was read in the Council on 12 September.[38] Again, there is no record of the contents of that communication, but, writing from Cascais on board the *George* in August, Blake said that he understood that Maynard had been dismissed by the king without any answer but that the king would send a reply by a minister of his own.[39] If that is indeed what happened to Cromwell's agent, then it was a churlish reception. It also made it plain that the Portuguese intended nothing but delays, now that England had become committed politically to an anti-Spanish policy.

A warrant was issued on 25 September 1655 for the payment to Maynard of £200 in remuneration for his services and to cover his expenses.[40] In November, he was reporting shipping movements to Thurloe from Plymouth, and he took the opportunity to ask that if and when the peace was concluded with Portugal, he should be given the place of consul and be made responsible for the repair of any ships of the fleet in need of it in Portuguese waters.[41]

The need to ratify the treaty became even more pressing because, committed to the Western Design, the government was also facing considerable economic problems. There was trouble in the fleet, several captains laying down their commissions and refusing to act any more. There was difficulty in manning ships: the crews of Blake's fleet, for example, had received no pay in twenty months' sea service; sums due to wives and families had not been paid either. Even prize money stayed with officials or was detained in the service of the state. Merchants complained bitterly of having suffered great financial losses by reason of ships attacked by privateers, especially in the Straits and near the Bay of Biscay.[42] At the Council meeting of 23 October, Cárdenas was told to leave the country within four days, and England declared war on Spain.[43] On 13 December, the Council decided to advise the Protector to send another agent to Portugal, and on 19/29 February, they recommended for the post Philip Meadows, one of Cromwell's secretaries.[44] It was intended that he should go to Portugal to persuade the Portuguese to pay the £50,000 due under the terms of the Six Articles, and to obtain the ratification of the treaty. Ten to fourteen days later, a great fleet was to be sent out to add naval pressure to his persuasive powers.[45] A fleet of forty-eight ships (about a third of the navy) was assembled under the command of Generals Robert Blake and Edward Montague, later Earl of Sandwich. The size of the fleet showed the importance placed by the Protectorate government on a ratification of the treaty. The fleet sailed on 16/26 March and arrived off Cabo da Roca, to the north of Cascais, on 5/15 April 1656. From there, a frigate carried a friendly letter from Cromwell to John IV, to be given to him by Meadows, who had sailed to Portugal some five days earlier than the fleet on the frigate *Phoenix* from Plymouth.[46] The fleet then sailed on immediately to harry shipping off Cadiz.

On 6/16 April, Meadows wrote to Cromwell, enclosing a reply from John IV, declining to ratify the treaty or to pay the £50,000 without further discussion, and expressing the wish to refer Articles 6 and 14 to the pope.[47] These were the two articles of which the Inquisition disapproved. Article 6 was really designed to ensure that seamen, of which there was a great shortage, did not abscond in Portuguese ports. Seamen knew that if they declared that they wished to become Catholics, the Inquisition would not allow them to be returned to heretic vessels, so when desperate they frequently resorted to that ploy. It was also designed to stop the Portuguese from poaching English seamen. Perhaps because Penaguião understood the true reason for the article, he had agreed to it in his letter to the Council of 20 April 1654.[48] Article 14 gave Englishmen the right to enjoy Protestant worship on their ships and in their homes, and the right to a burial ground. That article had never been specifically agreed by Portugal until the actual signing of the treaty on 10/20 July 1654. Both Articles had been discussed and commented on by various religious bodies in Portugal in 1653/4, when all agreed that they were unacceptable.[49] Penaguião had constantly averred that John IV did not have the power to give such a concession. None the less, Portugal needed the alliance desperately, and Penaguião signed the treaty on the king's behalf, having been instructed to do so, perhaps, by the Marquês de Niza, John IV's ambassador extraordinary.[50] Penaguião's credentials show that John IV gave him all power to act for and in his name, to negotiate, contract and assent to and sign a treaty of peace with the Republic, on terms and conditions and in the way he thought fit; such treaty to be firm and valid as if made by himself, notwithstanding any laws, rights, directives by Cortes and customs which might be considered to be superseded thereby.[51] To people in England these powers appeared to be comprehensive; however, it should be noted that no mention was made in the credentials of conferring on Penaguião power to deal with religious matters. In 1656, with excommunication impending, the king could not afford to anger the Inquisition even more. By declining to ratify the treaty without further discussion, and by asking that Articles 6 and 14 should be referred to the pope for approval, John IV was intimating that he would not ratify the treaty as it stood. There was, after all, no pressure on Portugal to ratify, because since July 1654 the advantages of the English alliance had been enjoyed, and the £50,000 was not payable until after ratification. Committed by the treaty to an anti-Spanish alignment, Cromwell had been out-manoeuvered. It is understandable that he was enraged.

Meadows wrote to the Generals-at-sea of the difficulties which he was experiencing. He reported with evident irritation '. . . the shiftings and delays used here upon a pretended impossibility on His Majesty's part to firme these articles in the treaty relating to religion, as being a matter exempt from his secular jurisdiction'.[52]

The 'shiftings and delays' were more genuine than Meadows realized. In addition to the pressure being put upon him by the Inquisition, John IV was being urged to stand fast by Dom Francisco de Sotomaior (1590-1669), bishop of Targa *in partibus infidelium*, who was very important in the Portuguese ecclesiastical hierarchy, even if he was only a titular bishop of a non-existent diocese. The pope had not recognized Portugal's independence or John IV's right to the throne since 1640. As Portuguese bishops had died, new ones had been appointed by the king and chapters of sees, but this was not canonically correct and made it difficult to ordain priests. By 1656 the bishop of Targa had been for eleven years the only canonically instituted Portuguese Bishop. He wrote to John IV from Elvas on 12 April 1656, saying that the people of Portugal would embrace war and hostilities with the English for the purity of the faith, with joy, and peace with sadness.[53] The majority of men in his council urged the king not to ratify the treaty without alteration. The first three commissioners appointed to talk with Meadows were the secretary of state, Pedro Fernandes Monteiro, the Marquês de Niza and Penaguião. The last would certainly have been familiar with the details of the treaty, but was perhaps not the happiest of choices. These commissioners demanded guarantees against any attack on the Brazil fleet before negotiating further. Meadows replied that if they ratified the treaty the fleet would be secure; until then, it would remain at hazard. The commissioners said that unless they received the required guarantee, they would deny the fleet access to Portuguese ports. Meadows told them that would be considered an act of war.[54]

On the crucial point of religion, the Portuguese suggested that either the pope should ratify the religious articles, or Articles 7 and 17 of the 1642 treaty should be substituted for Articles 6 and 14 of the 1654 treaty.[55] To resolve the deadlock, the commissioners were replaced by the Conde de Odemira and commissioners better disposed towards the English. With good will on both sides, differences were narrowed to two points. Article 6 would be acceptable to the Portuguese if the clause compelling the return of Catholic seamen were omitted. Regarding Article 14, the Portuguese suggested that the clause 'that the English demeane themselves modestly without scandal' should be inserted. John IV assured Meadows that 'scandal' would not be extended to pervert or enervate the sense of the article: it would only apply to overt and deliberate blasphemy of the Catholic church. He maintained that if the change were not accepted, the people would expect the English to live up to it anyway, and the practice would have to be the same. When consulted by Meadows, the merchants in Lisbon agreed to both the changes. For these concessions and a promise that the fleet would not attack, John IV agreed to ratify the treaty and Preliminary Articles; accept the figure of 23% in the Secret Article; give an authority to Meadows to take back to England £50,000 and, also, £20,000 for freight demurrage of shipping. The latter sum was to be paid within two months after the exchange of instruments of ratification, and not from the half custom, as previously enacted under his *alvará* of 21 January 1655.[56]

While these negotiations were in progress, on 1/11 May, Meadows was attacked and shot in the hand whilst returning home from the Conde de Odemira's house. Because Commonwealth envoys had been murdered in Madrid and The Hague, Meadows conveyed the news to Blake and Montague merely in a postscript to his letter of 3/13 May, sending a message of caution by a merchant emissary.[57] John IV apologized to Cromwell and did what he could to trace the attackers, but they were never caught.[58] Meadows was clearly pleased with the way in which the negotiations had gone, when he wrote to the generals-at-sea on 13/23 May that he had agreed the peace. He asked them to satisfy the king of their peaceful intentions to him and his dominions, for he had engaged his faith with John IV that such security would be given to him.[59]

The difficulties inherent in poor communications were to disrupt the harmony achieved, for on 18/28 May, before any reply had been received from the generals to any of his letters, the *Sapphire* arrived in Lisbon with Maynard on board. He brought with him a letter from Cromwell with new instructions for Meadows, which he decided to issue on receipt of John IV's letter, written just after Meadows's arrival in Lisbon. The instructions in question ruined everything that had been agreed. Meadows was told to ratify the treaty taken with him to Portugal, without alterations, and to give the king five days for his reply. As he pointed out in an unhappy letter to the generals, dated 25 May/4 June, the five days were already past and he was not likely to get any satisfaction of his demands.[60]

Cromwell's reasons for sending those instructions are set out in a letter he enclosed with his instructions to generals Blake and Montague, also carried on the *Sapphire*. Referring to John IV's wish to refer Articles 6 and 14 to the pope, he wrote: '. . . we cannot have it; whereby he would bring us to an owning of the pope, which, we hope, whatever befall us, we shall not, by the grace of God be brought unto'. He considered that any alteration of Article 6 would be 'a colour for any knave to leave his duty or for Roman Catholics to seduce our men'. Accordingly, he told the generals that, consistent with the condition of the fleet under their command, they were to take, arrest and seize upon the fleet or fleets coming from the East and West Indies belonging to the king of Portugal or any of his subjects, with their guns, cash, goods and merchandise. They were to keep and detain without breaking bulk or 'imbezilment' all these things in satisfaction for the wrongs and damages which England had suffered at Portugal's hands. If the Portuguese fought, the generals were authorized to fight too, and to kill and destroy and burn. If Mr Meadows gave them assurance that satisfaction had been obtained, then these instructions were to be regarded as void.[61]

Happily, Meadows was able to advise the generals that the instruments of ratification had been exchanged at Alcântara on 31 May/10 June.[62] The whole fleet returned on 3/13 June[63] and the agreed £50,000 was despatched to England in three ships, together with the sum of £20,000. Meadows also recovered a sum of £20,000 owing to Mr Bird, an English merchant in Lisbon, in respect of the debts the Conde de Penaguião had accumulated in London.[64]

It was without doubt the threat to the Brazil fleet which persuaded the Portuguese to accept Cromwell's ultimatum. The fleet comprised 139 ships, including 36 men of war, with 4,268 soldiers and sailors and 795 guns. On board the merchantmen were sugar, tobacco, amber, ivory, slaves, ginger, gold and brazilwood, worth 9,000,000 *cruzados* (£1,500,000).[65] John IV's Armada Real was in Lisbon harbour with seven or eight warships, under the command of the Count of Vila Pouca de Aguiar, when he learned of the ultimatum.[66] He had to decide, very quickly, whether to risk all the wealth of the Brazil fleet by fighting the English fleet with the armada, or, obtain security at the price of £50,000 and ratification of a treaty with unacceptable religious clauses.

Although John IV decided to ratify the treaty, he continued to try to evade and alter Articles 6 and 14. His Jesuit confessor, Father André Fernandes, provided instructions in the art of prevarication. He suggested that the treaty should be ratified with blanks for both Articles 6 and 14 in some of the copies. For this purpose new Latin copies should be drawn up, besides the one which would go to London with the king's signature. The trusted English merchant, Christopher Warren, would carry a confidential explanation to the Portuguese resident in London and a final diplomatic effort would be made to get Cromwell's acceptance. In any case, Portuguese ecclesiastics could be shown the amended Latin copies, duly signed by the king, and given to understand that the treaty in its original form had not been and would not be accepted. The Portuguese translation of the Latin could be made to sound as innocuous as possible.[67] John IV was a willing pupil, for Portuguese manuscript versions of the treaty extant in England and Portugal, whether in Latin or in Portuguese, show that Father Fernandes' advice was followed. They contain alterations, additions and omissions, as well as spaces left for additions in the religious Articles 6 and 14.[68] No copies of the treaty were admitted to be available in Portugal to settle arguments and those which were available were considered by the then agent (1670), Francis Parry, to be scandalous, because they were so inaccurate.[69] Authenticated copies had to be obtained from London.

John IV coupled this double dealing with a further direct approach to Cromwell, to whom he wrote on 24 June 1656, saying that he could not be committed to Articles 6 and 14 as they stood. He explained that he preferred the version of the treaty suggested during the negotiations with Meadows. He wanted the removal of the phrase in Article 6 which required the compulsory return of seamen to their ships even though they claimed to be Catholics. In Article 14, the clause guaranteeing freedom of worship to merchants 'together with their families', should be extended to read 'of the same nation and religion'. The reason was that freedom of worship could not be given to Portuguese wives of English merchants or English men and women who had been Catholics. Once a Catholic, a person would ever be liable to judgement by the Inquisition, and could not revolt from it. Lastly, he wanted a scandal clause added.[70]

Cromwell replied to that letter in August 1656. He hoped that the alliance between the two countries would beget a mutual confidence, greater every day. He would be quite willing to enter into a particular treaty in order to settle the matter, either in Lisbon or in London, but '. . . the league, being now confirmed and duly sealed with the seals of both nations, to alter any part of it would be the same thing as to annul the whole; which we are certainly assured your majesty by no means desires to do'.[71] In the circumstances of 1654, it had been open to Cromwell to commit England to a Spanish alliance, a Portuguese alliance, or to remain neutral. Had he accepted the Spanish offers, or remained unaligned, it is doubtful whether Portugal would have continued to exist as a separate nation for very long. It appeared to England that John IV had accepted the treaty in 1654 to obtain Commonwealth protection for Portugal, but with no intention of ratifying it.

In Portugal, according to William Mettam, it seemed incredible that with the £50,000 ready waiting in the house of an English merchant to be despatched, Cromwell would stand out for a 'punctilio in religion'.[72] Portuguese Catholics could not understand that Protestants felt as deeply about their religion as the Portuguese did themselves, even though some of the merchants in Lisbon might not value it 'a straw'.

John IV died on 6 November 1656. He was succeeded by his son, Afonso VI, who was a minor, retarded and partly paralysed. Queen Luisa was appointed Regent, and was immediately persuaded to cancel the hated *alvará* of 6 February 1649. She and her ministers were afraid of the Inquisition and clergy who, generally, were of the Spanish faction, and they did not feel able to publish the treaty in case the religious put the people in an uproar.[73] This view was confirmed by Consul Maynard who considered that the Portuguese were delaying the publication of the treaty in the hope that Cromwell would grant them their desire for an alteration of Articles 6 and 14, because they feared the Inquisition beyond measure. 'God make them sensible of their slavish condition and give them spiritte to cast of that Yoake', he wrote.[74] The peace was not published in Lisbon until 25 March/4 April 1657, after it had been decided to send an ambassador to England.[75]

The Portuguese have generally considered themselves humiliated by this treaty.[76] To the extent that they were forced to ratify it by an ultimatum, they have reason for thinking so. Portuguese and Lusophile historians who subscribe to this view, however, have never assessed England's role in the making of the treaty, other than in the context of Portugal's needs and aspirations. John IV was a realistic, stubborn, astute and devious monarch. Portugal needed such a king at that time. In England his prevarication and double-dealing were not appreciated.

What can be called the 'treaty era' had an inauspicious beginning. The provisions of the treaty were seldom honoured by the Portuguese in practice, unless it suited them to do so. None the less, it became what was later called the Magna Carta[77] on which English traders depended for their mercantile and personal privileges in Portugal and its dominions. That this was so, was in great measure due to the work of Thomas Maynard, who, for thirty-four years as Consul (1656-60) and Consul General (1660-89) in Lisbon, was to press continuously for the rights of the English nation in Portugal within the terms of the treaty.

6

Portugal and England 1656-1660

The immediate responsibility for seeing that the terms of the newly ratified treaty were observed fell on Thomas Maynard, who was appointed Consul by letters patent dated 27 August /6 September 1656, with powers to act as Agent.[1] In the letter of credence, Cromwell asked that Maynard should be given the privilege of free admission to the king, not only regarding matters of trade, but also in connection with other affairs of interest to the Protectorate.[2]

Maynard arrived in Lisbon with his wife and family, on board the *Phoenix* frigate, on 9 January 1657 (N.S.). Two days later, he was visited by the Conde de Odemira, followed by many nobles and courtiers, who went to congratulate Cromwell on his success against the Spaniards. Five days after his arrival he had an audience with Queen Luisa, the regent.[3] Maynard had begun what was to be thirty-four years of service to the English community in Portugal and its dominions, at a time when Lisbon was considered to be one of the most remunerative consular posts available.[4]

As agent between 1657 and 1660, Maynard was fulfilling a role akin to that of a present-day chargé d'affaires. England was at war with Spain, and Maynard was given a cipher to use in making reports. His main concern on arrival in Lisbon was to establish channels whereby he could obtain accurate and quick information regarding the condition and movements of the Spanish fleet.[5] He managed to place an informant in Faro, at a cost of something over £400 per annum.[6] The Conde de Odemira promised to keep him informed of any news which he received from Spain. De Ruyter and a Dutch fleet of nine ships were based on San Lucar de Barrameda, ostensibly to fight Algerian pirates, but according to the Spaniards, they were there to supply and assist the Spaniards.[7] The ten-year truce between Portugal and the United Provinces had lapsed in 1651, and in 1654 the Dutch had been expelled from Brazil,[8] so although they were no longer at war with England, their relations with Portugal were very strained. It was in the interests of the Dutch to assist Spain against Portugal, but they were to show that they did not wish to become directly embroiled in Spain's war with England. Maynard told the Conde de Odemira that their late war with England was still too fresh in their minds for them to attack the English fleet.[9] None the less, the Dutch fleet remained a threat. Of more immediate consequence to the Portuguese government, however, were the disruptions caused to Portuguese trade by the Spanish fleet. That fleet continuously posed the possibility of invasion from the sea, while Spanish armies constantly threatened invasion by land all along the frontiers. It is not surprising that the Portuguese government was very happy to have General Blake and his fleet based on Faro, in spite of the Portuguese detestation of the 1654 treaty. Indeed, so important to Portuguese security did the British fleet seem to the queen regent, that she summoned Maynard in March 1657 to assure him of the fact. She offered to pay towards the charge of victualling the fleet if she could thereby be sure that it would remain off Portugal.[10] In June 1657, General Blake succeeded in destroying sixteen sail of galleons which had arrived in the Canaries from the West Indies. The queen expressed her appreciation by sending Blake a present of twelve oxen, a thousand sheep, four hundred hens, forty turkeys, twenty pipes of wine, eight canisters of sweetmeats, and twenty-eight of saletting and green pease, for distribution to the fleet.[11] In order to further good relations with England, in March 1657 the queen decided to despatch an ambassador to London, Francisco de Melo (1620-67), 'a soldier with little of the scholar in him', according to Maynard.[12] He sailed to England in one of the ships of Blake's fleet towards the end of July 1657, to take up his new appointment.[13]

Both the open and secret instructions given to Melo underline the importance placed by Portugal on having the English naval squadron based on Portugal.[14] In the open instructions, he was told to try to include Portugal in a league which, it was (wrongly) believed, was being concluded between England, France and Sweden. Failing that, he was to make a league or offensive-defensive alliance with England alone. It was emphasized that whatever happened, it was essential that the English fleet should not be taken away from Portuguese waters. 'Este cabedal de ter aqui armada poderosa será o maior efeito com que haveis de procurar entre a Inglaterra neste tratado.' ('The advantages of having such a powerful armada here would be the greatest benefit of any treaty which you conclude with England.') In his secret instructions, Melo was authorized to offer up to 80,000 *cruzados* per annum towards the cost of victualling that fleet. If he succeeded in making the required treaty, he was to inform Frei Domingos do Rosario,[15] who was then, it was thought, in France, on a mission from Portugal. Queen Luisa had continued John IV's policy of putting Portugal's major diplomatic efforts into obtaining a league with France. It was hoped to marry the Infanta Catherine to Louis XIV, and it was to further that marriage that Frei Domingos had been sent to France. Mazarin's policy, however, had always been directed to an eventual peace with Spain. To obtain this on the best possible terms for France, he encouraged Portugal with assiduous diplomacy, but gave them the minimum amount of help; just enough to enable the Portuguese to keep Spanish troops stationed on the Portuguese frontier.[16] Unfortunately for Melo's mission, on the night of 14/24 July 1657, the eve of his departure, the Queen was obliged to write to him and cancel the instructions concerning the offer to assist with victualling the English fleet.[17] The reason for this was the unexpected arrival in Lisbon of Frei Domingos do Rosario, accompanied by the Comte de Cominges, who came as a special envoy from Louis XIV to congratulate Afonso VI on his accession to the throne. Not only did he disappoint the Portuguese by bringing no assent to a marriage between the Infanta and Louis XIV, but he came with a request that the Portuguese should pay France 2,000,000 *cruzados* merely to enable France to maintain an army in Catalonia.[18] Portugal could not pay both France and England, so before he sailed, Melo was instructed to carry out his other instructions without making the offer of an annual payment towards the cost of victualling the British fleet stationed off Portugal.[19] Thurloe had already been advised of the offer, made by the queen through Maynard, so when commissioners were appointed in October 1657 to treat with Melo, they naturally expected that Melo would make the offer formally during their discussions. They were greatly surprised, therefore, when he said that the Spanish attacks on Portugal were caused because of the presence of the English fleet![20] Later, so inconceivable did it seem that an ambassador should be sent to negotiate empty-handed, that it was even suspected the ambassador was in fact contravening his instructions.[21] On 5 May 1658, Melo had a long conference with Thurloe, who told him frankly that unless Portugal assisted England financially, England could not enter such an alliance as Portugal desired. Melo reported that Thurloe said:

> . . . that the treaty we want was out of the question, unless your majesty helped, because they did not have the wherewithall to continue keeping a fleet against Spain, and that a league without joint effort would not be considered . . . everything would come to nothing without that.[22]

In September 1657, when Melo had been in England a month, the Dutch blockaded Lisbon in an effort to obtain compensation for the loss of Dutch property in Brazil.[23] Portugal refused to accede to Dutch demands and the Dutch declared war on Portugal in October 1657.[24] The Dutch then began actively assisting the Spanish at sea; both British and Portuguese shipping suffered as a result of the covert assistance given to privateers, nominally Spanish, but really Dutch.[25] The Dutch also helped to convoy Spanish West Indian fleets from the

Canary Islands to Cadiz.[26] Although Cromwell was not prepared to embroil England in another war with the Dutch, he was not insensitive to Portugal's problems.[27] Melo grew to like and respect Cromwell, and to fear that his death would be bad for Portugal; in him the queen had a great enemy of Spain, not just because of what he considered to be the interests of England, but because of his own inclination.[28] Cromwell died on 3 September 1658, and was succeeded by his son Richard.

The war against Spain on the Portuguese frontier had not been successful. Jealousies between Portuguese nobles and the treachery of some of them were, Maynard said, a major part of the problem.[29] The year 1659 was to prove a year of disaster for Portugal. The Portuguese ambassador to The Hague, D. Fernando Teles de Faro, left his post and gave his allegiance to Spain, causing negotiations with the Dutch to founder.[30] Portugal's darkest hour came on 7 November 1659, when Mazarin finally concluded a peace with Spain. Instead of marrying the Portuguese Infanta, Catherine, Louis XIV married the Spanish Infanta Maria Theresa, his mother's niece. At the end of 1659, therefore, Portugal was still fighting for independence from Spain in a war which had continued for nineteen years. Portugal was also at war with the Dutch and had been deserted by France. No longer would Spain be fighting in Catalonia as well as on the Portuguese frontier: all its efforts in Iberia could be directed against Portugal. Portugal had become politically isolated, and even the pope had not recognized its independence. Thus, more than ever before, Portugal's survival as a nation depended on her relations with England, although their treaty was only a commercial one. Melo continually urged the queen to see that the terms of the 1654 treaty were kept by Portugal, writing on 24 December 1657: 'It is important that we do not have embarrassments with England, which is so necessary to us'.[31] By 1659, both the queen and her secretary of state, Pedro Vieira da Silva, also fully understood the extent of Portugal's problems. During the summer of that year, da Silva wrote to Melo: 'During the last two years we have witnessed the full effects of God's punishment'.[32] In October, the queen instructed Melo to ensure that the English never doubted Portuguese good faith. 'You must make that understood at all costs', she wrote. 'It is very important'.[33]

But this realization of England's importance to Portugal on the part of Melo, the queen and da Silva, was certainly not general in Portugal. In the summer of 1657, when Portugal's dependence on the protection of the British fleet was realized by the Portuguese government, William Mettam, Thurloe's intelligencer in Lisbon, wrote: 'The English, as everywhere, so here, purchase terror and honour, yet are generally hated by this nation'.[34] Maynard reported in January 1657 that justice for Englishmen was only obtained with 'abundance of trouble', because inferior ministers pretended ignorance of the articles of peace.[35]

In Melo's open instructions, he was told to take over from Francisco Fereira Rebello the matter of the settlement of the claims of the merchants and seamen, resulting from the 1650 confiscations (under Article 25 of the treaty), as Maynard had complained that more than £30,000 was due to the English nation for goods taken and that the customs in Aveiro and Viana were withholding the half custom entirely, because all customs in those ports were normally paid to particular persons and institutions, such as friars and nuns. Other ports, too, had failed to hand over sums due to the appointed treasurers.[36] On the margin of his instructions Melo jotted a few questions. One of them was to ask what he should do if the English would not hear of a league without specific mention being made of the necessity to recompense the merchants. The secretary of state replied, also in the margin, that on no account was he to break the 1654 treaty or desist from entering a league or making a new treaty for that reason.[37]

In August, the consul asked Thurloe to make the Portuguese ambassador sensible of the continuing abuse. No money had been made available for the merchants, and Mr Bird (perhaps he was treasurer of the factory) had advised Maynard that 50,000 *cruzados* were now owing.[38] The matter was brought to the attention of the ambassador, who wrote to the queen on 24 December 1657 (N.S.), complaining that although the amount of money paid by Englishmen in customs duties had been great, the half custom had not been paid to the entitled recipients. It was making it hard for the commissioners on both sides to deal with the outstanding claims. He suggested that it would be better if the treasurers of the Portuguese customs were to give receipts for customs paid. He emphasized again the importance of not giving the English cause to complain.[39] This had little effect in Portugal. On 21 May 1659, he again wrote asking the queen to see that the tribunals and ministers executed punctually what the Portuguese were obliged by treaty to do[40]

Melo was in an extremely difficult position. He was trying to negotiate a desperately needed treaty, empty-handed except for commercial privileges which had been granted previously. When English merchants complained, with reason, that Portugal was not keeping the 1654 treaty, and when it became clear that they were being listened to by the government in England, it was difficult for Melo to make any headway. The English government was entitled to infer that if Portugal did not keep the articles of the treaty already extant between the two countries, it was not likely to keep the articles of any future offensive-defensive alliance. Because of this, Melo embarked on an unusual policy for a Portuguese ambassador: he began to woo the Portugal merchants in London. He was astute enough to realize that at the root of merchants' complaints lay the desire for greater opportunities to trade, so that it was in their own interests to assist him in his dealings with the government. Not only did he do what he could to insist on the terms of the 1654 treaty being observed, but he made a point of getting to know the merchants personally, entertaining them, even on occasion using them to try and advance the diplomatic process. As has been seen, Edward Bushell's influence with the English government was great. He became one of Melo's principal advisers in his treaty negoti-ations, and advised Melo 'on what was possible and how good Englishmen did things'. In return for this assistance, Melo begged the queen to see that Bushell's procurations under the Six Articles should not be continually questioned.[41] An arrangement had apparently been reached by 1660, whereby merchants still operating in or to Portugal or its dominions could receive their payments out of their own customs duties payable during a period of four months.[42] That arrangement did not, of course, help the many seamen, merchants who had failed, or widows and children of merchants and seamen who had died during the intervening ten years.

Richard Beere, who was married to a Portuguese woman (he had been imprisoned in 1650), became a personal friend of Melo's and was involved in a more specific diplomatic initiative.[43] When the rump of the Long Parliament returned to power in May 1659, Melo asked Richard Beere to call on Charles Vane, brother of Sir Henry Vane, who had great influence in Parliament. Beere was to sound out the pos-sibilities of a further treaty with Portugal. Charles Vane, however, had obviously not forgotten the treatment he had received in Portugal. He told Beere not to worry about any treaty with Portugal, because Por-tugal had up to then done nothing but deceive England, being far more interested in friendship with France. Negotiating with Portugal was all right, but what England needed was 'peace and more peace with Spain'. That was a view shared and widely canvassed by the pro-Spanish lobby.[44]

After the signing of the Treaty of the Pyrenees, Portugal was forced to realize where she stood with France. This helped Melo, and events in England were to help him even more. The unsettled political and economic situation made it possible for General George Monck (1608-70), in charge of the army in Scotland, to march gradually southwards, with his troops. He crossed the border early in January 1660, reaching London on 3/13 February. His handling of the members of Parliament and the City of London was masterly. When the Rump government came to an end, Monck became a member of the newly formed Council. It was in the midst of these stirring events that Melo at last managed to agree a treaty with England. He had sent his interpreter, João Milles de Macedo, to compliment Monck when he first arrived in London, and to ask if he might have a meeting. The request was refused at that stage, but an interview was granted Melo on 28 February/9 March, at which Monck promised to intercede with the Council to negotiate with Portugal.[45] At that interview, according to Sir Robert Southwell, writing in 1698, Melo told Monck that he would not presume to enquire if Monck had good will for the king's return, but he wanted to convey the intelligence that the Spaniards had resolved, if Charles II attempted to return to England, to stop him leaving Flanders until he had promised to return Dunkirk to the Spaniards.[46] On 19/29 March, Monck secretly met his kinsman, Sir John Grenville, a prominent Royalist, and declared himself for the king. Through Grenville, he advised the king to leave Brussels and go to the United Provinces immediately. This was doubtless because of the information received from Melo. Charles followed that advice and arrived in Breda on 4/14 April, from which town he issued the Declaration of Breda outlining what his policy would be if he returned to England. The Convention Parliament accepted the Declaration on 27 April/7 May 1660 and on 5/15 May, he was invited by them to return. He landed at Dover on 25 May/4 June 1660.[47]

There is no doubt that one of Monck's chief worries was to find employment for men in the army, which would have to be disbanded when the king returned. Portugal needed soldiers, and so commissioners were quickly appointed to meet Melo, who was received in audience on 2/12 March 1660.[48] Melo stressed the commercial reasons for a further treaty: that the Portuguese colonies and ouposts were important to England because of the importance of trade to the nation; Portuguese colonies were a protection against pirates, and points at which ships could victual and water in long distance hauls – to the Levant, for instance; Portugal was in the habit of freighting English ships, and whereas Portugal allowed English ships to trade with her colonies, Spain never did. Melo also emphasized the privileges enjoyed by the English under the 1654 treaty.[49] The outcome of the ensuing negotiations was the Treaty of Westminster, signed on 18/28 April 1660,[50] which was never ratified because of the Restoration. It was to be superseded by the far more important marriage treaty of 1661.

Although the Treaty of Westminster concerned the employment of English soldiers in Portugal, the first article confirmed the Six Preliminary Articles and the treaty of 1654. Articles 2, 3 and 4 allowed the king of Portugal to enlist up to 12,000 soldiers from England, Scotland and Ireland, in three equal contingents of 4,000 men. He could also purchase up to 2,500 horses for his war against Castile. All the officers, both cavalry and foot, were to be selected from the same three nations (Article 5), and Portugal could freight up to twenty ships at current rates. The masters and men of these vessels had to be English, but the

Portuguese minister in England had the right to select and approve them (Articles 6 and 7). Article 8 provided that the Portuguese agents could buy arms and ammunition as needed. Troops were to be transported to Portugal at the latter's cost; the men could be engaged by the colonels chosen by the Portuguese minister, but all troops had to swear never to fight against the Republic or its allies (Articles 9-12). Under Article 13, the troops were to be allowed the free exercise of their religion as agreed in Article 14 of the 1654 treaty. The mention in Article 2 that the troops were to be recruited for the defence of Portugal against Spain was very unusual. Bordeaux, the French ambassador in London, told Melo that he would only believe that when he saw it, so Melo gave him a copy for Mazarin.[51] Melo specifically pointed out to the queen that the wording of Article 5 would enable her to select only Irish Catholics as officers.[52] It had been hoped to include the words 'without scandal' in Article 13, when allowing the practice of their religion to the troops. That this became impossible was due to the 'affair of the consul'.[53] This was a reference to events which occurred in Lisbon earlier in the year 1660, and nearly caused the failure of Melo's mission. They are recounted in the next chapter.

7

The Affair of the Consul

Although the Lisbon Inquisition Process No. 7522 and an undated, unfinished letter to Melo from Queen Luisa have both been commented on elsewhere by historians, their true significance in connection with Maynard and Anglo-Portuguese relations has only become apparent with access to the archives of the Condes da Ponte.[1]

From Process No. 7522, we know that a young Catholic girl of eighteen, Margaret Throckmorton (Margarida Troquemorton in the Process),[2] accompanied another girl to Lisbon in the spring of 1659, with the intention of entering the Convent of St Brigid. Before entering the convent, however, she moved into the Maynard household, where she was converted to Protestantism by the chaplain, Zachary Cradock, who resided there.[3] The Inquisition decided to act. Maynard and Protestant Englishmen tried to protect Margaret from being taken from Maynard's house by the familiars,[4] but Maynard himself was imprisoned by the Inquisition from 3/13-9/19 February 1659/60. According to the Inquisition records, Maynard told the Inquisition that any infringement of the articles in the 1654 treaty would bring about a break-down in the negotiations in progress between England and Portugal in London. Our information as to what happened next comes from the queen's letter. The consul, she said, had been imprisoned by the Inquisition because he had failed to keep his promise to take Margaret to a Portuguese house, where she could be arrested without offence to his (Maynard's) rights. The queen said that she had asked the Holy Office to treat the consul well and allow him to speak with whom he would. She and her ministers would do their best to make Maynard modify his attitude, and that of the Englishmen who were advising him. The English, she wrote, were very restive and many of their ships were in Lisbon harbour; men on those ships could spread untrue and inflammatory reports when they returned to England. She had been advised that they had already sent word to England by a frigate which sailed under a French captain's flag. Apparently, the English in Lisbon were claiming that in conformity with their Articles of Peace, no vessel of the Protectorate could be detained or molested in Portugal on account of a religious question and that their consul had immunity from arrest, both of his own person and that of anyone of his house. The queen said that she had told the English that the Articles of

Peace did not specify anything regarding English Roman Catholics, who, by reason of their Catholicism, were subject to punishment by the Inquisition. (This was one of the reasons put forward by John IV for changing the wording of Articles 6 and 14.)[5] The treaty only referred to those English people who had never been Catholics. Even Englishmen who did not account themselves subject to the Protectorate were also excluded from the treaty, she maintained. (This last is an interesting interpretation.) The queen told them (correctly) that consuls did not customarily enjoy immunity as to their persons or their houses. Finally, she emphasized that she had no authority over the Inquisition or its laws. Queen Luisa further told Melo that the consul was being well treated; that he was being given the unheard-of-privilege of having his wife and sons to dine with him, but that he was threatening to embark for England as soon as he was freed. She feared that in England he would be heard with prejudice to the privileges enjoyed by Melo himself, so Melo was advised to hide his papers. Should there be disturbances in England because of the affair, she considered that it would be best for him to remove to the French embassy or wherever he though fit, even to France or Holland, if he considered that to be advisable.

The queen was referring to the use made of the Portuguese embassy as a centre for Catholics, and to disseminate Catholic propaganda. In the embassy itself, the ambassador had a staff of over thirty persons, including a chaplain.[6] It must be remembered, however, that clerical staff would have included religious. In addition, Richard Barton and Joseph Simonis, both Jesuits, formed part of Melo's 'family'. Richard Barton was no less than the Provincial for the Society of Jesus in England; Joseph Simonis, who had been educated in Portugal, was running a clandestine Jesuit college in London. Melo referred to him as the 'Rector' of the college. From various references in Melo's letters, Senhora Castello Branco believes that the college was actually in the embassy, or an adjoining building.[7] Melo himself confirmed that 600–800 English people had been communicating publicly in the embassy on Sundays and saints' days.[8] In so doing, they were breaking the law of the land, but the government was allowing it. Such privileges went far beyond normal diplomatic usage at the time, which allowed a chaplain on the staff of an embassy, and facilities for practising their religion only to the nationals of the embassy living in that country, and, of course, they went far beyond the diplomatic usage tolerated at the time in respect of the English minister of state in Portugal. It is reasonable to assume that if Maynard had visited England in 1658 or 1659, he would have called at the Portuguese embassy in London. He would have known the members of the English College there, at least by sight, and he may also have known Joseph Simonis. In any case,

English Catholic merchants in London attended the embassy masses. It may have been this knowledge of the proselytizing activities of the Portuguese embassy in London which encouraged and emboldened Maynard to stand firm against the Inquisition regarding Margaret Throckmorton's conversion whilst she was living in his house in Lisbon. Given the circumstances, it was an act requiring great courage, and Maynard clearly had the support of the Protestant merchants.

Melo had repeatedly asked to be recalled, as he thought that that might spur the English government to sign the treaty being negotiated. He was also short of money. Instructions from Portugal were eagerly awaited, but when he did receive a letter, it was to tell him about the affair of the consul. His chagrin and irritation are evident in the letter he wrote to the queen on 16/26 March 1660, complaining of neglect, and warning that unless he obtained a signature of the treaty within thirty days, Charles II would be in England and all the negotiations of the last two and a half years would have to begin again.[9] He told her that by imprisoning the consul, not only his person, but the persons of all Catholics in England, had been put at great risk. The English, he maintained, were an insolent people, without God, without law, who hated Catholics. He anticipated that as soon as the news arrived, the embassy would be the butt for their fury.

On the following day (17/27 March), he was sent a memorandum from the Council of State, signed by the president, Sir Arthur Annesley. Sir Arthur was a friend of Portugal, for he was a cousin of the embassy interpreter, João Milles de Macedo, as well as a personal friend of Melo's. Their friendship had grown because they were both bibliophiles.[10] The memorandum stated that they had received a report from Maynard, which they considered to be of grave importance.[11] As reported to them, on 2/12 February Dom Jorge de Melo and Dom Manuel de Sousa, familiars, had gone to the consul's house with fifty armed men and had asked him in the name of the Inquisition to hand over Margaret Throckmorton, who was staying in his house. This Maynard refused to do, but the next day Maynard was requested to go to the Inquisition headquarters to discuss the matter with the inquisitors. He did so on the following day and was promptly imprisoned and shut up, without being allowed to even send a message to his wife or to the merchants who had accompanied him. The gaoler had told him that messages were not allowed and he would have to learn to take the only possible medicine, patience. He had been kept there for six days, until the Thursday of the following week, when an Inquisitor had arrived and told him he was free to go. On return to his house he had been told that on the previous day four hundred men had been sent by the inquisitors, who had broken into his house, forcing doors, looking everywhere.[12] The memorandum concluded by informing

Melo that the Council was greatly injured by the dishonour done, not just to an Englishman, but to a public minister of state, against human rights and the articles of peace. Melo was advised to make representations to his king of the consequence of such actions. Crimes of that nature had to be punished. The Council trusted that the prudence and sense of justice of His Majesty would make exemplary reparation, and that no tribunal, no matter how holy, would be allowed to break human rights held sacred by all. Only if such reparations were made could the countries continue to be friends.

Melo made no attempt to reply to the Council of State's memorandum at the time. On 20/30 March he wrote to the queen again on the subject of 'that hardworking and, unhappily, successful consul of the English'. He advised that he had sent his interpreter, João Milles de Macedo, to Whitehall that day to ask Oliver Fleming, master of ceremonies, to discover whether the news had yet reached the City. As soon as the latter saw Macedo, he looked black and thunderous, clutched his neck band and said:

> Wretched Portugal, miserable negotiations, unfortunate ambassador! England was Portugal's last hope. What can I say to these men? Even if the consul were treated well, by what right, divine or human, was he imprisoned by the Inquisition? A consul who had left England with credentials, too. What am I to say if I am told that Portugal has broken the peace? What will the friends of Spain do in this instance? What will the Dutch not say against the Inquisition? What will the people do? Tell the ambassador we have a conference tomorrow, if it is not cancelled because of the news. Because of what happened you need not expect much of England.

That, Melo told the queen, was the state of things at 10 p.m.[13]

On the following day he wrote that he had discovered that most of the Portugal merchants had been to the Council of State between 7 and 8 p.m., to complain that the Portuguese crown had broken the peace and allowed human rights to be violated. They had suggested that Melo be made prisoner until everything in Portugal had been satisfactorily settled and the culprits punished. The Council had answered that the matter was being seriously considered. That morning, Edward Bushell and others had gone to the Exchange, making trouble and urging that the queen be forced to do away with the Inquisition before England treated with Portugal. However, that day also, Melo had had a conference with the commissioners negotiating the treaty, and although the proposed religious article was discussed, not a word was said to him personally about the matter of the consul. He was thus adopting a policy of continuing to be friendly to everyone.[14] The discovery that the Council was prepared, through the commissioners, to continue negotiating, must have been a relief to Melo, even if he were being greeted in an increasingly less friendly fashion by ministers.[15] Doubtless the importance of finding employment for soldiers if they were disbanded was great enough to overcome the opposition of the Spanish lobby and the incensed Portugal merchants. Protests and negotiations proceeded together from then onwards, but not without plain speaking on the part of the Council. Melo believed that the core of the London accusations was that the queen had ignored their representative's rights by allowing the Inquisition to imprison the consul, and that the ministers of the Holy Office were working against the crown in Portugal. He visited his friend, the Swedish ambassador.[16] Through him and others, he let it be known that the idea that the Holy Office was working against the crown in Portugal was being spread by Jews, and was quite untrue. Maynard, he said, was in fact no longer entitled to be called a consul, because in Portugal consuls had to be reappointed every three years and Maynard had not been reappointed.[17] When Cromwell died, Maynard should have received another patent, and after Richard Cromwell retired from the government, he should have received another from Parliament. On every occasion he should also have received credentials from the crown of Portugal. When this reached the ears of the Council, they informed Melo that such an argument showed bad faith on the part of Portugal. Unless Maynard had been recalled, they maintained that it was clear that he continued under the aegis of the government at that time in England. Melo himself had constantly suffered from lack of credentials being sent to him from Portugal at the right times. He was accustomed to preparing his own when needed, just as if they had come from Portugal.[18] It is no wonder, therefore, that he wrote: 'Please Your Majesty, see that there are no more accidents. Do not let it be said in Portugal that he was not a minister. It is enough that I say it'.[19] At a conference, the English ministers told Melo roundly that they were not prepared to put up with the fact that he allowed Englishmen to attend mass at his house and exercise the Catholic religion. Englishmen were as zealous in their religion as the Portuguese were in theirs. He was informed that guards would be posted at the embassy to prevent attendances at mass, but he judged that to be just noise and fury, directed at improving religious privileges for the English in Portugal, or at making it easier for England to make peace with Spain by not completing the new treaty with Portugal. Peace with Spain was what England wanted most, and he assumed it would be automatic when, and if, Charles II returned. Begging to be recalled to keep the peace, he wrote: 'Preserve me from the zeal and faith of the inquisitors, who in this instance dealt with the realm of Portugal as they did with the consul'.[20] Later he heard from his spy on the Council that it had been decided that if any English man or woman were taken in Portugal by the Inquisition, he himself would be put in prison, and war would be declared immediately.[21]

On 3/13 April, Melo replied officially to the Council's memorandum. He stated that Maynard had not been in the prison of the Inquisition, but only in the 'escolas geraes', which was a place for penitents, where there was no keeper and where his wife and friends could be with him. Margaret Throckmorton was an intended religious and a practising Catholic. The Inquisition only wanted to see her in the house of a third person, an Englishman or *fidalgo*. He pointed out that the king of Portugal, even if a sovereign prince, had no power at all over the council of the Inquisition, as the ministers of that council were ministers of the pope, maintained, supported and nominated by him. The king not only had no jurisdiction over them, but believed he could not have such jurisdiction. Nowhere else would a Catholic prince have done what Her Majesty did for Maynard: that was the extent of her love for the English. Maynard had lacked a valid patent, and proof of that fact was that a new patent had been procured for him by a petition of the merchants a day or so earlier.[22] Under Article 7 of the peace, the consul was entitled to the same privileges as other consuls in Portugal (France, Sweden, Holland, Denmark, German Principalities, Venice, Genoa and Florence). None of them had religious meetings in their consul's house, but only in the privacy of their own families. The consul of England had exceeded that permission, having big meetings, not only of English people, but of other nations, which were never stopped.[23] Only ambassadors and grandees of the realm were allowed into the chamber near the Queen Regent's cabinet, but the consul, held in affectionate tolerance, was allowed to enter without permission, at any time, as he wished. Melo maintained that Maynard was not a good public minister, because he had not tried to be conciliatory. If the Council were to ask Englishmen from Spain, they would be told how kind the Portuguese were. In two hundred years, there had not been a case of the Inquisition interfering with Englishmen, who had always been free to worship without scandal, and without taking third parties from the path dictated to their conscience.[24] These facts should be pointed out to Maynard. Finally, Melo hoped that the equity and generosity of the council would not heap afflictions on a prince and realm which had shown such affection for England, by preferring it above other countries.[25]

The consequences of the Throckmorton affair were serious for Anglo-Portuguese relations, that much is clear. It also seems clear that Maynard's account of events, as presented to Melo by the Council, was substantially correct, for it was corroborated by the queen. What is strange is that the Inquisition reported the matter to the queen at all.

Normally, they proceeded in their affairs, brooking no opposition, as is illustrated by the case of the arrest of Duarta da Silva, who was a man of great importance to the crown.[26] Though not mentioned in the process, it may be that Maynard had pointed out to them that religious privileges at diplomatic level were reciprocal, and that if the English lost theirs in Portugal, the Portuguese ambassador would lose his in London. The Inquisition could not have afforded to have it be known that they, the upholders of the faith, had been the cause of so many English Catholics losing the opportunity to practise their religion. The break-down of diplomatic negotiations would not have troubled them. As the Conde de Miranda[27] (who was despatched to the United Provinces as ambassador after the treachery of D. Fernando Teles de Faro), commented to Melo in a letter of 2 April 1660 (N.S.) the members of the tribunal of the Holy Office were not concerned who won the war against Spain, for they would continue their work no matter who was sovereign.[28] The assertion in the Council's memorandum that Maynard had been imprisoned without letting him send a message to his wife or colleagues was also probably correct, for it was in accordance with the normal procedure. It was without doubt the intercessions of the queen that caused him to be moved to the *escolas geraes*. He had to be kept incommunicado until the Inquisition had succeeded in extracting Margaret, because the Inquisition could not have allowed it to be seen by the populace that a foreigner and a Protestant had worsted them. Maynard and the Council were correct in asserting that he was a public minister, because besides being a consul he was an agent. The curious thing is that neither in the letter from the queen to Melo, nor in Melo's approach to the problem, is there any mention of Maynard's being an agent and therefore a minister of state. There appears to have been a divergence of opinion between England and Portugal as to what constituted an agent: in England, an agent was looked upon as a minister of state, albeit a low ranking one; but in Portugal, it seems that an agent was synonymous with a factor or trade agent, thus greatly inferior to a consul. Because the king of Portugal's factors were Jews or New Christians, their diplomatic standing was nil. They had no credentials and were regarded as less than consuls ('quaes reputamos menos que consuls').[29] It may be that Maynard found it preferable to build up his image in Portugal as a consul with special privileges, rather than to be known as a mere factor. In 1670, when Francis Parry was appointed agent, Prince Pedro, the regent, made difficulties about giving him full diplomatic status and Parry could not present his credentials.[30] To solve the problem, Parry was sent new credentials as a commissary instead of agent,[31] but he was not received in audience for another four weeks.[32]

The majority of the merchants in Lisbon cared greatly about their religion, and so did their principals in England. At a time in England when dissension in politics raged; when it was assumed that Charles II was returning; when the members of the Council did not know how they themselves would be treated by the incoming victorious faction, the affair of the consul was still able to raise a great stir and command their support. Indeed, had Monck himself not been virtually in control of England after 21 February (before the news from Portugal reached England), it is likely that reaction would have been greater.[33] It would certainly have given Sir Arthur Heselrige, Sir Henry Vane and other prominent republicans on the Council an excuse to engineer a break with Portugal and make peace with Spain.

Meanwhile Maynard, who had been released by the Inquisition at the queen's personal request, had been to Queen Luisa and offered to go to England in order to assist Melo in his negotiations with the new government. According to the queen, Maynard thought he might be of assistance because he was a good friend of Monck and because Monck was his wife's first cousin. The queen understood that Maynard was also related to one of the counsellors of state (presumably the Serjeant, Sir John Maynard). This information was imparted to Melo by the queen in cypher,[34] when she advised him that she had decided to accept the offer because she knew Maynard to be a man who really cared about the affairs of Portugal. He had lived in Portugal for many years, and the fact that he was proposing to leave his wife and children behind in Portugal while he was away, had persuaded her that he was really prepared to serve her. She asked Melo to listen to him and deal with him to the best advantage of her service, letting her know whether he behaved as she expected him to do. It was important to Maynard personally that he should obtain a fresh patent from the king, and he would have realized that on his return to England, Charles II would be inundated by petitions from those who felt that they were entitled to rewards for services given in the Stuart cause. Maynard's own allegiance to the king had been conducted very secretly, for safety reasons. Without a doubt he thought that by serving the cause of Portugal in helping to bring about an alliance between the two countries, he would not only obtain a free passage to England and back, but would have an opportunity to serve his own interests as well.

Maynard returned to England via The Hague, where he kissed hands with Charles II.[35] He may have formed part of Charles's train to England, for he joined in and contributed to the celebrations for the king's return at the Portuguese embassy. Melo reported early in June that Maynard was doing much to gain friends for Portugal, although the court was wholly Castilian.[36] As for Margaret Throckmorton, no records have yet been found which throw light on her movements after her expulsion from Portugal.

8

The Treaty of 1661

i *The Merchants and the Marriage Treaty*

There is no doubt that Portugal was the chief instigator of the Marriage Treaty, just as it was with the 1654 treaty. Portugal's position was worse than it had been in 1659, because in 1660 it was certain that England would make peace with Spain. Apart from the strong pro-Spanish lobby, Charles II had been sustained by Spain over a number of years and the royalists who returned with him to power were largely pro-Spanish. Before returning to England, the king had refused to see the Conde de Miranda, the Portuguese ambassador at The Hague, so Melo had little expectation that the treaty he had just completed would be ratified.[1] Maynard reported to Melo that Monck had assured him that it would be ratified, even though the king would certainly make peace with Spain, but everyone with whom Melo had discussed the matter were of the opinion that it would be wrong and ungrateful of the king to ratify it, after having been supported financially by Spain for so long.[2] Melo also feared that because he had negotiated with the Protectorate, he himself might not be acceptable as ambassador. The United Provinces had recalled Niewport, the Dutch ambassador. France had sent new credentials to Bordeaux, but he had been told that he was *persona non grata* when he tried to present them, because he had negotiated the 1657 treaty between France and the Protectorate. According to Melo, though, the real objection was not that Bordeaux had negotiated the treaty, but that, on orders from France, he had called on Monck and told him that France would support him personally, if he wished to govern England.[3]

Melo's own requests to be replaced were ignored by Lisbon, so he set about the business of making an alliance with Restoration England by means of a two-pronged policy: he made a determined effort to gain friends for Portugal among men in power, and he continued to encourage the Portugal merchants to lobby for a further Portuguese alliance, whilst continuing to advertise loudly the benefits of Anglo-Portuguese trade. In pursuit of this policy, he made use of Maynard and Father Richard Russell of the English College, who became his official interpreter when Milles de Macedo returned to Portugal early in May. These two men, who were basically opposed to each other, worked together for Melo because they had one need in common: their interests were bound up with the survival of Portugal.

Father, later Bishop, Russell (1630?–95), had entered the English College in Lisbon as a servant in 1642 and become a student in 1647. He had been sent to Douai and Paris for further studies, being ordained before returning to Portugal as Procurator at the College in 1655.[4] William Mettam, writing to Thurloe from Lisbon on 3/13 July 1657, had reported that Russell had accompanied Melo to England:

> . . . a certain English priest, no great politician for witt, yet was a great informer against the late treatie of Mr. Meadowe at that time, taking all advantages against the repute and interest of England, especially with the Inquisition. He is a short fatt man, by name Mr. Richard Russell, whom the said ambassador hopes to keep for his confident intelligencer . . .[5]

It is curious that Melo had never mentioned his name in correspondence with Portugal before 1660, although he frequently wrote of the various Jesuits in his house in London. Perhaps, as Castello Branco has suggested, Russell did not travel with Melo after all, preferring not to voyage in Blake's fleet.[6] It may be that whilst Melo judged it safe to mention the Jesuits, being aware of the *de facto* liberty of conscience allowed under the Protectorate, he knew that anyone engaged in working actively for Charles II's cause would not be tolerated. In a modern brochure published by the English College, it is stated that Russell aided and abetted the secret supply of arms and ammunition provided by Portugal to the royalists (presumably in abortive plots, such as that of Colonel John Gerard), and was the only safe go-between of Charles and his supporters.[7] The unknown writer of that brochure was clearly not perfectly informed,[8] but it may well be that Russell acted as a go-between for Charles II, the Catholic gentry and other royalists in the course of his pastoral duties. The college annals state categorically that Russell was recalled to England and travelled in the company of Francisco de Melo, and that he remained with him at the embassy in London for three and a half years, until November 1660.[9] In whatever capacity he had operated before 1660, after April of that year, he worked as interpreter and confidential assistant to Melo. It is clear, too, that he knew personally, and was known by, all the prominent royalists. As early as 4/14 May 1660, Melo wrote asking that the queen reward Russell, because of all the help he had given with the making of the treaty of Westminster.[10] By September, Melo was eulogising Russell: the Apostolic Pronotary, Richard Russell, served her cause well; he knew all the ministers, the king, the secretaries, and had secretly distributed Melo's bribe presents; his knowledge of languages and his ability were of the utmost help and essential to the embassy at that time.[11]

In his attempts to discover whether or not he would be acceptable to the king as Portugal's ambassador, Melo sounded out some of the members of the former government who continued in power, and who were already his friends, such as Sir Arthur Annesley, former president of the Council of State. His friendship with Monck became more intimate after the arrival of Maynard. Knighted on 26 May 1660 (O.S.), and created Duke of Albemarle on 7 July 1660,[12] Monck promised to speak to the king about receiving Melo as soon as his new credentials arrived.[13] Promises of support came from Edward Montagu, Earl of Manchester (later Charles II's Chamberlain), General Montagu (later Earl of Sandwich), Lord Fairfax, Sir John Temple and William Morice. The latter, who was to become a secretary of state and was a friend and relative of Monck's, was won over to Portugal by Maynard. According to Russell, Morice said that he was a man with many children, but of good will and straightforward, and that he had no scruples in receiving money from Portugal, because he knew that he would be serving both the king of Portugal and the king of England. Melo thought that the minimum he could give him would be £1,000 in gold, and he promised to give this to Morice as soon as he had had his first audience with the king.[14] Russell took a letter from Melo to Sir Edward Hyde (later Lord Clarendon), who refused to see Melo, but said that he would speak to the king, because he loved England and because he believed that England's interests lay with Portugal.[15]

With the promise of such support, Melo once more prepared his own credentials; the new ones, dated 15 June, did not arrive until after he had presented his forged ones.[16] He was obliged to work fast because Spain, too, was distributing largesse. Melo distributed a total of 40,000 *cruzados*, whereas Spain boasted of having spent 400,000 *cruzados*.[17] A present of Spanish horses was sent to the king and a man named Ramirez, who brought them to England, also distributed large sums among the ministers and royalists who had been with Charles in Flanders, on the pretext that the sums were payment for services to Spain when they had been on the continent.[18] The arrival of an ambassador from Spain was expected soon. Early in July, Melo had distributed a memorandum to the new ministers, in which he pointed out that the convenience and interests of England demanded that Portugal should not be allowed to fall into the hands of her old enemy Spain. Portugal's aid to Charles I was recalled, and the fact that John IV had aided Prince Rupert for Charles II's sake, involving Portugal in a war for which it was still paying England. Commercial and religious privileges were also recalled, and England was asked to remember its debts to Portugal.[19] It was a diplomatic *volte face* on the part of Portugal which, during the Interregnum, always maintained that it was not responsible for Rupert's actions. If Sousa de Macedo's behaviour had been detrimental to the making of the 1654 treaty, it provided excellent support for Portugal in making the 1661 treaty.

Meanwhile, Melo laboured with the Portugal merchants, and on 3/13 July, a delegation presented a petition to Charles II with two hundred signatures. Melo sent the queen a translated copy, under cover of his letter of the same date, in which he told her that the document had required a lot of hard work and money, but that it would be worth it if it were to bring the desired result.[20] The chief points made in the petition were that trade with Portugal was worth in the region of £200,000 a year, whilst English merchants in Portugal and the Islands normally held a like sum among themselves there in Portugal. The chief items of trade were enumerated and the importance of the fish trade from Newfoundland was stressed, as occupying fifty to sixty ships a year, giving employment and training to seamen. English ships not only traded with Portugal, but also between Portugal and her dominions, as well as along the Portuguese coast. Portugal was in the habit of freighting English ships, and all this brought employment and profit to Englishmen. Debts owed by Portugal (because of the confiscations in 1650) were being repaid by Portugal from the half custom of the English merchants. If that were to stop, it would mean ruin and famine for the poor families and orphans of many sailors and merchants. Finally, the petition reminded the king of the privileges enjoyed by the English in Portugal, both with regard to trade and to the exercise of their religion, by the terms of the 1654 treaty, and pointed out that if Portugal were to be re-absorbed by Spain and if, later, England were to be at war with Spain, England would no longer enjoy the benefit of the Portuguese ports on the journey between the French ports and the Straits.

The reference to the dependence of so many families on the payment of the half custom is a pointer to the extent of the damage done to English trade and shipping by the confiscations and imprisonment of 1650. As has been seen, even when compensation was paid, it was paid only after much soliciting, costly in itself, and probably not in full. Doubtless the poor families were able to obtain credit on the strength of the terms of the treaty. The debt gave Portugal an enormous hold over many Englishmen. Indeed, so powerful was the desire to obtain the half custom payments, that Melo suggested to the queen that if she were to withhold all payments of the half custom until the Treaty of Westminster had been ratified by Charles II, then it would be ratified very quickly. If it had not been for the money owed to the merchants, he said, there would certainly have been a war over the affair of the consul.[21]

That letter was written on the same day as Melo was finally received in public audience by the king. On that occasion, he was informed by the master of ceremonies that he must understand that the king could not treat with anyone who had dealt with the Protector, but a week later, on 30 July/9 August, he was received in private.[22] Charles and his ministers, however, were not prepared to negotiate unless they received assurances from the merchants that they were obtaining satisfaction in Portugal and being given all that they had been promised. This presented Melo with difficulties, because at that time the merchants were complaining of a number of serious matters, in addition to their long-standing grievances. The merchants in Aveiro were being badly treated by officials, and an English ship had been lost in Setúbal harbour because of the uncalled-for personal animosity of the town's governor.[23] The Inquisition was not releasing, from the sequestered estates of the Portuguese merchants that it had imprisoned, payment of debts owed by those prisoners to Englishmen, under the terms of Article 5 of the 1654 treaty. Rowland Hill, from Oporto, had gone to the king and complained about the non-payment of 5,000 crowns owed to him personally under the terms of Article 5. Melo and Maynard eased the situation by seeing Hill. Melo promised, in the name of the queen, that she would order justice to be done.[24] Consul Cobbs of São Miguel had suffered grievously at the hands of that island's governor. Melo saw Cobbs personally, and obtained his promise to keep quiet until Melo heard from the queen after she had discussed the matter with Maynard, who was returning to Portugal.[25] Further, the English had a just complaint with regard to the treatment of one of their ships in Angola, and there was also the matter of the non-payment for the freighting of a ship called *Calpaper* (Culpepper?), master, Jack Reynolds, which had been lost in the king of Portugal's service. As Melo pointed out to the queen later, if compensation was not paid for ships lost fighting for Portugal in time of great necessity, when Portugal was obliged to use and freight English ships, the English would not take such commissions again.[26] Melo took it upon himself to promise the merchants, in the name of the queen, that they would be given satisfaction: 'Prostrate at your feet, I beg your majesty to order that the treaty be kept exactly'.[27]

Three days later, Melo explained the reason for this somewhat desperate plea and the promises he had made in the queen's name. Perhaps unaware of the serious complaints of the merchants, and wishing to be helpful, Morice, who was by then secretary of state, had sent for Russell on 18/28 August and told him that the king would not allow Ormonde and his pro-Spanish faction to dominate the Council. All was going well for Portugal, Morice reported, but the commissioners selected to negotiate with Melo just wanted to call a few merchants for questioning. Morice asked Russell which merchants Melo thought would be most likely to further Portugal's aims, so that they could be sent for, among others, including the consul, whom he had been instructed to call. Russell gave him four names, but asked Morice not to send for them until Melo had a chance to speak with them. Morice agreed to this. The merchants in question were dined by the ambassador, who informed them of the negotiations, and made suggestions about what they should say at the meeting. It was agreed that the consul should be their spokesman. When they eventually attended at Whitehall (the exact date is not available), they went in the ambassador's coaches and were accompanied by Russell. Melo had discovered that the other merchants being called wished to cause difficulties by bringing up the matter of the Inquisition, so Russell hurried off to warn the Earl of Manchester, who was waiting in an antechamber with Morice, and persuaded them to stop this. At the meeting, the consul handed in a paper in support of ratification of the treaty. The merchants were asked two questions: had they anything to say? and had Portugal kept the articles of past treaties? The merchants agreed that all was well, but one man, named Adams, had the courage to complain of the Inquisition. The commissioners merely told him that the consul would look into his complaint on another occasion. Adams's complaint had disquieted a number of his fellows, however, seeing which Russell persuaded them to go to Melo, who 'turned their minds to more practical matters by thanking them for their services to the queen'.[28]

Though an influential body, the merchants were not proof against the machinations of diplomats and ministers. Portugal's hold on the merchants was the money Portugal owed them, and if Portugal could gain prestige by the ratification of a treaty, then the merchants could be more assured of their credit, and so of their livelihoods in their risky calling. Maynard's position (and this would apply to other unnamed merchants present at the meeting) was difficult. His wife and family were in Portugal and, like all Protestants, they were at the mercy of the Inquisition. Furthermore, all his assets and livelihood were there. Maynard had also specifically journeyed to England to promote Portugal's interests and his passage had been paid for by the queen. Men who earned their bread in the Portugal trade were dependent not only on good relations between England and Portugal, but upon good relations between themselves and the Portuguese. They had overwhelming reasons, therefore, to support Melo's negotiations.

On the 10/20 September, the Prince de Ligny arrived in England as Extraordinary Ambassador from the king of Spain, and he was accompanied by Baron de Batteville, who was designated resident ambassador. They brought with them a great train and 160 coach horses, and they were received with artillery salvoes, peace with Spain being proclaimed. There was to be a cessation of hostilities and a renewal of friendship, effective from Charles II's return to England. Confiscated goods were to be returned. For Portugal, this meant that there would no longer be an English squadron to help protect her shores.

Before the arrival of the embassy, however, Portugal had begun to negotiate for far bigger things than the ratification of the Treaty of Westminster, namely, the marriage of their infanta, Catherine, to Charles II.[29] According to Portuguese sources, it was Dom João da Costa, Conde de Soure, Portuguese ambassador to France, who first suggested the marriage when he knew of the coming restoration. He had written recommending the idea to both Melo and the queen. The latter had eagerly accepted the idea and had written to Melo suggesting that not only should Charles marry Catherine, but that Princess Henrietta, Charles's youngest sister, should marry Afonso VI. However, she sent no bargaining instructions.[30] Soure, who regarded Portugal's need of England with great distaste ('esta ma correspondencia', 'this bad alliance', he called it),[31] none the less suggested that since the queen had once been prepared to offer two million *cruzados* and to cede Tangier for the marriage of the Infanta to the king of France, then Melo should proceed with these as bargaining counters in the English case.[32] The negotiations for the ratification of the treaty of Westminster and those for the marriage proceeded separately. The first negotiations were conducted openly, but the second were carried on secretly with the king, through Manchester, to whom Melo first proposed the matter on 1/11 September. Only Russell at the embassy was privy to the secret.[33] By the end of October, the marriage treaty was ready except for guarantees, and to obtain these, Melo embarked for Portugal on 21/31 October.[34] In order to prevent disquiet in the city of London, because of course Melo's reasons for returning were only a matter of conjecture to those outside the secret negotiations, the king issued a proclamation on 6/16 October, declaring the confirmation of the treaties with Portugal and the continuance of the amity and commerce between the two crowns. '. . . We have thought fit to publish and declare to all our loving subjects that they may without fear or apprehension, continue their trade and concern in Portugal . . .'.[35]

ii   *The Articles of Marriage*

The Articles of Marriage between His Majesty and the Lady Infanta of Portugal were signed on 13/23 June 1661. Details of the negotiations for the marriage can be found in Senhora Castello Branco's *Vida do Marquês de Sande*. They properly belong to a history of the diplomatic rather than commercial relations between the two countries. However, the treaty was not purely diplomatic in content.[36] It is significant that

Article 1 confirmed and ratified all treaties made since 1641 between England and Portugal, and those treaties were to receive 'as full force and ratification by this treaty as if they were herein particularly mentioned and inserted word for word'. Thus, in a sense, the Articles of Marriage were also a commercial treaty, for they confirmed and re-ratified the treaties of 1642 and 1654. The 1661 treaty contained even more of commercial interest. Four families of British subjects were to be allowed to live and enjoy privileges and immunities which the Portuguese themselves enjoyed in order to trade in each of the cities and towns of Goa, Cochim and Dio (Article 12), and Bahia de todos os Santos, Pernambuco and Rio de Janeiro and all other of the king of Portugal's dominions in the West Indies (Article 13).

It was hoped in England that the cession of Tangier (Article 2) would prove beneficial as a base from which a fleet could protect commerce through the Straits to the Mediterranean and the Levant, but the maintenance of a garrison there, and the building of a mole, proved too costly. Tangier was abandoned in 1684. By Article 11, Portugal had also ceded Bombay 'so that the king of Great Britain may be better enabled to assist, defend and protect the subjects of the king of Portugal in those parts'. Article 14 allowed Britain to keep any territories which might be re-taken by her from the Dutch or others, if they had belonged to Portugal in the past, with the exception of Muscat, which was to be Portuguese. Should the island of Ceylon be taken by either England or Portugal, then Colombo was to be reserved to Portugal, and Galle to England, and the cinnamon trade divided between them. The price for these concessions (Article 15) was that the king of Great Britain, with the consent and advice of the Council, promised that he would defend the interests of Portugal and its dominions by sea and land, even as he would Britain itself. Further, Charles II was to send to Portugal two regiments of horse, each regiment consisting of five hundred men, and two regiments of foot, each consisting of a thousand men. The cost of equipping and transporting them was to be met by the British king but, once landed, they were to be paid by the king of Portugal. Replacements were to be the charge of the king of Great Britain.

Under Article 16, Charles was to send ten good ships of war, manned and victualled for eight months, to sail under the orders of the king of Portugal, to protect the coast of Portugal as and when requested. Should the ships be required for more than six months, then the king of Portugal was to be responsible for victualling them. If Portugal should be specially pressed by enemies, then all the king of England's ships in the Mediterranean and Tangier were to obey orders from the king of Portugal and no charge was to be made by England for their use.

Queen Catherine brought with her a dower of 2,000,000 *cruzados* (£353,000), besides Tangier and the port and island of Bombay. It was specified in Article 5 that half the money was to accompany her to England.[37] In whatever form the money was put on board (whether jewels, sugar or merchandise), it was to be sent to the king of Portugal's agent in London, and then paid by him to the king within two months in English money. The other half of the dower was to be paid within a year of the arrival of Catherine in England. Articles 6 and 7 concerned the cost of the Infanta's transport and her freedom to exercise the Catholic religion in England. Articles 8 and 9 concerned her jointure and her household officers and servants, while by Article 19, Catherine was not required to renounce either her rights or those of her heirs to the Portuguese throne, or her portion as her father's daughter.

There was a secret article to the treaty. By this, the king of Great Britain promised to protect all the conquests or colonies belonging to the crown of Portugal against all its present and future enemies; to mediate a good peace between Portugal and the United Provinces and all companies of merchants subject to them; to defend with men and ships the dominions and conquests of the king of Portugal if such a peace were to prove impossible; to oblige the Dutch to a full restitution of any Portuguese territories which they might take after 1 May 1661, and, finally, the king of Great Britain was to send, the next monsoon ensuing the ratification of the treaty, convenient succour to the East Indies, proportionable to the necessity of Portugal.

Therefore, in return for re-ratification of an existing commercial treaty, a queen with a dower of two million *cruzados*, Tangier and Bombay, Great Britain was committed to onerous and expensive promises to protect Portugal for the unspecified future. Portuguese historians are given to being critical of the treaty.[38] They tend to generalize it, saying that Portugal ceded Tangier and Bombay and freedom of commerce, as well as paying the biggest dower ever paid before, for their princess's marriage to Charles II. They minimize or totally ignore what Portugal received in exchange, and they overlook the fact, made explicit in the instructions given to Melo,[39] that one million *cruzados* of Catherine's dower was considered by the Portuguese Council of State to be in payment for the assistance with defence, the cost of which, to England, in the end was arguably far more than one million *cruzados*. Senhora Castello Branco has suggested that the wording of Article 5 may have been because English ministers did not want this fact made public, or, perhaps, because Charles wanted to have the money at his own disposition.[40] After the first dower payment in 1662 of not quite one million *cruzados* (£176,500), of which, according to the Treasury, one hundred thousand *cruzados* were used to cover the cost of Sandwich's embassy to convey the Infanta to England,[41] no payments were made until pressure was brought to bear in 1668, after peace was made with Spain. Then the Portuguese maintained that the *cruzado* had been over-valued in their previous sterling payments and also claimed a further variety of deductions, which they maintained reduced the second million *cruzados* to 669,093. It was agreed that payments were to be resumed in 1670.[42] Because of successive devaluations of the Portuguese currency, by 1680 the *cruzado* was only worth 2s 7¼d. compared with 3s. 6d. in 1662.[43] Thus the sterling value of the dower was shrinking. When Charles died in 1685, £24,000 still remained to be paid to his successor, but £11,000 or 85,000 *cruzados* of that was used to cover the cost of Charles Fanshaw's embassy to Portugal to arrange the final payment.[44] To the last, there was constant cavilling on the part of the Portuguese about minutiae and every penny was disputed. Even when the money was packed and ready for shipment, difficulties were made about issuing a licence to cover its export, because of the restrictions on exporting bullion.[45]

The basic reasons for Portugal defaulting on its monetary obligations were the country's great poverty, and its inability to sustain the expense of the war for independence. In addition it had to find the wherewithal to make expensive treaties and to dower Catherine with two million *cruzados*. According to Maynard, even before the signing of the articles of marriage, the tax burden of the mass of the Portuguese people was nearly intolerable. The *fidalgos*, of course, paid nothing.[46]

None the less, as Professor Boxer and Senhora Castello Branco have pointed out, contemporary informed opinion in Portugal and elsewhere was virtually unanimous in considering the alliance a great diplomatic triumph for Portugal, most of all because it signified Portugal's re-entry into the comity of nations.[47] Portugal's standing and credit rose in the commercial world. By the treaty, England openly guaranteed Portugal's survival as an independent nation. Maynard summed up the position of Portugal during the negotiations when he said that a good peace (treaty) with England was 'the only thing under heaven left them to keep them from despair and ruine'.[48] The treaty certainly astounded Rome. The Portuguese currency rose on the Roman Exchange, and Cardinal Orsini, Portugal's Protector in Rome, reported that the pope had spoken with more respect regarding Portuguese affairs, which previously Orsini had thought to be lost.[49]

There was, however, a considerable body of uninformed opinion in Portugal which was very critical of some aspects of the treaty. This arose in part from the mystical attachment which the mass of the Portuguese people felt for their conquests, acquired at so great a cost of men and materials. There was considerable resentment at having to part with Tangier and Bombay, so great in the case of Tangier that Queen Luisa ordered that all reference to it be omitted in the final reading of the treaty before the Council of State, because she feared that the inhabitants of Lisbon would hear of it and oppose it.[50] A

seaport of Morocco, on the Straits of Gibraltar, fourteen miles east of
Cape Spartel, Tangier was of great strategic importance in guarding the
entrance to the Mediterranean and as a base for protecting shipping
from Moorish attacks. In 1437 a Portuguese expedition led by Henry
the Navigator had failed to take the town, and the Infante D. Fernando
had been left there in prison as a hostage for the return of Ceuta, which
had been taken by Portugal in 1415. He was never redeemed because,
as the expedition had been undertaken on papal advice, the archbishop
of Braga held that Ceuta could not be surrendered without the pope's
consent. This was never given, and Fernando died in Fez in 1443. He
was popularly canonized as the 'Infante Santo'. Tangier had ceded
from Spain at the Restoration in 1640, but became a drain on Portugal's
meagre resources. Certainly, the port was of little help to Christian
shipping. After Tangier was transferred to England, Lord Sandwich's
fleet transported the eight hundred Portuguese inhabitants who wished
to leave to ports in the Algarve. All Catholics who wished to remain
were given complete freedom to practise their religion. A mole was
built for shipping; the upper castle was repaired and an arsenal and
many redoubts were constructed against constant Moorish attacks. In
1664, 470 men and the governor, Lord Teviot, were killed, and from
1679 the town was under permanent siege. In 1680 the outside forts
were lost.[51] It is not surprising, therefore, that Britain abandoned the
port in 1684. It is certain the Portuguese could not have defended it
either. By then it had been found less costly in men and materials to
make treaties with the Moors (as was explained in Chapter 1); nevertheless the abandonment of Tangier was much resented by the Portuguese.
   In the case of Bombay, its value to Portugal was chiefly sentimental.
The Dutch had not considered it worth taking when they seized Muscat
and Ceylon. The so-called Bombay 'fortress' was only two small bul-
warks, some earth and stones. As for the island, 'the king of Portugal
has neither house, fort, ammunition nor foote of land on it'. 'Bombay
doth not answer our king's expectation by 4/5th of what was rep-
resented to him'.[52] The Portuguese governor of Bombay, António de
Melo e Castro, was actually conveyed to Bombay to effect the transfer
of the island to England in an English five-ship squadron, which sailed
from Lisbon on 10/20 April 1662 under the command of James Ley,
3rd Earl of Marlborough. En route, Melo e Castro quarrelled bitterly
with the English commanders and on arrival in Bombay he did everything possible to antagonize Portugal's allies. He refused to transfer the
sovereignty of the island, saying that Marlborough's credentials were
not in order, even though they had the broad seal on them. Further, he
actually boasted of his policy in his letters to Portugal.[53] Lisbon disas-
sociated itself from his policies and had to recall him in disgrace and
England only obtained possession in 1665. Meanwhile, the English

troops had died in great numbers for lack of shelter and accommodation, and so when the Dutch drove the Portuguese out of most of their positions on the Malabar coast and defeated them at Cochin, there was no one to oppose them.[54] It is no wonder that Charles II felt 'in the last resentments against this usage that can be imagined'.[55] Maynard said that the local people in Bombay were reported to have been convinced that Afonso VI did not really want to hand over Bombay and had only done so because he had been ill-advised by his ministers.[56]

Commenting on the Portuguese lamentations regarding Tangier and Bombay, the Portuguese historian Virginia Rau asked some valid questions: if these places had not been ceded, would they still have been in Portugal's possession in 1941? Would Portugal have been capable of developing them?[57] England, an ally of Portugal, was able through the East India Company to develop Bombay and offer some effective opposition to Dutch and, later, French, inroads in the Far East. England never attacked Portuguese interests in the Far East after the 1661 treaty, thus Goa, Daman and Diu remained in Portuguese hands until they were occupied by India after independence, in December 1961.

The cost to England of the fleet sent to take possession of Bombay had been high, the expenses being agreed at £229,862.14.0d,[58] allowances being made for Portugal's poverty. Charles never asked for compensation, doubtless because he knew Portugal could not pay. No record of payment of agreed expenses has been traced, but, strangely, no envoys even appear to have asked for it. The debt was not added to the dower. In 1669, Charles ceded Bombay to the East India Company. The latter asked Sir Robert Southwell to obtain permission for them to trade in cloth with China or, at least, to be able to fit and repair ships at Macao.[59] Although a source of friction between allies and a disappointment at first to England, Bombay was to prove of great value to England in the eighteenth century and its cession was the first step in the East India Company's investment in India which, later, became a part of the British Empire.

In 1661, Portugal had been negotiating a peace with the United Provinces. The Dutch were insisting on obtaining the same commercial privileges as those given to England in 1654, or, alternatively, what they considered to be adequate monetary compensation. It was customary for the Portuguese ambassadors in Europe to keep each other informed of their negotiations. Melo wrote to the ambassador at The Hague remonstrating against the settlement which the latter proposed to the Dutch. Such concessions were most inconvenient at a time when his treaty with England had been agreed, but not yet signed. Portugal had no other remedy than England, and England might well cancel the treaty if the clauses of the Dutch-Portuguese treaty were to be diametrically opposed to what the English considered to be the most important aspects of their treaty with Portugal, the trade concessions.[60] Charles was to show himself consistently sympathetic to Portugal's difficulties, however, and he consented that the crown of Portugal should grant the Dutch (who were Britain's chief commercial rivals) the same commercial privileges as those enjoyed by the English, in view of the urgency felt by Portugal in concluding peace with the States-General, but he asked to be compensated for this kindness in some other way.[61] This concession on his part ended the chief advantages enjoyed by the English merchants in Portugal by the treaty of 1654. In what way Charles was ever compensated is difficult to say. In 1667, Portugal granted the same privileges to the French, and by the end of the century, they were enjoyed even by the Spanish.[62] The Portuguese did not proclaim their treaty with the Dutch until 27 April 1663. The treaty was unpopular in Portugal, for besides granting the Dutch commercial privileges, Portugal agreed to pay them four million *cruzados* in compensation for the loss of their Brazilian territories, as it had actively assisted those who had rebelled against Dutch rule in Brazil.[63] This had to be paid chiefly in salt from Setúbal, which meant that there was no revenue coming into the treasury from one of the chief exports at a time when Portugal was still at war with Spain. The Dutch took Cochin and Cananor early in 1663, and by May 1664, even before Bombay had been ceded, the Portuguese were asking Charles II for assistance in recovering them (in accordance with the Secret Article of the 1661 treaty), maintaining that the delay by England in agreeing to allow the Dutch equal commercial privileges in the Luso-Dutch treaty had been the cause of their loss.[64] That England was not able to do anything about Cochin and Cananor at that time is not surprising, in view of Charles' own financial straits;[65] his 'last resentments' against the Portuguese treatment of the Earl of Marlborough and the force sent out to take over Bombay, and his costly concessions regarding the Luso-Dutch treaty. Moreover, it should be remembered that in 1665, when England was again at war with the Dutch, Portugal did nothing to assist, because the war with Spain was not concluded. The plague in 1665 and the great fire which devastated London in 1666, left England with few reserves. By January 1666 England was also at war with France.

It needs to be said in this connection that despite Portugal's financial defaulting, Charles made constant efforts to mediate a peace between Portugal and Spain.[66] He also fulfilled his obligation to protect the Portuguese coast, by maintaining a fleet off it for the protection of maritime trade in general, and of the Brazil fleets in particular. English warships in Portuguese waters for three successive summers (1661-3) certainly prevented a Spanish invasion by sea[67] and, as Maynard pointed out, the arrival of Lawson's squadron in May 1663 enabled veteran troops to be drawn from garrison duty at Lisbon, Setúbal and other ports, for the reinforcement of the army in the Alentejo, which contributed to the Portuguese victory at Ameixial in June 1663 and ended the long stalemate on the frontier.[68] The English auxiliary forces sent out to Portugal were ill-treated, and their pay was grossly in arrears, so much so that they had to be paid from the dower money.[69] When requested, Charles sent out reinforcements. There is no doubt that Charles fulfilled his treaty obligations in these instances, and he certainly did not do it for financial gain.

iii Queen Catherine

Queen Catherine's thirty years in England cannot have been a happy experience for her; sadly, she never seemed able to adapt herself to her new country or to the English, and never won their affection. Further, because there was no heir from her marriage, she was a great disappointment, for few people were happy at the prospect of Charles II's Roman Catholic brother, James, becoming king.

Catherine was born in Vila Viçosa on 15/25 November 1638. She had been taught that submission and unworldliness were the greatest virtues, and she was brought up in a court where life was monotonous and austere, with iron etiquette.[70] It is no wonder that Maynard believed her to be shy and retiring, as well as of 'incomparable virtue, excellent parts, and very beautiful though of indifferent stature'.[71] Despite her education, Catherine was not docile and malleable. She was a woman of strong character and determination and, like her brothers, lived in constant rebellion against her mother.

Nothing illustrates her dislike of governance more than her attitude to Portugal's Ambassador to London, Francisco de Melo (Conde da Ponte, 1661 and Marquês de Sande, 1662), who was placed in charge of her on the voyage to England and asked to advise her when she arrived. Before leaving Portugal, she was forced to make what amounted to a public apology to Melo and on the voyage to England, Catherine and her retinue completely ignored him. When she reached England and discovered that Lady Castlemaine, the king's mistress, was to be one of her ladies-in-waiting, she refused to listen to Melo's advice to be tactful. Charles was consequently cool, and it was Chancellor Clarendon who finally persuaded Catherine to accept the situation.[72] As far as Melo was concerned, she still bore a grudge in 1666. From a letter Melo wrote to Russell from Paris, it is clear that he and Catherine were barely on speaking terms.[73] Whilst it was understandable, her attempted stand against Lady Castlemaine appeared gauche and unsophisticated in a royal princess of twenty-four.

One of her difficulties was that, in spite of English lessons, she never mastered the English language, and she spoke little and bad French. She and Charles always conversed together in Spanish, which must have lessened her rapport with English people. She adhered to the Portuguese fashion in court dress, whether from choice or on the advice of her Portuguese ladies is not certain, but the result was that she was ridiculed at court.[74] She was a great card player and gambler, and enjoyed these amusements even on Sundays, which scandalized Protestant Pepys.[75]

Catherine failed to accommodate herself to major trends and forces in English life, and never succeeded in passing herself off as someone fully committed to the welfare of her adopted country. The most glaring instance of this was her characteristically Iberian attitude to advancing Roman Catholicism. Even before she left Portugal, it was agreed between her and her extensive ecclesiastical retinue that her chief task in England was to provide a base for the restoration of Catholicism in that country.[76] Her staff of priests was brought to England not just to minister to her and her household, as specified in the articles of the treaty, but to secure the conversion of influential persons at court, to meet the needs of English Catholics, and to provide cover and support for Catholic missionaries. Her 'family' and chapel staff included many English, Irish and Scottish Roman Catholics, and it was her overt involvement with assisting English Catholics which explains the attacks made on her at the time of the popish plot. More circumspection in the operation of her chapels would have lessened suspicion.

Charles II could have done more to guide Catherine, because she grew to love him sincerely. Although a convinced Catholic himself, he was astute enough to know that if he were to openly acknowledge this, he would have been sent 'on his travels' (in exile) again. Only on his death-bed did he accept conversion. None the less, he firmly supported Catherine during the plot fever between 1678–81.

The great pity about Catherine's apparent lack of understanding was that she had great goodwill towards England, and fully realized the value to Portugal of the English connection, as is obvious from the letters she wrote to her brother, Pedro, the Prince Regent.[77] Even after 1668, when the alliance was of less value to Portugal, she continued to work for Anglo-Portuguese friendship.

Catherine's lasting legacy to England was to make tea-drinking fashionable.[78] It has been said that she introduced marmalade to England, but that is unlikely. What she probably did introduce was 'marmelada', made by boiling quinces and sugar. Perhaps oranges were more generally obtainable and, cooked by the same method, became English marmalade.

After the death of Charles II in February 1685, Catherine did not return to Portugal immediately, as she was involved in a law suit against her former Chamberlain, Henry, Earl of Clarendon. She was still in England at the time of the revolution in 1688. She finally left for Portugal in March 1692, travelling overland through France and Spain and arriving in Lisbon in January 1693. There she became the chief spokesman in Lisbon for the traditional policy of alliance with England. She was regent for her brother, King Pedro II, in 1704–5 and when she died at Bemposta on 31 December 1705, she told her English doctor that she had never tried to introduce Roman Catholicism into England, but had just tried to do her duty in accordance with the marriage agreement.[79]

PART II:
THE ENGLISH NATION IN PORTUGAL 1650–1690

9

Trading in Portugal

i   The Consul, his Consular Duties, the Factory and his Charges

The office of consul originated in twelfth-century Italy. A consul was a president, judge and spokesman for his fellow citizens living in a foreign country.[1] Seventeenth-century consuls had a more difficult task than diplomats at that time, because they did not enjoy the protection of the law of nations, and were subject in civil and criminal matters to the jurisdiction of the place of residence.[2] In 1649, the Council of State had asserted its right to approve all consular nominees,[3] for it depended on consuls for political intelligence and assistance to the fleet. However, consuls were not paid by their own government, which issued their letters patent, nor by the foreign prince or government which concurred and assented to their appointments, but by the merchants. Normally, seventeenth-century consuls in English service received a ¼% cut on all goods and merchandise imported by English subjects into the country to which they had been appointed. In the case of Maynard, by his patent of 27 August/6 September 1656, he was to receive ½% on all goods and merchandise imported into Portugal by the subjects of the Commonwealth, for as long as he combined the consulship with being an agent as well. Out of this salary, but only as long as he received the ½%, Maynard had to pay a Protestant minister 400 *milreis* per annum and allow him a sufficient diet. Any monies voluntarily contributed to the minister's maintenance by the merchants and factors resident in Portugal were to be deducted and allowed to Maynard out of the 400 *milreis*.[4] In Charles II's reign, the crown not only enjoyed a free consular service, which was the universally accepted practice at the time, but used appointments to the office of consul as a means of rewarding friends and supporters, without even consulting the merchants, whereas the Commonwealth did consult them. This power of appointment Charles II jealously and successfully guarded against the efforts of Commons and merchants to make such appointments subject to mercantile approval.[5]

Maynard's consulship was remarkable, not only for the initial terms of his remuneration. He was one of the very few consuls to keep his post after the restoration of Charles II. He had remained secretly a king's man throughout his consulship under the Protectorate, and, as will be seen, he worked astutely to retain his post. He received a new patent as consul general which was dated 27 June 1660.[6] This granted him four crowns on every ship entering the place where he resided, or any other place or places within the limits appointed to him, 'from Caminha northwards unto Castro Marim southwards in ye maine and ye islands of ye Azores, Maderas, Porto Santo and ye Algarves and frontier towns in Barbary'. Maynard was entitled to collect his percentage from all Englishmen, Irishmen and Scotsmen importing goods into Portugal, and on goods sent to Portugal by merchant strangers residing in England, Scotland and Ireland. He was also to receive ½% on all freights made to Brazil and the East Indies on all ships and vessels belonging to British subjects or any merchant strangers resident in His Majesty's kingdoms. Out of his revenue Maynard was to pay the Protestant minister the sum of 300 *milreis* per annum for his salary, diet and lodging. That sum was half the minister's salary; the merchants paid him the same, and thus had the right to appoint to the benefice.[7]

In order that the consul should not be defrauded, and to prevent contentions and differences, the patent enjoined all merchants, owners and purveyors of ships and others whom it might concern to show the consul, or his deputies and assigns, their books or bills of lading, contents, qualities and quantities brought into ports, so that he could levy his consulage according to the value declared by the officers of the customs house of the king of Portugal. In the case of goods which paid no duty, such as corn, butter and grain, consulage was to be levied on the price for which the goods were sold. This gave ample opportunity for dissension, because a merchant's books were sacrosanct. The consul was more often than not a merchant himself, and he usually had a business of his own.[8] Indeed, merchants and factors preferred to have a consul who, because he was one of their own kind, understood their needs and problems; the disadvantage as that he, too, knew the tricks of the trade and the art of avoiding the payment of customs duties. By seeing their books, he would learn the 'secrets of their trade'. The system led to many battles between dissatisfied merchants and their consuls, not only in Portugal. Consul Martin Westcombe of Cadiz, for instance, was required to go to England and answer charges brought against him by the merchants before the Privy Council.[9] The Levant Company solved the problem by ruling in 1624 that once a merchant was elected to be a consul, he was no longer allowed to trade for himself.[10] The Levant Company, however, was a regulated company enjoying the monopoly of trade in the Levant, and there was no such company in Spain or Portugal in the second half of the seventeenth century. A prohibition on the consul's trading would have meant higher fees being paid by the merchants, or the consul being paid from the Exchequer. Neither was practicable at the time.

The consul's remuneration came from ship-owners as well as mer-

chants and factors, so the masters of ships pressed for consulage to be
levied solely on the value of merchandise carried, whilst merchants and
factors pressed for a blanket charge on every English ship, which
would fall on ship-owners and merchant companies alike. The consul
naturally wanted to be paid a percentage value of goods, a tax on the
ship and a percentage of freights. Everything really depended on the
strength and personality of the consul, for there was nothing which
effectively bound the masters or merchants and factors to pay anything
if they did not wish to do so, for, as the patent stipulated, the pain of
disobedience was to be according to royal prerogative. That was so
distant as to be of no effect. The only lever available to a consul was that
he could refuse to clear goods through the customs until his demands
were satisfied, but he could only do that when he himself was resident
in the port in question.[11] In 1683, for instance, the Oporto merchants
disapproved of what Maynard wanted, so they just withheld payment
of his dues.[12]

It was the consul's duty to take up and decide all contentions and
strife that arose among the British subjects in Portugal and the Portuguese Dominions, which could be conveniently ordered without any
further proceeding at law, and, if those subjects suffered damage or
injustice at the hands of the Portuguese nationals, he had to endeavour
to obtain reparation by complaining to the Portuguese sovereign. In
default of redress, he had to advise the Secretary of State in England
and the British representative in Lisbon, if there should be one at the
time. If any merchants died intestate, authority was given in the patent
for the consul, and merchants whom he called to his assistance, to seize
and take into their possession all the goods and chattels, wares and
merchandises, monies, books and evidence; to make an inventory and
true valuation, and dispose of perishables by sale or otherwise, for the
benefit of whomsoever they should belong to. If the deceased left a will,
the consul was to follow the same instructions, until the legatees (often
in England) could give orders for disposing of or taking possession of
the goods. If any factor, agent or apprentice or servant of a merchant
misdemeaned himself, putting the estates of merchants and other
subjects in danger, Maynard, or his deputies, had to take the estates of
such merchants into safe keeping, until the owner should give orders
for disposing of them, and to send the offending party to England.

The consul had overall control of the poor box, which by 1721 had
become known as the contribution fund. This was used to help
Englishmen in extremity because of shipwreck, pirates, sea-rovers or
other disasters. The consul could levy and collect money for this at his
discretion from the estates of the merchants and factors, in order to
have sufficient funds to return the distressed to their own country with
all convenient speed. For this purpose he normally collected four *reis*

per *milrei* on the valuation of goods in the customs house at Lisbon.[13] In practice, this fund was administered by the Treasurer of the factory, but, as was usual with factory matters, there was much dissension; as, for instance, when the Treasurer arbitrarily extracted four hundred *milreis* to buy plate for a departing envoy.[14]

In addition to the tasks mentioned in the patent, it was customary for the consul to help merchants to fulfil their customs formalities, clear ships and collect debts. He determined disputes between merchants and masters of ships, and between masters and their seamen. He assisted English masters in rounding up their crews after shore leave and prevented, whenever possible, masters of foreign vessels from luring English seamen into their service. He had to secure for Englishmen all the civil and religious rights to which they were entitled by treaty or by the Law of Nations. In wartime, apart from making regular reports to the Secretary of State, he had to report the movements of any enemy in the vicinity; warn English merchantmen of the dangers they might encounter in nearby waters; induce them to wait for convoy; issue passports; commission privateers; assist in the disposal of prizes that might be brought into the ports over which he had charge, and give all possible assistance to the English fleet in Portuguese waters.[15] In addition, it would seem that during the Protectorate, Maynard undertook to fulfil further responsibilities with regard to the fleet. The victualling of the English fleet was apparently in the hands of a Mr Amory, but Maynard pointed out to Thurloe that all the provisions which Blake obtained from Portugal were subject to customs duty. This was unnecessary, he said, because in the past the Commonwealth's enemies had been able to buy provisions free of tax. He asked Thurloe to let him have instructions to ask for the same privilege. He also asked to be allowed to have the management of the victualling of the fleet. 'I will be faithful', he wrote.[16] It would seem that his request was granted, for on 4 December 1657 (N.S.), Maynard wrote to Thurloe saying that Mr Amory was leaving for England on the *Lamport*, with a 'fair estate gotten in twelve months' time'.[17]

As consul, Maynard was, therefore, expected to be the leader and representative of all Englishmen in Portugal and its dominions, but because he was dependent on the merchants for his living, they were the most important of his charges. Like the merchants of other nationalities in Portugal, the English merchants were organized in a factory, an assembly of merchants and factors. There was no act or decree authorizing the factory; its growth had been gradual and built on custom and usage. Research into the organization and trade of the English merchants in Portugal is hampered by lack of source material. When the French invaded Portugal in 1807 during the Napoleonic wars, it is known that the factory minute books, or journals of proceedings from 31 July 1715 to 1807, were in existence. Those covering the period 31 July 1715-17 February 1749 were laid before the factory by John Bell, the pro-consul general, at the first meeting of the factory after the expulsion of the French, held on 15 November 1808. They have disappeared. The other journals were entrusted to James Gambier, the retiring British consul, to be taken to England for safety.[18] They were said to have been lost by ship-wreck on their way to England, but there has been no evidence to support this statement. Gambier himself arrived safely, later, in Rio de Janeiro, but the journals have not been found.[19] The factory itself was abolished by the Treaty of 19 February 1810, between Great Britain and Portugal, which was signed in Rio de Janeiro.[20]

There is no record of any constitution having ever been drawn up for the factory, but much can be deduced from extant records, chiefly correspondence. It is known, for instance, that not all merchants and factors were members, because eligibility depended on the quantity of goods imported and on commercial and social reputation. Membership was only open to British nationals. The consul was an ex-officio member and he levied the dues assessed by the factory officers. Membership of the factory had a business value and brought commercial and social prestige, besides a vote in the election of officers of the factory, some of whom were paid salaries whilst others held honorary positions. More important, membership meant having a voice in decisions taken to facilitate the clearing of goods through the customs; redressing the anomalies in valuation of goods; drafting new tariffs and helping to secure space in the customs house for landed goods, which was extremely important in Lisbon.[21]

Professor S. George West has shown that residence in Portugal was not a statutory condition of membership.[22] It may be that factors who returned to England maintained their interest, either by continued membership, or by proxy. Perhaps another member of the family would go out to Portugal to represent a business, not necessarily with the same name, for he might be a relative by marriage. He would still have been, however, part of the same family group or 'house'. Another possibility is that a retiring factor, or his remaining partner, might have been able to nominate a successor.

To determine the actual number of members in the factory presents difficulties, because it is not known whether membership was limited to any given number. By comparing a list of factory members given by Captain James Jennifer of the merchantman *Saudades* in 1672/3,[23] with the names said to be those of all the members of the factory by the signatories on a petition sent to the bishop of London in 1686,[24] Professor West has come to the conclusion that on both occasions there were thirty-three members.[25] The petition to the bishop of London, however, was made as a result of the imprisonment of Maynard and the Chaplain, Michael Geddes, by the Inquisition. In the circumstances of 1686, no Catholic would have dared to sign the petition to the bishop of London for redress against the Inquisition, and it is known that Catholics were not excluded from membership of the factory. Indeed, William Colston, listed by Captain Jennifer as being Treasurer of the factory in 1672/3, was a Catholic.[26] Because of the rifts caused by political and religious differences and local animosities, it would be unwise to identify membership of the factory with the signatories to the many merchants' petitions preserved in the Public Record Office and the British Library. It is also more than probable that membership increased or decreased in accordance with the economic climate. Finally, there is the uncertain position of the twenty-one merchants stated by Captain Jennifer to be resident in Oporto.[27] Whether they were, or could be, members of the Lisbon factory is not known. The Oporto merchants were governed by a consul, who was within the appointment of the consul general in Lisbon.[28] The same arrangement applied to groups of merchants in other ports in the kingdom. A percentage of consulage dues paid in those ports was paid over to the consul general in Lisbon. Oporto later had its own factory.[29]

The factories became not only the business and organizational centres of the merchant communities but also the social centres for all British nationals. To what extent this applied in the seventeenth century is difficult to judge. It is known, however, that the English merchants had a meeting place in the Travessa do Espirito Santo, a narrow lane running up hill from the Largo do Corpo Santo, which had been given to them by a former king.[30] Such a gift was not unusual. The English merchants in San Lucar de Barrameda had been given a house in which to meet, land on which to build a church, and the right to a consul and judge of their own by the Duke of Medina Sidonia in 1517.[31] Factory affairs, on the other hand, were transacted at the consul's house. In a letter to Sir Robert Southwell, dated 28 May 1670 (N.S.), Maynard stated that five or six days previously he had summoned all the factory to meet at his house 'according to the ancient custom of the place'. It is interesting to note that he further said that 'all twenty of the merchants met'.[32] It is clear from the Hospital Minute Book that even in the nineteenth century, factory meetings were held at the consul's house.

Merchants operated singly or in partnerships. The partnerships were usually not permanent, but for specific ventures only. It was essential to spread risks.[33] In a business house, one partner would sometimes remain in England, whilst other partners might be in Lisbon or Oporto, operating independently. Such partners generally belonged to the same family, by birth or marriage, because until there was a law of limited liability, it was safer that way.[34] Not all merchants were factors. Factors were agents, sometimes apprentices nearing the end of their apprenticeship, sometimes just trading for themselves, serving several merchants. They all had to have a knowledge of book-keeping (such as it was at the time), and bills of exchange, and they had to keep their principal/s up to date with the current information on trade and diplomacy, sending copies of their letters by different ships or overland as well as by sea, in order to ensure safe receipt of at least one copy. If apprentices, they were generally allowed to trade on their own account. They received either a salary or factorage, but they were bound to answer for losses caused by exceeding their commission.[35] The merchants in Portugal did not belong to a regulated company, so it was up to individual merchants to pay their factors as they pleased, and it appears that payment was generally made on a commission basis, 2% being the minimum.[36] Maynard said that 11% was the maximum profit a merchant ever made on a transaction. It is not clear from the context, however, whether he was referring to the principal's profit or that of the factor, but it was more than likely to have been the former.[37]

Merchant houses in England did not necessarily use their own nationals as factors in Portugal. One of the reasons for this was that by not doing so they avoided the payment of the four *reis* in the *milrei* levied on the valuation of goods exacted by the factory for the benefit of distressed British seamen and others in need.[38] The practice of avoiding levies by consigning goods to other nationals grew so great that the factory wanted all goods from Great Britain and Ireland exported to Portugal and its Dominions to be leviable regardless of the nationality of the consignee. They wanted to be able to levy any sum not exceeding 200 *reis* per ton on tonnage of goods, except wheat, barley, rye, coals, timber, boards or lumber, and 100 *reis* on the excepted goods, as well as 15% on freight of other goods. These dues were to be paid by all masters or commanders of ships.[39] It is not known whether merchants of other countries trading to Portugal used English factors to avoid payment of their factory dues, but it seems that all English business in Venice in 1665 was in the hands of Italians and Dutchmen, and half the goods exported to Livorno from England were in the hands of foreigners, although the English factory there comprised fifty members.[40]

Many of the factors and merchants were sober, responsible people; many were married men, living with their wives, children and servants, but some of the younger men were extremely difficult to govern and keep in order. According to Sir Robert Southwell in November 1668, William Peachey, Major Randolph, Richard Stanley, Joseph Dorny, Edward Colson and Humphrey Benning were 'factious unquiet spirits and delight in debauching all young men to make up a party', who wanted to 'shew themselves . . . Free borne subjects, and to uphold the

Liberties of the People, which is their mutinous dialect'.[41] In another letter he describes them as being: '. . . for the most part young men who, having been bred up in the Licentious Principles of the late bad Times have not as yett mended their manners nor their operations'.[42] Neither political nor drunken debauchery would have endeared Englishmen to traditionalist and abstemious Portuguese people, making it harder for the consul to redress any wrongs done to the sober, responsible members of the community.

After the consul, perhaps the most important person in the factory was a Portuguese, the judge conservator, or *Conservador*. He was not a member of the factory and had no vote in proceedings, but the merchants and factors often valued him more highly than they did their consul, for he was the means of giving them speedy justice in the courts without in any way interfering, or being suspected of interfering, in their affairs. Since the privilege had first been granted in 1367, the conservator had always been a petty judge who was overseer of the customs house in Lisbon (*ouvidor da alfândega*), and had been changed triennially according to the laws of Portugal.[43] He was empowered to constitute a court and bring cases before him in the first instance and to determine in a judicial capacity all causes, disputes and contracts concerning Englishmen, whether or not they were members of the factory.[44] These were many, because the various privileges which the English had received over the years had led to jealousy and animosity on the part of the native merchants. Cloth and other merchandise belonging to English merchants and stored in the customs house were liable to be stolen, and fines were exacted for technical omissions on papers and affidavits. In addition to adjudicating on complaints of this sort, the conservator was responsible for the collection of debts for goods sold to Portuguese who refused to pay or whose heirs sought to avoid payment after death.[45]

The English merchants had no choice in the selection of their conservator until after 1656, when the 1654 treaty was ratified, and their privilege of having a conservator became a right under the treaty. It seems that they then decided that it would be preferable to have a man of their own choosing. This was granted. Only once was their choice refused, and that was when they selected António de Sousa de Macedo, who was then a judge.[46] The post was highly sought after because the conservator was paid a retaining fee or salary by the factory, and the salaries of local officials were mostly in arrears.[47] Under the new system, the conservator was not changed triennally but held office for life. All went well until one, Luís Alvares Ribeira, who had been chosen by a bare majority vote, had had his appointment confirmed by Prince Pedro, the Regent.[48] He proved a most unsatisfactory conservator; lived too long and did not prove sufficiently zealous in pressing the affairs of the English nation. Charles II wrote to Prince Pedro to ask that the conservator should be replaced, and that the merchants should be allowed to select a man for a three-year term. The Regent would not agree, unless there was a return to the old system of using the *ouvidor da alfândega*. The merchants had thought that if they could choose a man triennially from among the judges of the supreme court, the authority of his person would add vigour to his dispatches, and the hope of being re-elected would make him favourable to them.[49] The matter was not settled until the death of Luís Alvares Ribeira in 1678, when it was agreed that there should be a return to using the services of the *ouvidor*.[50] The consul and twenty-six merchants voted for the change on the grounds that the judge of the customs house gave audience three times a week near the merchants' houses, whilst a superior judge would give audience only two times a week and his court would be further away. In addition, the judge of the customs house was replaced triennially and was dependent on the merchants for his gratuity.[51] There were no further complaints about the conservator in the seventeenth century.

Another important member of the factory was the chaplain. The advowson and gift of the cure of souls was in the English merchants in London trading to Lisbon, though the bishop of London issued the ecclesiastic licences, as until 1867 all foreign plantations, colonies, factories and other places abroad were in his diocese.[52] The first chaplain to be appointed was Zachary Cradock, a Fellow of Queen's College, Cambridge, who was recommended to Thurloe by Dr Ralph Cudworth, Master of Christ's College and brother-in-law of Edward Bushell.[53] Maynard's patent of 1656 made it quite clear that he was to act as Agent in the absence of an accredited envoy, so it became the custom for religious services to be held in his house, the Casa dos Caídos, in São Paulo parish, every Sunday. All the Protestant members of the factory and their wives and families attended. When there was an envoy, everyone met in his house.[54]

Religious dissension in England was reflected among the merchant community in Portugal. There were those who strongly supported Nonconformist Protestantism and those who wanted an Anglican chaplain. When Cradock returned to England in December 1659,[55] there was disagreement with regard to his successor. Some merchants wanted another Presbyterian, but Maynard wrote asking that a Church of England 'conformable' man be sent out, 'well versed in controversies'. He considered it essential that a chaplain should be appointed; without one, 'young men will take too much liberty and growe more Extravagant in their vices if they be not restrained'.[56] While there was no chaplain, the merchants wanted that part of Maynard's salary payable to a divine to be applied to the factory's common stock for charitable uses, in order to ease them and their principals in London, but as Sir Richard Fanshaw pointed out, if that were allowed, the living would never be filled and the privilege would be lost. Sir Richard suggested that the stipend should be held over for the next incumbent.[57]

Thomas Marsden, Sir Richard's own chaplain, went to Lisbon in 1663, and a letter from him to Sir Richard soon after the latter's departure for Madrid in 1664, throws an interesting sidelight on the factory: '. . . Immediately on my being deprived of the protection of your presence, I thought it needful to put more sweat into my sermons than formerly I did, least any might watch for an occasion to say that my pains were not equal to my pay'. He goes on to say, however, that all the Englishmen in Portugal were so anxious for him to stay that they offered to augment his salary, or give him leave of absence for ten or twelve months for settling his affairs in England before his return.[58]

In the absence of an accredited envoy, services continued to be held in the consul's house in Lisbon until 1686, when the then chaplain, Dr Geddes, and Maynard, were both taken up and questioned by the Inquisition because of this.[59] From then on, when there was no envoy, there were no services. The position was difficult, because although Maynard's patent from Charles II did not specifically say that he was to be an agent in the absence of any envoy (which would have given his house the necessary diplomatic privilege to have services held there), it is clear that he in fact always acted as an agent on those occasions, and was expected by the king so to act.[60]

In Oporto, the English merchants had a chaplain from 1671. The first man to be appointed was a Mr Brawler or Brawlard. It appears that Maynard obtained a letter of favour for him from the Portuguese Secretary of State at that time, the Conde de Miranda (later Marquês de Arronches).[61] In Oporto the services were held in different houses each Sunday, to which the church box had previously been taken. The host entertained the congregation to dinner and a game of whist after the service.[62] The chaplains had to remain incognito, for the Portuguese government always insisted on unobtrusiveness in the worship of Protestants, to avoid scandalizing the people.

As consul general, as agent, as a merchant in his own right and as president of the factory, Maynard had a sufficiently difficult and onerous task. However, he had more than merchants and seamen to contend with: he had overall responsibility for all the people of his nation in Portugal and its dominions. Regrettably, it is virtually impossible to estimate the number and quality of those people with any accuracy, but a list of British residents living in Lisbon at the time of the 1755 earthquake gives some idea of their diversity. The list comprised all British residents living within the 'cortes' or official area of Lisbon and lists 155 men with business interests; 13 widows connected with business houses, 15 persons unconnected with business interests, but who were 'worthy of every consideration'; 165 people connected with eating houses, shops, inns, etc., as well as a number of hairdressers, carpenters, tailors, shoemakers, teachers of writing and accounts, and even a mustard maker. It was calculated that at the time of the earthquake there must have been a British population of several thousands in the city,[63] including those who had settled in Lisbon for religious reasons.

Considerable numbers of Catholics left England during the seventeenth century to avoid the recusancy laws, preferring to live abroad in Catholic countries, and some found their way to Portugal. If they wished to enter religious houses in Portugal, arrangements were made for them to stay in the houses of nobles and *fidalgos* until they had learnt the language. For instance, Margaret Throckmorton stayed in the house of Dom Manuel de Souza.[64] The Portuguese state paid small pensions to persons suffering exile and poverty because they had become Catholics. Thus, Allen Hutchinson applied for and received, in 1679, a pension of 120 *milreis* a year by claiming that he was the first cousin of Queen Catherine's Lord Chamberlain, and that he had left England and large estates in order to be converted.[65]

Queen Catherine's will throws some light on the English-speaking religious houses in Lisbon. She left 3,000 crowns each to the Convent of St Brigid; the Convent of Bom Successo (which housed Irish Dominican nuns) and to the Irish Friars of Corpo Santo. In addition, she left 1,000 crowns to the English Seminary, the College of St Peter and St Paul (always known as the *Inglesinhos*, or little Englishmen), and a like sum to the College or Seminary of St Patrick, run by Irish fathers.[66] The Brigitine nuns, who by the nineteenth century were back in England, had originally left England on the accession of Queen Elizabeth in 1558, and, after many wanderings on the continent, arrived in Lisbon in 1594. They were given pensions by Philip II and by the City of Lisbon. Philip also gave them thirty-six quarters of wheat annually to be paid for from the revenue of the fens belonging to the crown at Santarem. These they enjoyed until they returned to England in the nineteenth century. The number of sisters is only known for the year 1622, when there were twenty-eight, which number included three Portuguese and two Dutch women. Their church and convent were burned down in 1651 and when they were rehoused in 1656, they became chiefly a lay foundation.[67] It is interesting to note that when Portuguese girls entered the convent, feuds occurred, so that it was necessary to rule that only girls born English subjects could be admitted. Apparently, any English girls left destitute in Portugal by parents who were unsuccessful in business or trade, or wanted to come and join them from Great Britain, were accepted.[68]

The Convent of Bom Successo had been founded by Frei Domingos

do Rosario (Father Daniel O'Daly, 1595-1662) who became rector of
Corpo Santo Monastery in 1634. In order to obtain permission to found
the convent, he had to recruit Irish soldiers for the Spanish army. Bom
Successo was dowered by Dona Irene de Brito, Condessa de Atalaya,
and housed forty nuns.[69] It is not known how many Dominican friars
there were in the Corpo Santo, but Frei Domingos was appointed
confessor to Queen Luisa, and he was employed on diplomatic missions
by John IV and Queen Luisa, when Regent. He was made Bishop of
Coimbra in 1659, but was not consecrated, because no Portuguese
bishops were consecrated between 1640 and 1670 as the pope had not
recognized Portuguese independence.[70]

With the exception of one instance, when the Corpo Santo Monastery disseminated anti-Protestant propaganda,[71] none of the foregoing
establishments, except the *Inglesinhos*, is known to have given the
consul any problems. The English College of St Peter and St Paul was
quite another matter. Not only did its members very actively carry out
missionary work in England, and among the English community in
Portugal, but the college's close ties with the Portuguese crown and the
court of St James made it a great force in the fight which English
Catholics made to obtain a return to Catholicism in England. It was the
source of many of Maynard's difficulties in Portugal. The college was
only closed in 1973. All its records are now housed at Ushaw College,
Co. Durham, where they are currently being catalogued. Because of
the important part played by the college, it will be dealt with separately
in Chapter 12.

ii   *Vicissitudes of the 1654 treaty*

During her regency, Queen Luisa had always tried to ensure that the
unpopular treaty with England was observed by Portugal, because she
realized Portugal's dependence on the English alliance. Owing to
Afonso VI's defects, however she made plans in 1662 to supplant him
in real power by his younger brother, Prince Pedro. Her plans were
foiled by Luís de Vasconcellos e Sousa, Conde de Castelo Melhor, First
Gentleman of the Bedchamber to Afonso VI. Castelo Melhor forced the
queen to retire and became, in reality, the ruler of Portugal. Sousa de
Macedo, Portugal's former representative in London between 1642-5,
was appointed secretary of state. Castelo Melhor was ousted and exiled
by Prince Pedro in 1667. Pedro forced his brother to withdraw from
public affairs and assumed the regency of Portugal. Only on the death
of Afonso in 1683 did he become king, with the title of Pedro II.

It is from the time that Queen Luisa retired that the State Papers,
Portugal, in England contain constant complaints about the non-observance by Portugal of the terms of the 1654 treaty. There was certainly

substance in the complaints, for succeeding English envoys, who were not merchants but spent considerable time in Portugal, substantiated them. Further, even before the multiplication of complaints in English records, the papers of Francisco de Melo show that he was aware that the 1654 treaty was not being observed in Portugal. He was constantly exhorting the queen to see that the articles were kept, and where he knew that the Portuguese government had virtually no real control, as in matters concerning the Inquisition, he went to considerable lengths to keep the facts from being exposed. This was demonstrated in his manipulation of the Portugal merchants at the time he was negotiating the 1661 treaty.

The normal procedure was for merchants' complaints to be dealt with in the first instance by the consul, or by the English representative in Lisbon when there was one. When complaints became too numerous, or if redress proved impossible, then the complaints were listed and Charles II was asked to intervene. Overall, an impression is gained of a stubborn resistance on the part of the Portuguese to a treaty they resented. Unfortunately, in this they were aided by bad drafting of the treaty as far as England's interests were concerned. The Commonwealth negotiators were not experienced, and clearly they were not able to match the diplomatic subtlety of Penaguião. It is no wonder that John IV was prepared to authorize Penaguião to sign the treaty in 1654. He knew that unless Portugal so willed, there was sufficient loose drafting in the commercial and legal sections to make it of little effect in practice.

Merchants were forced to pay many more taxes than those specified in the treaty. This was particularly the case in ports other than Lisbon, and in the islands of Madeira and the Azores. The wording in Article 2 was the cause of this. Dealing with the geographical extent of permitted trade, the clause ended with the words 'saving nevertheless all the laws and statutes of each place'. As individual ports and towns were governed by local charters or *forais*, this gave those places virtual freedom to do and charge what they pleased. Article 10 regulated trade with Spain through what were called the *portos secos*, or dry ports. The article had been drafted during the war between Spain and Portugal and forbade trade across the border, but there was nothing in the wording to say that trading could be resumed when the war was over. When the war ended in 1668, merchants wanted to renew their old habit of trading over the frontier. The Portuguese made them pay an extra 10% tax and told them they were lucky to be able to carry on the trade at all, as it was forbidden in the treaty. This kind of treatment may have been instigated by the secretary of state, because all customs revenue from the *portos secos* was specifically allocated to pay pensions of secular priests. The secretary was himself a priest and had formerly been a deputy on the Inquisitorial Tribunal.[72]

Another continual cause for dissatisfaction was the refusal of Portugal to honour Article 25 and make over payments of the half custom to the appointed treasurers on behalf of the merchants, mariners, widows and orphans in compensation for the confiscations in 1650. Portugal never honoured its financial commitments under the 1654 treaty. In the words of Charles Fanshaw (envoy, 1680-6), 'every farthing comes from them like drops of blood'.[73]

Much trouble was caused by the long-lived conservator, Luís Alvares Ribeira, who was lazy and did not look after English interests. Englishmen had to use the Portuguese courts and found them to be corrupt and in some cases biased against Protestants.[74] It is not surprising that the non-observance by Portugal of so many of the articles in the 1654 treaty, led to English dissatisfaction with the treaty as it stood, and a wish to renegotiate it. When Maynard arrived in Lisbon to take up his post in January 1657, he warned Thurloe that inferior ministers in Portugal pretended ignorance of the articles of peace, because they had not been published or printed in Portuguese.[75] Curiously, this need seems never to have been met during the seventeenth century, giving Portuguese officials ample opportunity for non-compliance on the grounds of ignorance. After Castelo Melhor came to power, Maynard was obliged to put constant pressure on secretary of state Sousa de Macedo, not only on behalf of the merchants, but also on behalf of the auxiliary forces which had been sent out to Portugal under the terms of the 1661 treaty. These complaints so irritated Macedo that he used more abusive language 'than became a minister'.[76]

Whilst it is perhaps not surprising that the Portuguese should conveniently not have copies of the treaty available for reference, it does seem surprising that even in England copies of the treaty were hard to obtain. In 1666 Southwell wanted to obtain a copy of the treaty, but could not do so. In the end he sent his man of business, Mr Floyd, to the secretary of state's office in Whitehall to take a copy of the treaty and ask Arlington to attest it. Mr Floyd must have obtained a copy, as one is to be found among the Southwell papers.[77] Before the treaty could have been published in Portuguese, however, the attested copy would have had to have been agreed by the Portuguese, and then translated. After that, the English would have had to agree the translation into Portuguese. This gave too many loopholes to the Portuguese for evasive action, and Southwell had no more success than Maynard in persuading the Portuguese to observe the Treaty. When Southwell returned to Portugal after a visit to England in 1668, he came with instructions to complain about the way the Portuguese were observing the treaty of commerce and to seek to have it renewed. In any renewal, he was to preserve privileges and amend ambiguities; to enlarge the privileges as advised by the merchants and, if possible, to try to activate the payment of the half custom in compensation for the sequestrations (Article 25).[78] Within six months, the projected negotiations were shelved pending clarification of Prince Pedro's title, and the attitude of Spain and France in the matter of recognizing the new government after the deposition of Pedro's elder brother, Afonso VI.[79]

Nothing further seems to have been done in the matter of renegotiating the treaty until 1670, when, in reply to a request from Arlington, Maynard summarized what he considered to be the principal ways in which the merchants could be helped. He said that, firstly, it was necessary to print the articles of peace in Portuguese; secondly, if the treaty were revised, then the merchants would like their grievances redressed by the Council of State in Portugal and not be obliged to have their complaints referred to government tribunals; thirdly, that the Prince of Portugal should give orders to all courts of judicature, municipal chambers and customs houses in all parts of his dominions, that they were to comply with the treaty, notwithstanding that it might contradict ancient laws of the kingdom.[80] This last was one of the chief points made by Parry (agent and later resident 1670-80) when he forwarded his recommendations for a possible new treaty in 1671. This was necessary, Parry said, because of the clause at the end of Article 2 of the treaty which was used by the Portuguese as an excuse to disregard any articles in the treaty which they did not wish to observe.[81] As Parry pointed out, however, the Portuguese could not reasonably pretend to amend any of the articles, whether the privileges were explicitly or implicitly granted, by any law made either before or after the signing of the treaty, because, unless every article of a treaty did supersede every law of the land that contradicted it, the prince that made the treaty would have no power over his own laws, and, consequently, insufficient authority to make a treaty at all. The Portuguese were using the wording of Article 2 not only to avoid observing the 1654 treaty, but also to take away from the English privileges which they had been granted by former kings of Portugal. Parry blamed the faulty drafting of the articles of the treaty.[82]

One of the difficulties inherent in the redrafting of a new treaty was that privileges granted by successive kings by *alvará* did not always apply generally throughout the Portuguese dominions. For instance, the privilege of having a conservator did not extend to Oporto until 1698,[83] and other towns and islands never had one. Privileges enjoyed under *forais* had been granted by individual cities, so they varied from place to place. Parry was often asked to provide proofs of what were old *foral* privileges when making complaints to the authorities. He recommended that the privileges formerly granted by kings and *forais* should be confirmed specifically in the body of any new treaty, instead of being expressed generally.[84]

There is no doubt that by 1670 the English merchants in Portugal and the islands were being subjected to many difficulties and abuses. Parry asked Williamson in that year to try to ensure that Charles II told the Portuguese ambassador in London that he was sensible of the great hardships being suffered by the English merchants in Portugal.[85] He told Arlington at the same time that the grievances and impositions put on them, contrary to the Articles of Peace, had much decayed their commerce and impoverished them. Without speedy remedy, England's trade with Portugal would be totally destroyed and the traders ruined. Again, he advised that the merchants were pressing for the articles to be printed in Portuguese. That was particularly important in places other than Lisbon.[86] In the following month articles of the treaty were printed in Portuguese, but Parry said that they were 'scandalous' in their inaccuracy. When he complained about this to the Portuguese secretary of state, he was informed that the prince did not want friction, but the English should be aware that the French also wanted the same privileges.[87] The English merchants were not likely to have been reassured by this reasoning. Parry was remitted from one tribunal to another and begged for support from England.[88] Maynard wrote to Arlington complaining of the 'insufferableness' of the Portuguese and asking that pressure be brought to bear from London to have the treaty printed in Portuguese.[89] He also pointed out that he was himself unpopular with ministers because they knew that he knew what was in the treaty, for he had been there when it had been ratified. It was proving impossible to obtain an authorized copy of the treaty in Portuguese, and this meant that it was virtually impossible to have it observed in outlying places.[90]

In order to cope with the situation, the merchants had been driven to acquire their own copies of the treaty. A cry for help arose in 1672 when the Portuguese ministers invalidated all copies used by merchants in the courts of law. It had even become impossible to find an authenticated copy of the 1661 treaty in Portugal.[91] Parry wrote to Arlington two weeks later about the urgency of having authenticated copies of the 1654 treaty published, and said that the Portuguese ministers were now maintaining that there could never be any re-ratification of a treaty made by a rebel and traitor (Cromwell).[92] Maynard sent Arlington a summary of the privileges granted to the English by former Portuguese kings, which had been confirmed by John IV in 1647.[93] Parry forwarded a detailed project for a new commercial treaty, framed so as to eliminate all doubts and ambiguities and including all the privileges claimed by the English. He inserted a few new ones which would be helpful in a worsening situation. He also had a translation from Latin to Portuguese of the 1654 treaty made by two able lawyers, which he forwarded to Arlington, presumably because he knew it would be better if the renegotiated treaty were in Portuguese.[94] Charles II had appointed a committee to deal with the Portuguese ambassador about a treaty of commerce, but the exercise was fruitless because the Portuguese never sent their ambassador in London any instructions to negotiate.[95]

Six years later, in 1678, Parry told Coventry of the obstructive attitude of the Portuguese secretary of state to all the complaints and representations made by him on behalf of the merchants, and of the impossibility of ever obtaining any redress from him.[96] Parry sent a copy of that letter to Williamson, saying that he considered that unless Charles told the Portuguese ambassador that he would take all further delays for peremptory denials, no new treaty would ever be negotiated.[97] The fact that Parry thought such a proceeding might be effective, shows that he lacked appreciation of the true position. The motivation in Portugal for an English alliance had disappeared. Unlike the position in 1654 and in 1661, England was now the seeker after a treaty, not Portugal. Parry emphasized to Coventry that the merchants were concerned less with an extension of privileges than with a clarification of existing privileges, in such a way as to stop false interpretations. They wanted a renewal of the treaty to obtain the same freedom of trade as was enjoyed in fact by the Dutch and the French, who, by treaties with Portugal had obtained rights equal to those which the English had obtained in 1654. England paid Portugal more customs and exported more of Portugal's products than all other European countries put together,[98] but, as will be explained in a succeeding chapter, Portugal was at that time endeavouring to build up her own cloth manufacture, and so remained indifferent to that fact. Indeed, when the consul made a complaint to the Portuguese secretary of state in 1679, he was told that the English should avenge themselves by not sending any more goods to Portugal.[99] Parry told Sunderland in April of that year that the prince did not want to alter the treaty because a genuine clarification would render Portuguese violations too manifest. 'I cannot think they here designe anything less than to beat us out of our trade hither', he concluded.[100] In June, Coventry was still reporting to Parry that the ambassador had not received any powers to treat.[101] By inferring in Portugal that renegotiations were essential, and then blocking their possibility by not sending instructions to their ambassador to treat, the Portuguese were able to hold the status quo, which suited them perfectly.

Finally, in June 1680, the prince, through the secretary of state, definitely rejected English proposals to negotiate a new treaty. All he wanted, as he had said in 1678, was to retain the 1654 treaty, merely substituting Charles II's name for that of Cromwell.[102] Because all hope of renegotiating the treaty had gone, Parry asked for permission to return to England. He left Portugal in the autumn of that year and Charles Fanshaw replaced him as envoy.[103] Fanshaw actually obtained from the prince a promise to negotiate a new commercial treaty in Portugal, but he doubted the prince's sincerity because the Portuguese were all so averse to it.[104] Even though commissioners were appointed to treat with Fanshaw, negotiations were continually stalled and it was impossible to obtain any concrete advance towards a new treaty or to gain any redress for non-compliance of the 1654 treaty in Portugal. Fifteen months later, Fanshaw advised that he regarded his efforts to renegotiate a new commercial treaty to be at an end.[105]

Portugal had always resented the 1654 treaty, and had soon forgotten the desperate straits which had led her to seek it in the first place. The bad drafting of the treaty had anyway enabled Portugal to disregard its provisions when it suited her to do so. In practice, therefore, the 1654 treaty never gave the English the trading advantages so often claimed by many Portuguese and other historians to be the cause of Portugal's economic decline. The French and Dutch were given treaty rights equal to those of England, and, arguably, because their treaties were better drafted, they enjoyed more advantages than the English.

It also seems evident that with the accession of Charles II, the English merchants in Portugal did not enjoy the political protection they had enjoyed during the Commonwealth and Protectorate. As his reign progressed, Charles called fewer parliaments, thus restricting the merchants' opportunities to exercise pressure upon government.

ILLUSTRATIONS

*The Editors are grateful to Dr Manuel Cadafaz de Matos for his advice and help,
and to Michael Eltenton for his assistance in gathering illustrations from sources in
Lisbon.*

Endeavours to reestablish a Minister at Oporto. I
have given him the best information I am able
of all the passages that have happened in Relation
to that business: which I hope may stead him in
some stead.

When the Treaty was first made betwixt England
and Portugal it was agreed that there should be a
Minister sent over to the Merch[ants] notwithstanding
it was not inserted in the Articles, as I was allways
told and your hon[our] may be informed by Mr
Edward Bushel, a Merchant now liveing in London
or Hackney, who was commissionated by Cromwell
to treate and conclude the peace with the Portugal
Ambassador; and one Mr Thorogood a Minister
was made choice of to come over with me, as Minister to the Merchants: but I being posted away, he
could not be ready to come with me, and some
dispute falling out betwixt the Merchants and him
after I left England they elected Mr Cradocke, one
provost of Eaton College; to be Minister of
this Factory; I arrived here the beginning of January
16 5/7 and Mr Cradocke in September of the same
year, who lived in my house and preached there
where the whole Factory and others assembled
all the while he was in Portugall, which was
about two years and a halfe, without haveing
any publicke minister in this Kingdome all that
time; tho these people doe now affirme that the
Liberty of haveing a minister was never consented
to any but the Kings publick ministers. but very
lately about the month of February 165 9/60 Doctor
Cradocke returned to England and I was clapt into
the Inquisition, where I met with very rude and
severe treatment for six days togather for protecting
an English Gentlewoman (that came over to be a
Nun, but turned protestant in my house) from
their

Plate 2. The Inquisition Chamber (Artist unknown)

Plate 3. Auto-da-fé: the Act of Faith (Artist unknown)

Plate 4. Auto-da-fé: the Grand Procession (Artist unknown)

Plate 5. Auto-da-fé: the Execution of the Condemned (Engraving by
B. Picaret 1722)

Plate 6. King Dom João IV. His attempts to develop Portuguese trade with the help of the New Christian merchants were severely hampered by the persecutions of the Holy Inquisition (17th century, artist unknown)

Collection and photograph: Dr Manuel Cadafaz de Matos

Celeberr.^{us} P. Antonius Vieyra Soc. Jesu Lusit. Ulyssipon.

Plate 7. Fr António Vieira, Jesuit missionary and most famous of Portuguese preachers, opposed the Dominican Inquisition's persecutions of New Christian merchants, which left additional opportunities for foreigners to profit from Portugal's overseas trade (17th century, artist unknown)

Collection and photograph: Dr Manuel Cadafaz de Matos

Plate 8. This map of the world, shown also on the dust jacket and endpapers, was drawn by António Sanchez in Lisbon in 1623.

At that time the crowns of Portugal and Spain were united, as the shields on the map attest. Iberian power is shown as world-wide – all new and future discoveries having been allocated by Papal decree to the two countries, following the Treaty of Tordesillas (1494), Spanish to the West, Portuguese to the East, of the line shown on the map.

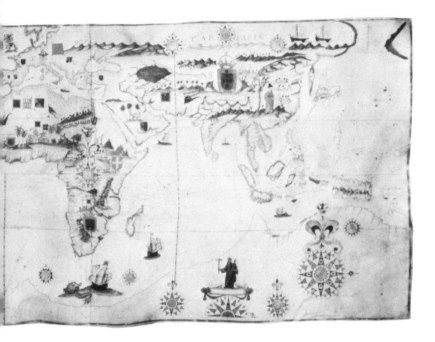

Iberian, and especially Portugese, power is here shown as insepar-
able from the missionary activity of the Catholic Counter-Reformation.
Illustrations on the map include the Madonna, the Portuguese-born St
Anthony of Padua in his Franciscan habit, a Dominican of the Holy
Inquisition, the Portuguese knight who commissioned the map (at
prayer by the crucified Christ) and a Chinese mandarin presumably
awaiting conversion. The map declares that the world beyond Europe
is Iberian and is or will be Catholic.

Plate 9. Lisbon in 1705, then the greatest entrepôt in Europe, where the rich trade with Asia, Africa and Brazil was handled (Engraving by I. Otero)

Plate 10. The Royal Palace in Lisbon, destroyed by the great earthquake of 1755 (Artist unknown)

Plate 11. Departure of Catherine of Braganza from Lisbon to join her husband, Charles II (Engraving by Dirk Stoop)

Plate 12. Arrival of Charles II and Catherine of Braganza at Hampton Court (Engraving by Dirk Stoop)

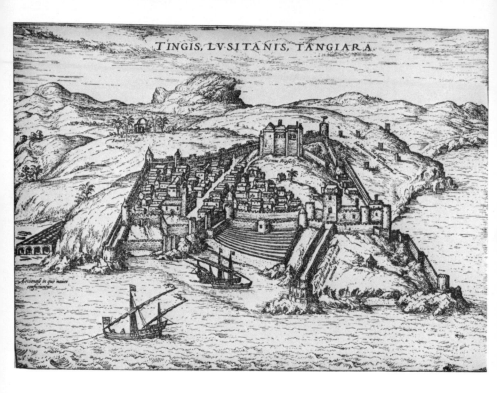

Plate 13. Tangier (17th century engraving)

Collection and photograph: Dr Manuel Cadafaz de Matos

Plate 14. Bombay in 1670. Both Tangier and Bombay were parts of Catherine of Braganza's dowry. Charles II, constantly short of money, abandoned Tangier in 1684; Bombay – the first possession of the English Crown in India – he leased to the East India Company in 1669. By then the Portuguese had been there for 150 years. Other Portuguese possessions on the same coast – Goa, Diu, Bassein – were more important at the time, but Bombay was handed over with the greatest reluctance, the Portuguese Viceroy foreseeing future British expansion in the region. (Contemporary engraving in Baldeus' *Voyage*)

Plate 15. Charles II (After P. Lely)

Plate 16. Catherine of Braganza (Studio of J. Huysmans)

Plate 17. The English College in Lisbon, formally opened in 1629, to train English Catholics to reconvert Protestant England and to minister to its Catholic population. The College was finally closed in 1948 (Drawing by W. Raeburn-Little, 1946)

Drawing taken with permission from the papers of the English College, Lisbon, now at Ushaw College, Co. Durham (Librarian: Father Michael Sharrat, S.J.)

10

Religious Tensions and the 1654 Treaty

The religious differences between England and Portugal were highlighted by the difficulties experienced when ratifying the 1654 treaty. Articles 6 and 14 were the chief reason for this. There was, however, another article (5) in that treaty, regarding New Christians, which was of great concern to English merchants in Portugal. All three of these articles will be commented on in this chapter.

i New Christian (Jewish) Debtors

The descendants of Jews who had been forcibly baptized in King Manuel's reign were known as New Christians. When they were processed by the Inquisition for allegedly following Jewish practices, they were called Jews. To simplify matters, all people of Jewish race will here be referred to as Jews.

Article 6 of the 1642 treaty and Article 5 of the 1654 treaty concerned the repayment of debts owed to Englishmen by Portuguese imprisoned by the Inquisition. In the 1642 treaty, the court of the Inquisition was given one year in which to effect payment to creditors out of confiscated estates, whilst in the 1654 treaty, it was given six months, with the proviso that if any *specie* was sequestered, it was to be paid over to settle the debts immediately. The reason for the inclusion of these articles in commercial treaties was the manner in which arrests were effected by the Inquisition. Familiars or bailiffs of the Inquisition not only arrested prisoners, but sequestered all their property, wherever it might be. Prisoners' families were turned out on the streets. The latter could not complain, for that would be criticism of the Inquisition and invite arrest too. Dwelling houses owned by prisoners also passed into the ownership of the Inquisition. One of the first things that a prisoner was told to do was to swear that the list which had been compiled of his property was complete.[1] Lists in Inquisition records show that the Jewish merchants were owed large sums by *fidalgos*, religious institutions and the state.[2] On the other hand, no note was taken of debts owed by prisoners. Prisoners were told by the Inquisition that they were 'forgiven' their debts.[3] Foreign merchants in Portugal were wholesalers, and they sold their wares to local retail merchants, who were mainly Jews. Because of the credit system in trade, every time a Jew was imprisoned by the Inquisition, he was certain to have debts owing to Englishmen or other foreign merchants at the time of imprisonment. These were the debts which were forgiven, and thus not even noted on the carefully prepared lists made of the prisoners' property, signed by the prisoners. Merchandise confiscated, even if not yet paid for, was always registered as having been owned by the prisoners. Everything so shown to belong to the prisoners was registered and deposited with the *fisco*, an office whose judge owed his appointment to the inquisitor general. Because the existence of debts was not registered with the *fisco*, it was always impossible for any English merchant to make a claim through the *fisco* to recover what was due to him. The only proofs of the debt were in his own records. Even if there had been witnesses to a business deal, they would not have dared to come forward. Thus, the Inquisition never objected to Articles 6 (1642) and 5 (1654), because it knew that it would be impossible to prove the debt, and therefore there was no reason for concern.

There is no record of any complaints regarding non-payment of such debts by the Inquisition until Maynard became consul. This is probably because he was the first Protestant consul: it is unlikely that a Catholic consul would have had the courage to petition the tribunal for payment. The amounts involved in the debts were quite considerable. It will be remembered that in 1660, Rowland Hill of Oporto complained to Charles II and to Melo that he was owed 5,000 crowns under the terms of Article 5 of the 1654 treaty. The undated complaints of the English merchants among the documents for 1662 in the State Papers, show that over 40,000 crowns was owing to the English merchants for goods sold on credit to Portuguese merchants imprisoned by the Inquisition. Some of the claims were said to be over five years old.[4] A list of grievances dated 8 June 1664 stated that three years previously the *mesa grande* of the Inquisition had confirmed that the English merchants were not entitled to receive anything from the sequestered estates of New Christians. The consul obtained a letter from the king, which was read at the *mesa pequena*. The Inquisition claimed to know nothing of any articles of peace between England and Portugal. (This was, of course, quite untrue. What they perhaps meant was that they did not acknowledge even the existence of the 1654 treaty because in 1656 the treaty had been ratified against their wishes.) The Inquisition said that it was not concerned with any articles of peace, because it had a law and constitution of its own. Maynard again complained to the king, but was told that nothing more could be done, and if the English could not be content with such justice as was administered by the tribunals of the kingdom, they should get it where they could.[5] This was a reply showing nothing but irritability, for they knew, and

Maynard knew, that only the judge of the *fisco* was competent to deal with the claims being made.

In 1671, when writing to Arlington about the improvements which should be made in a possible new treaty, Parry suggested that the wording of Article 5 should include:

> The debts which shall appeare by such proofs as are Allowed to be sufficient in any other Court or Judicature, shall be fully paid out . . . without molestation from the Inquisition, their judges or ministers or from any officers or judges of the *fisco*.

He explained that the Inquisition was insisting on such proofs as were almost impossible to be given, and the judges of the *fisco* were just as guilty. Parry also thought that a clause should be inserted to ensure that the quittance given by the Inquisition of a prisoner's debts, did not absolve the debtor from paying those debts, if or when he might be discharged by the Inquisition and continued to trade.[6]

During the 1670s, increasing pressure was brought to bear in Rome by New Christians, and all proceedings of the Portuguese Inquisition were held up by the pope. Prisoners remained incarcerated, although *autos da fé* were stopped. It was only early in 1683 that the Inquisition was able to operate with renewed vigour.[7] Maynard reported that he was once more in contest with the Inquisition. Many Jews, or people said to be Jews, had been apprehended, some being the chief merchants of the city of Lisbon. Many had fled, seventeen of them via the *Rebecca* of London. Those imprisoned were indebted to members of the factory to the extent of 49,000 crowns at least. When Maynard had applied (to the *fisco* for repayment, he was told that he must recover the debts by law, meaning that he must put up a legal case to be tried by the judge of the *fisco*. Maynard replied that the treaty was made to prevent law suits and that he would petition the king and, if necessary, ask the envoy to do the same.[8] There is no more documentary evidence available as to the outcome of the affair.

It paid English merchants to aid the Portuguese merchants to flee, because once in England or the United Provinces they could be expected to start to trade again and repay their debts. There is no record of debts owed by prisoners of the Inquisition ever having been recovered. It is clear, therefore, that Articles 5 (1654) and 6 (1642) were never observed, because the Inquisition disavowed the debts or any knowledge of treaties, and the crown of Portugal was unable and unwilling to intervene.

ii *Seamen*

Article 6 of the 1654 treaty differed from Article 7 of the 1642 treaty in an important respect. In both articles, it was stipulated that the captains, masters, officers and mariners of the ships of Great Britain were not to procure any trouble against the said ships, nor against other Englishmen, for their wages or salaries on pretext that they wished to become Roman Catholics, or to join the service of the king of Portugal. Article 6 of 1654, however, states that such men are not to separate themselves from their ships, and if they do so, they must be compelled by the magistrates and officers in Portugal to return. If they could not be found, it would be lawful for the master of their own ship to detain their clothes, goods, or wages, for the repair of damages. Portugal was very content with the 1642 treaty, but, as has been seen, Article 6 of the 1654 treaty was one of the reasons which held up its ratification for two years. This was because no magistrate would have dared to order anyone who had once professed the Catholic faith to return to a Protestant ship: the Inquisition would not have allowed it. To the English, however, the professing of the Catholic faith was not the main point of the article. They wanted it in order to assist in the control of a scarce commodity, English seamen, when their ships were in Portuguese ports. It was because seamen sometimes pretended to Catholicism if they wished to abscond in Portugal, knowing that they would then be assisted, that the clause was included. For the English, these two articles had to be considered in conjunction with the references to seamen in Articles 9 (1654) and 10 (1642). These stipulated that neither the king of Portugal nor any of his ministers was to detain, arrest or attach any merchants, masters of ships, captains or mariners or their ships, merchandise and goods, without the permission of the Protector/ king having first been obtained. All were to have complete liberty to depart from the Portuguese dominions without hindrance. They were not to be diverted to the use of the king of Portugal. Articles 7 and 10 (1642) and 6 and 9 (1654) were not reciprocal.

These articles provided room for conflict. Seamen were scarce in Portugal as well as in England, and the Portuguese had as much interest in diverting English seamen to Portuguese service as England had in preventing it. The scarcity of seamen made the temptation to poach so great that it is difficult to take statements from either side at their face value. No record has been found of English ships poaching Portuguese seamen in Portugal, but there is evidence of English tavern keepers in Lisbon who sold English seamen into service on foreign ships. Another problem is to determine what was genuine desertion by English seamen and what was deliberate enticement or snatching by Portugal. For example, in February 1664, Maynard reported having assisted in the rescue of eighteen English seamen from a Portuguese man-of-war, who had cried out for help to the *Advise*, an English naval frigate which was preparing to sail. He and Captain Poole of the *Advise* had rescued them. There had been five or six other English seamen left on the Portuguese ship because they said they wished to serve the Portuguese king.[9] The Portuguese version of the affair states that Maynard took only six or seven English seamen off the Portuguese war ship.[10] With no record or statement from an independent witness, it is impossible to say with certainty how many seamen had deserted and how many had been poached. Maynard and Captain Poole were carrying out instructions received from England, for proclamations had been issued in 1575, 1636, 1639, 1647, 1662, 1664 (when the incident occurred), forbidding English seamen to serve foreign princes.[11] Before rowing away from the Portuguese frigate, Captain Poole had warned those remaining on board that if he met with them at sea, they would be forcibly taken. A proclamation of 1675 even went so far as to declare those not obeying the proclamations to be rebels. English seamen were also taken off foreign ships in the Downs, the Channel and Malaga in accordance with those proclamations. It must be emphasized that at the time it was the practice of all seafaring nations to press both merchant ships and seamen into service, but Portugal was specifically committed by treaty with England to return English seamen to English ships.[12]

In the same year, 1664, when the Portuguese were preparing eight ships to escort in the expected Brazil fleet of seventy ships, they took 120 English seamen, mostly by constraint, to man their own ships.[13] They were taken from merchant ships in Lisbon harbour and even from a naval vessel. A Major Holmes, commanding a naval ship, complained to Maynard that twenty seamen had been taken from his ship to one belonging to the king of Portugal. Castelo Melhor maintained that the men in question had received money from the king of Portugal to the value of eighty *milreis* (£30), which Maynard paid in order to obtain their release, though the men themselves said that they were not indebted to the king, in fact were owed money by him for the services they had been forced to render.[14]

One of the chief methods of obtaining English seamen used by the Portuguese was reported by the Portugal merchants in London to be the use of 'several licentious houses which are kept by H.M. (of England) subjects wherein seamen are first debauched and then in a manner sould into forraigne service for ye payment of ye debts they are drawne into'. The merchants maintained that because of this, English ships were delayed and sometimes had to cancel their voyages, to the great detriment of commerce. They suggested that these houses should be licensed by the conservator and certified to him by the consul, and should be closed at 9 p.m., under penalty of ten *cruzados* or three months in prison with removal of licence. No English seamen should be allowed to take service with the Portuguese without a certificate from his last master or the consul to say that he had been freely discharged.[15]

Maynard considered that the conservator, the long-lived Luis Alvarez Ribeira, had become 'most horridly impudent in debauching of seamen and selling them into the king of Portugal's service'. This, he said, in May 1670, had led to many 'disgusts' between the court in Lisbon and Sir Edward Spragge, then in command of the English fleet off Portugal.[16] A month earlier, Maynard had explained to Arlington in more detail that a number of seamen had been taken to the Portuguese East India fleet by certain Englishmen and Irishmen in town who kept debased houses. He had told the Portuguese that, if it were necessary, Spragge would recover his men at sea. Spragge sent two of his captains with Maynard for a further interview with the authorities. The prince sent six soldiers with them to the East India fleet, with orders that the men should be returned. The East India captains would not comply. Another visit to the palace the following day obtained an order from the prince that the seamen were to be returned on pain of the East India captains being lashed if they did not comply. As the ships were ready to sail, Maynard was too wary to go aboard himself, and insisted that the men be put ashore. They were. Dutch ships in Lisbon harbour at the same time also lost a number of seamen, but they were not able to get their men back.[17] Following these happenings, the Portuguese envoy in London, Gaspar d'Abreu, sent three memorials to Charles II, complaining of Sir Edward Spragge's rudeness in insisting on the return of men he claimed were deserters. D'Abreu asked that orders be given to prevent such high-handed and arrogant behaviour by naval commanders in the future.[18] These complaints were rejected, it would seem, by the Duke of York, who was in charge of the navy. The State Papers contain a memorandum from Mr Wrenn, the 'Duke's mind', in draft form, recommending Charles II to reject the Portuguese protests. The duke recommended that orders be sent to Spragge and all commanding officers to retake English seamen in foreign vessels. The memorandum also suggested that the king let it be known that he expected the same privileges in this respect as other nations enjoyed in Portugal.[19] In any case, it was a treaty obligation.

It seems that in cases of genuine desertion by English seamen, they would do anything rather than return to their ships, and they were then prepared to say that they would become Catholics. In March 1682, for instance, the storm-tossed *Golden Fortune* (sometimes called the *Golden Providence*) arrived in Lisbon bound from London to Virginia.[20] At that time the Portuguese were preparing a fleet to go to the kingdom of

Savoy. Twenty men from the *Golden Fortune* went over to Portuguese service. Maynard met four of them and had them imprisoned, but because they promised to do their duty and return to the *Golden Fortune*, they were freed. After two or three days, they deserted again, and again Maynard had them imprisoned. This time, they declared that they would turn Catholic. The Inquisition was told, and the men were made to renounce Protestantism. According to Maynard, they did not really want to do this, or found difficulty in doing it, so the Inquisition had them imprisoned in the common gaol.[21] Presumably this was done to persuade them to make up their minds. Maynard tried to get them freed, but was told that that was impossible without an order from the Inquisition.[22] Maynard complained to the secretary of state. Another eight English seamen went over to the Savoy fleet. It is not known whether or not they came from the *Golden Fortune*. These, the secretary of state said, would be returned later, but nothing could be done about those who had chosen to turn Catholic. The *Golden Fortune* could not sail without a crew, but Maynard was wary of opposing the Inquisition, because on the previous Sunday he had witnessed the first *auto da fé* in nine years, and had seen the renewed vigour with which the Inquisition was approaching its work.[23] Article 6 of the 1654 treaty meant nothing to the Inquisition and the ministers of the government were not prepared to enforce it. It seems that, by the end of May, there were six men altogether who had turned Catholic.[24] The remainder of the deserters had presumably been returned in accordance with Article 6 of the 1654 treaty. This is surprising, in view of the fact that Portugal was extremely short of seamen at the time and most of the men on board the ships of the Savoy fleet were foreigners.[25] Charles Fanshaw (the envoy) wrote to the prince asking that the six (Catholic) seamen should be returned to their ship.[26] The latter promised to comply, but did not send the necessary executive order until after the fleet had sailed,[27] thus showing willingness to comply with Article 6 of the 1654 treaty but, at the same time, giving no offence to the Inquisition.

The Inquisition also claimed authority over all Negroes. There were many of them to be found as crew on ships from the plantations, and they were Protestants. The Inquisition told Maynard not to allow them to go out of their ships, even if they belonged to subjects of Charles II. Maynard replied that slaves were a commodity, so by treaty it was lawful for English ships to carry what goods they pleased. However, Maynard had been warned privately by a friend to be very careful of the question of blacks, particularly in view of the fact that he housed the Protestant chaplain.[28] This could well lead to trouble for himself with the Inquisition. In 1671 the Inquisition seized a seventeen-year-old Negro called John Adue, who belonged to Richard Borthwick, and

Maynard sent out a notice to merchants warning that the Inquisition was claiming jurisdiction over all blacks, as they would not allow the prince's Portuguese subjects to be transported to England to become heretics.[29] The thinking behind this was, presumably, that by reason of the Donation of Constantine and the Treaty of Tordesillas, all Africans were subjects of the king of Portugal. From then onwards, the Inquisition began seizing any Negroes found on English ships, a practice that figured prominently in a list of complaints of 1676. English ships were kept below Belem at great expense, whilst searches were made for blacks.[30] In 1683, a black English subject, not a slave, was arrested and forced to become a Catholic.[31] Negro slaves were considered to be merchandise, by both the Portuguese and English, and they were entered in the customs in Portugal as such. Maynard could get no help from Portuguese ministers in this matter.[32]

In his suggestions for a new commercial treaty, Parry asked that a special clause be included, so that ships could keep black crewmen, even if they were Protestant.[33] With the evidence available, it is safe to say that such a clause would not have been acceptable to Portugal, and if forced upon her, would not have been observed any more than Portugal observed Article 6 of the 1654 treaty, where Catholic seamen were concerned.

iii   *The Practice of Protestantism in Portugal*
      under Article 14 of the 1654 Treaty

In Article 14 of the 1654 treaty, the king of Portugal promised that he would take care to provide:

a) that the English should not be molested by any person, court or tribunal for possessing bibles or other books;
b) that they should be free to observe and profess their own religion in their own private houses, together with their families, within his dominions, and the same to be true on board ships and vessels, and,
c) that a place would be allotted to them for the burial of their dead.

It was also stipulated that the English were not to exceed what was written in the article.

It will be recalled that the Portuguese had much preferred Article 17 of the 1642 treaty, because there it was only promised that the English would not be molested on the score of their conscience, provided that they gave no scandal to others. Further, it was specifically stated in that article that, although the king of Portugal acknowledged that he had no power to determine or dispose of faith and religion, he would take care that the English should have as much liberty regarding their religion as was enjoyed by subjects of other princes in his dominions. Such wording had been loose enough to ensure that English Protestants only enjoyed private liberty of conscience. They had no chaplain and families could not meet together for worship. The visitor of ships appointed by the Inquisition would not allow bibles to be taken ashore; there was no envoy until the arrival of Sir Henry Compton, whose wife was a Catholic and who only stayed in Portugal for less than two years in the period 1646-8. There is no evidence that he was accompanied by a chaplain.[34] The Dutch had been given liberty to practise their religion in their houses and on their ships in the ten year truce of 1641 with Portugal, but by 1651, there were no other Protestant nationals with whom the English could demand parity. If it is remembered that there was no English Protestant consul in Portugal until 1657, it is understandable why the English merchants pressed so hard for Article 14 of the 1654 treaty. They certainly never obtained all that they hoped for from Article 14 during the seventeenth century.

The promise to allocate a burial ground for the English Protestant dead was not forthcoming at that time. This is not surprising, in view of the fact that a religious *consulta* of 24 June 1654 ruled that a graveyard for Protestant Englishmen was clearly impossible.[35] No cemetery was allotted to the English in Lisbon until 1717, and then it was insisted that the site be surrounded by trees to hide the heretical burial ground from good Catholics.[36] To this day, St George's church and grounds are well hidden behind a high wall. Once through a gateway, it is difficult to find the church buried deeply among trees and gardens. In Oporto, there was no cemetery for English Protestants until 1787.[37]

Points a) and b) were better observed, especially at first. Indeed, the English nation in Lisbon enjoyed more than was specifically allowed in Article 14, in that from 1657 they had a chaplain who lived in the consul's house, and all English Protestants met regularly for divine service on a Sunday, either in the consul's house, or, when an envoy was resident in Lisbon, at his house. According to diplomatic usage at the time, only envoys (not consuls) could hold divine service in their residences. There is no doubt whatsoever that the king of Portugal and the Inquisition were well aware of the presence of the chaplain, and that services were held regularly on Sundays in the consul's house in the absence of an envoy. To begin with, Maynard's patents from Cromwell and Charles II both specified that he was to house a divine and that he had to pay half the latter's salary. Those patents were approved and confirmed by John IV and Afonso VI. The Inquisition clearly knew about it too, as is evident from reports it received in connection with the Margaret Throckmorton affair.[38] The latter demonstrated that, where the practice of religion was concerned, there was an unwritten understanding between the two countries. Maynard confirmed this in 1683, when he explained to Secretary Jenkins that at the time when the 1654 treaty was being negotiated, it was agreed that the English nation should be allowed to have a minister, but it was also agreed that this should not be written into the articles. It had been Edward Bushell, a merchant of London and Hackney, who had been commissioned by Cromwell to treat about this with the Portuguese ambassador. Mr Cradock, Provost of Eton College, was the first chaplain to go to Portugal.[39] It may well be that the quid pro quo given by England was to allow the Portuguese embassy, far in excess of diplomatic usage, to be used as a base for Catholic missionaries, the housing of the Jesuit provincial and as a centre not only for Portuguese, but also English recusants, to attend mass. It would have been impossible openly, in a treaty, to allow a Protestant minister in Portugal. Equally, it would have created a furore in England to have had the quid pro quo inserted. According to John Colbatch, a later chaplain, writing in 1696, the Portuguese authorities were so anxious to avoid trouble when the first chaplain, Zachary Cradock, held his services in Maynard's house in 1657, that initially they posted soldiers round it to ensure that the curious did not cause trouble when they observed large numbers of people arriving on Sundays.[40]

The ambassador Sir Richard Fanshaw (1662–3) and envoy Sir Robert Southwell (1666–9), had their own chaplains and, whilst they were in Lisbon, services were held in their houses, but during their absences, and between appointments, the chaplain celebrated divine service in the consul's house. It was only after the departure of Southwell that the foundation was laid for future trouble. In 1669, Southwell left behind his secretary, Francis Parry, to deal with outstanding matters to do with the collection of Queen Catherine's dower.[41] Parry was only appointed agent a year later. Meanwhile, the chaplain continued to reside and preach in Maynard's house. It will be remembered that Parry had difficulty in obtaining recognition by Portugal because he was designated an agent. Colbatch, whose informants were men who had known Parry personally, says that Parry, 'on some nice punctilios', alleging that it would be good for the factory's prestige, insisted on having the Sunday services at his house.[42] In all his ten years in Portugal, as agent and then as resident, he never housed the chaplain, nor did he pay a half of his salary. During his absences from Lisbon, services were held in Maynard's house. Charles Fanshaw arrived in Lisbon in 1680, when Parry left. According to Colbatch, Fanshaw tried to persuade the merchants to return to the use of the consul's house for services on a permanent basis, in case the Portuguese should question the nation's right to hold services there if, at some future date, there were no envoy.[43] This he foresaw would happen once the dower had been completely paid. Fanshaw's advice was not heeded, because Parry, during his years in office, did much to set the factory at odds with Maynard. How this was done will be explained in Chapter 13. It is not certain when Charles Fanshaw left Portugal. The last report from him in the State Papers Portugal, addressed to the secretary of state, is dated 18 December 1684 (N.S.), but he was received by James II at the end of his appointment on 12 May 1686 (O.S.).[44]

After the death of Charles II in February 1685, England was ruled by a Catholic king, James II. Both the Portuguese government and the Inquisition soon came to the conclusion that it was no longer necessary to observe the unwritten reciprocal privileges regarding religion, as Catholics in England were receiving every help and encouragement. Thus, on Thursday 2/12 September 1686, the consul and Dr Michael Geddes, who had been chaplain in Lisbon for eight years, were brought before the Council of the Inquisition. Maynard was taken first, alone, to the Council Board, and was asked by what right he had prayers and preachings at his house in the Portas de Santo Antão (situated very close to the Palacio das Estoas, the office and prisons of the Inquisition in Lisbon). Maynard could not say that services were held by authority of an unwritten agreement between John IV and Cromwell, so he replied that Article 14 was his authority. The Inquisition denied this. Maynard was in a difficult position, because of course Article 14 did not specifically grant that right. Maynard's answer was, therefore, to quote the first part of Article 14. He told the inquisitors that services were held by virtue of the fact that the article stated that since all commerce would be ineffectual if the king of England's subjects were disquieted for conscience sake, they should not be molested by any man, court or tribunal, but that they might freely, in their houses and with their families, being of the same nation and religion, exercise their religion without molestation in any part of the king of Portugal's dominions and possessions. An inquisitor told Maynard that such a provision had never come to the cognisance of the Inquisition, Maynard repled that he had been consul for thirty years and divine service had been held over many years in his house, so that statement was improbable. Then he reminded the inquisitors that many years ago the holding of services in his house had been questioned by the Inquisition, but that when informed of the authority (Maynard did not say which authority) by which the services were held, the services in his house had continued unmolested. The inquisitors told Maynard that he was mistaken in all he was saying, and that thenceforward there were to be no more meetings except in an envoy's house. Maynard was asked to sign a guarantee that no more meetings would take place. This he refused to do. When he was let out, he was not allowed to communicate with Dr Geddes, who was then led in for questioning by the board. On the following day, 3/13 September 1686, Maynard boldly went to see the inquisitor general, D. Verissimo de Lencastre, who told him that there was no reason or justice in persisting in the matter. Englishmen could pray privately in their houses by themselves. Maynard pointed out that there was no need for Article 14 for men to pray privately in their closets, at which D. Verissimo became enraged and said that neither he nor Dr Geddes should have been allowed to leave on the previous day. When Maynard, denying that he had committed any fault, rose to depart, D. Verissimo took his arm. 'Sit down', he said. 'I have known you for at least thirty years. You never wronged or scandalized any man, but are generally well reputed, though I cannot grant you this because it is too great a scandal to the people'. Maynard replied that the meetings were private and it was no scandal to serve God. Englishmen would try and meet without others seeing them assemble. D. Verissimo told him that he would have to apply to the king for an enabling order to assemble.[45] Maynard petitioned Pedro II,[46] but received a verbal answer in the negative through the secretary of state.[47]

On the same day that Maynard sent the report to the bishop of London, he also reported the matter to the Earl of Sunderland, the secretary of state.[48] Maynard and the leading merchants wrote to their principals in London.[49] Thirty-three members of the factory also sent a petition to the bishop of London by the same post. It was a duplicate of a petition sent a few days earlier, which, because a number of members were absent, did not have so many signatures. In this petition, the merchants pointed out that it had always been understood by the king of Portugal that the English might freely practise their religion with the families of their own nation, because of the £100 per annum which it was stipulated in the consul's patent had to be paid to the preacher who lived in his house. It was a slight to the English to be denied what the Dutch enjoyed.[50] This last statement is curious. It infers that the Dutch in Portugal were at that time holding Protestant services in their consul's house, although it is known that there was a Dutch resident in Lisbon between 1675 and 1695.[51] The latter may have been a Catholic.

By the time that these petitions reached the Bishop of London, he had been suspended from office.[52] With a suspended bishop, a Catholic king and a Catholic secretary of state (Sunderland), it is not surprising that the factory discontinued their religious observances until the arrival of Charles Scarburgh as envoy in the following November.[53] The latter did not see fit to interfere in the affair, as services in his own house were undisturbed.[54] Scarburgh was recalled in August 1689.[55] In January 1690 the chaplain, James Smallwood, wrote to Shrewsbury asking to be recalled, because the Inquisition had forbidden all further Protestant services to the factory.[56] Until the arrival of Sir John Methuen in 1693, the English were unable to practise their religion together.

It seems that the English merchants in Oporto also had a chaplain between 1672 and 1674. Services were held in the house of Maynard's daughter, who had married a merchant named Cooke. That chaplain's name was Brawler or Brawlard; he had left Oporto of his own free will and was not troubled by the Inquisition. Brawler's salary was met by a grant from the then Bishop of London, but when the latter died, Brawler's stipend was maintained by voluntary contributions. Maynard had obtained a licence from the Portuguese secretary of state to enable him to carry out his function. Why this was done is not explained.[57] This licence had been taken to the then governor of Oporto, the Conde de Miranda (later, the Marquês de Arronches), by the vice-consul, Walter Maynard, who was himself a convert to Catholicism, and several other members of the factory.[58] It is not known whether Oporto continued to enjoy the services of a chaplain, but on 12/22 June 1682, a divine named Samuel Barton arrived there, sent by the Bishop of London. He lived in the house of three merchants who were partners: Mr Peter Burrell, Mr Peter Baldwin and Mr Abraham Mayne. Only four English merchants did not attend his services. They were: Samuel Palmer, John Wrothesley, John Pickering and Henry Withingham, who had been converted to Catholicism by members of the English College in Lisbon.[59] Even the vice-consul, a man named Murcott, also became a convert.[60] Both Maynard and Fanshaw maintained that these converts were behind the insistance of the Inquisition at the end of 1682 that Barton should be deported.[61] In Barton's case, however, there is also a suggestion that he was not as discreet as he might have been, which would have enabled the Inquisition to accuse him of causing scandal.[62] On 6/16 December 1682, Barton was summoned to appear before the deputy governor of Oporto. He went accompanied by the vice-consul and Mr Burrell, and was told that the governor had received a positive command from the prince regent that Barton should leave by the next ship. As long as he did not practise, he was told that he could visit Aveiro and Coimbra on his way south to Lisbon, the vice-consul and Mr Burrell being his security.[63] He finally sailed from Lisbon on the *Palm Tree* on 5/15 February 1682/3.[64] Fanshaw thought that the Portuguese should be treated with a high hand over the matter,[65] and Maynard considered that the Portuguese were not impressed by reason, but only by force. He instanced how Blake's fleet had helped to obtain ratification of the 1654 treaty in 1656.[66] Fanshaw believed that the wording of the treaty extended to the general use of all the rites of the Protestant religion, which could not be performed without a minister. The phrase he quoted was: '. . . usque liberum sit populo hujus Reipublicae in privatis aedibus una cum familiis ex eadem gente oriundis intra quaecunque Dominia dicti Regis Portugallia Regionem suam observare et profiteri'.[67] (. . . and that it shall be free for the people of this Republic to observe and profess their religion in private houses, together with their families, within any of the dominions of the said King of Portugal whatsoever').[67] It is possible that a solution would have been found had circumstances been different, because the prince himself did not appear to object to Oporto having a chaplain. He even suggested to Fanshaw that he should connive at a chaplain being allowed to go to Oporto in the guise of a merchant. Fanshaw did not think this appropriate.[68] Unfortunately, at that time, the English were in ill odour over an alleged case of bullion smuggling,[69] and the Inquisition had recently recovered its former powers and was naturally anxious to be seen to have regained its role as the arbiter of moral rectitude and behaviour in a Catholic society.[70] The Marquês d'Arronches, who was powerful in the Privy Council and a good friend to England, emphasized to Fanshaw that even the Prince himself had no power over the Inquisition.[71] Fanshaw pointed out, to no avail, that deportation of a person in peace time, when he was not a criminal, was against the common law of nations and certainly contrary to the articles of peace.[72]

The question of a chaplain in Oporto seems to have been resolved temporarily, for it is known that Edward Hinde was there as chaplain in 1684. He had orders to officiate unobtrusively, for it was considered that the Portuguese would not tolerate him officially.[73] Hinde's last letter to the Bishop of Ely was probably written in the early autumn of 1686.[74] We know that he was deported by March 1687, for at that time Scarburgh presented a memorial to King Pedro II on behalf of the Oporto factory, because the Inquisition had banned the English Protestants from holding services and had ordered the chaplain to depart forthwith.[75] A month later, having received a refusal to allow a Protestant chaplaincy in Oporto, Scarburgh wrote to Sunderland and suggested that James II should take the matter up with the Portuguese envoy in London, as the government in Lisbon did not think James was in earnest. There is no record of James having followed this advice, so the Portuguese must have been correct in their surmise.[76]

The advent of James as king made it easy for Portugal to ignore the 1654 treaty and the unwritten agreement concerning the chaplaincies. Even the marriage of Catherine to Charles II had made Portugal's missionary zeal in England less dependent on the embassy in London. It was probably only Charles's apparent adherence to the Protestant faith that ensured that the agreements were observed. Article 7 of the 1661 marriage treaty gave Catherine and her 'family' the right to enjoy the free exercise of the Catholic religion and to have a chapel or place set apart for this in all the royal palaces where she might at any time reside. It is clear from documents extant in Portugal that it was always intended that she and her entourage should act as a focal point for English Catholics.[77] The planning of this task was approached with great fervour. Her religious household varied from time to time. Her confessor was a Jesuit, Father António Fernandes. Father Godden, formerly President of the English College in Lisbon, and Bishop Russell were also part of it. She had six Portuguese chaplains for her chapel in St James' Place, which was opened on 21 September 1662. Attached to the chapel was a community of six English Benedictines, whose task was to keep up the recitations of the Divine Office. Within five years she had also installed twelve friars of the obedience of St Peter of Alcântara (Arrabidos or Capuchins) and their father guardian, just to the east of St James' Chapel and cloisters, on land where now stands the entrance to the Guards Club and Marlborough House.[78] In addition the queen mother, Henrietta Maria, had a chapel in Somerset House, and when she left England in 1665, she exacted a promise from Charles that he would not close the chapel. She died in 1669 and Catherine moved her chapel into the larger Somerset House in 1671: St James' Chapel was never closed, and both chapels were open to anyone wishing to enter.[79] Between 1662 and 1678 the registers of the queen's chapel show that two hundred marriages were performed there. Nearly all those being married were English, and many lived outside London. Pepys visited St James' Chapel twice 'for the music'. Sermons were preached in English. The Duke of York maintained priests and, after he was received into the Catholic church in 1669, he, too, maintained a chapel and staff. Many of the Catholic nobility living in London had private chapels. The king employed lay Catholics and there were always many priests at court, such as Patrick MacGuin and Peter Talbot (in 1669 titular Archbishop of Dublin).[80] Anyone serving or purveying for the queen or her entourage was exempt from conviction of recusancy. An example of the latter was Daniel Arthur, a merchant, who acted as financial agent for many Catholics.[81] Catholics were, therefore, smiled upon and helped. Doubtless good Protestants thought these things were a 'scandal', too. Southwell, who was then secretary to the Privy Council, also spoke of the manifest indulgence to Catholics and the grief and scandal it was to many. The Commons Committee Report of 29 April 1678 spoke of the scandalous open practice of their religion by Catholics in Monmouthshire; the appointment of Catholic justices of the peace in Northumberland and recusancy fines being allowed to lapse.[82] The men on the Commons Committee were anxious about the militancy of Catholic priests in England, many of whom were fanatic crusaders, and secretary of state Coventry knew that there was a strong suggestion that one of Catherine's Capuchins, Paolino de Estrella, was involved in a plot against Charles II in 1678, at the time of the popish plot. Certainly, John Wrothersly and Peter Burrell, two Oporto merchants, had sight of a letter from Estrella which suggested that the Capuchins were a security risk.[83]

Whether Catherine produced an heir or not, Protestants all knew that their next sovereign would be a Catholic. It is therefore not surprising that in 1678 public opinion and the Commons forced Charles II to banish all papists from court, including his brother, James, who was sent abroad. It seems that in practice, however, none of these rulings made a great deal of difference to the accessibility and operation of the chapels.[84] Henry Compton, who became Bishop of London in 1675, was responsible for censorship of the press. In August 1676 his agents seized a large quantity of English translations of the Roman Mass at a printer's, and at the same time found that the licence for them had been issued by the Portuguese ambassador (D. Francisco de Melo). Compton reported the matter to the Privy Council. They called the ambassador to attend, but in spite of being at that time chamberlain to the queen, which was an English office, he maintained, in his capacity as ambassador presumably, that he could not answer at the Council Board without leave from his prince. He sent his secretary instead, who averred that the original licence had been issued for one hundred copies, but that this had been altered to nine hundred by an unknown person after signature.[85]

There is no doubt, therefore, that Portugal only observed Article 14 of the 1654 treaty in part. The unwritten agreement between the two countries was ignored by Portugal once England was ruled by a Catholic king, and there was little to encourage Englishmen in Portugal to hope for assistance from England. No matter what his private religion, Charles conformed to the Church of England publicly. On the other hand, under James, Catholics had licence to observe their religious beliefs publicly, and there was no more need to use the Portuguese embassy in London as a centre for the propagation of the Catholic faith. Given the changed circumstances in England and what they portended for English Protestants in Portugal, it is little wonder that so shortly after James II ascended the throne, the Inquisition in Portugal should have acted to put an end to Protestant services in Portugal, unless they were held in the residence of an envoy.

11

The Auxiliary Forces

The employment of auxiliaries was common in the seventeenth century, for it enabled one state to help another without committing itself to a formal declaration of war against that state's enemies, and without being involved in the expense of keeping a standing army.[1] Under the terms of Article 15 of the 1661 treaty, Charles II engaged to bear the expenses of recruiting, arming and transporting to Portugal two regiments of horse, each regiment consisting of 500 men, and two regiments of foot, each consisting of 1,000 men. Once landed, their pay was to be the responsibility of the king of Portugal.[2] Louis XIV had also allowed Portugal to contract for the services of French officers and technicians and to recruit some soldiers through the agency of Turenne, because he wished to help Portugal secretly against Spain.[3]

The auxiliary force which landed in Portugal on 7 July 1662 had been placed under the command of Murrough O'Brien, 1st Earl of Inchiquin, an Irishman and a royalist Catholic, who had been fighting in the French forces in Cataluña. He had been selected by the Conde de Soure, Portuguese envoy to France in 1649.[4] Under him were three major-generals: Christopher O'Brien, his brother; Sir John Talbot, a royalist; and Sir Thomas Morgan, who had helped George Monck at the time of the Restoration.[5] In an endeavour to keep the peace amongst such a mixture of Cromwellians and Royalists, a new clause in the articles of war forbade anyone to utter reproachful words to the disrepute of others among the garrisons or any person in them for former actions, on pain of punishment as incendiary. In spite of this, it was impossible to prevent insults between them. Colonel Molesworth, for instance, disheartened men suffering severe hardships by calling them 'Cromwell's whelps and rebels'.[6]

On arrival in July, the troops were marched straight to the front in the Alentejo. A month later, Maynard reported to Clarendon that the government had been forced to issue proclamations to the effect that the church was forbidden to protect and give sanctuary to Portuguese citizens murdering or wounding Englishmen.[7] Portuguese countrymen did not welcome foreign troops. The French already in Portugal had behaved badly, and Protestants were disliked.[8] The town of Beja rioted against the troops.[9] Sir Richard Fanshaw, Britain's ambassador in Lisbon (1662–3), pressed for public justice to be done to those committing such excesses, but without avail. He told the king of Portugal that the troops were being shown an invincible antipathy, never seen before (*aqui aya antipatia invencible y no antes vista*).[10] Inchiquin accused secretary of state Macedo of designing the destruction of the English troops by ill payment, ill usage and by slighting the general's person. He left for England and did not return.[11] The troops were then placed under the command of Marshal Schomberg (1615–90), whose mother was English and his father German. He was a Protestant and had served in the Dutch and Swedish armies until 1652, when he joined the French army. He fought with the Ironsides at the Battle of the Dunes in 1658 and he was liked and respected by the English Brigade.[12]

The troops' pay was one of the chief causes of friction between England and Portugal. The actual rate of pay had not been specified in the Marriage Treaty. In all probability this was deliberate, the necessity of getting them out of Britain being more important than delaying treaty negotiations whilst trying to find agreement. The troops clearly assumed that the Portuguese would pay them the same rates as Charles II, because of Charles's guarantee in the Declaration of Breda,[13] but they were wrong. Inchiquin was aware of the position, and he was so fearful that the men would make the sailors take them back if they knew the truth, that he swore his officers to secrecy.[14] The Portuguese troops were paid on a much lower scale and for only seven to eight months of the year, as they were mostly peasants and were sent home in the autumn to help with the harvest.[15] The English troops could not be sent home each autumn to relieve the Portuguese government of the necessity of paying them, neither had they any means of earning money in Portugal. The Portuguese government argued that to pay the English troops more would lead to jealousy and mutiny among their own troops. The French troops were paid somewhere between the two, and they simply took what they needed, as and where they could. Because of this, they were not forever demanding their pay and were more popular with the poverty-stricken Portuguese government.[16] There was the further point, made in a petition by the English officers to Clarendon during pay negotiations, that even if they were to be paid the Portuguese equivalent of their English pay at the time of their arrival in Portugal, because of the 'rise of money' (or devaluation), they would be receiving nearer half-pay only, because the Portuguese crown they received for the 6/3d. was only worth 3/6d. in England.[17]

These serious difficulties required constant negotiation with the Portuguese government. From his own and Fanshaw's correspondence in the State Papers, Portugal, it is clear that Maynard was involved in these negotiations from the outset, but it is not known for certain exactly when he was first appointed agent and negotiator general for the auxiliary troops in Portugal. There is a document so doing filed among the State Papers for 1660.[18] This may have been mis-filed, but it may be that Maynard obtained the appointment in 1660 when he was in England, in anticipation of a treaty being finalized. Certainly in September 1663, a declaration made by the officers of the English auxiliary forces in Portugal appointed Maynard as their representative in all negotiations with the Portuguese court,[19] and in December 1663, Charles II issued a warrant authorizing Maynard so to act.[20] Although Sir Peter Wyche, on the staff of Henry Bennet, (later Lord Arlington) accompanied the troops to Portugal as Paymaster in 1662, it appears that Maynard had obtained that post by March 1663.[21] In any event, from his many letters to England, it is clear that Maynard worked hard and cared greatly about the well-being of the troops.

Agreements about pay were negotiated, but not kept, by the Portuguese government. It is true that most troops in the seventeenth century expected that their pay would be in arrears, but after seven months in Portugal, the troops had only received one month's pay, and were 'daily mouldering away'. Their numbers were reduced to 250 horse and 1,400 foot by death and desertion.[22] Their condition was such that in March 1663, Charles allowed £6,000 from the dower money to make up the difference between Portuguese and English pay.[23] There is, however, no evidence of his having repeated the gesture. By 1666, Southwell was reporting that the troops' pay was six months in arrears. A year later, it was nine months in arrears and the men were starving.[24] Southwell told Williamson that the troops were being barbarously treated and unless Charles II helped them, they would be undone men.[25] It was the English merchants in Portugal who helped the troops most, by extending long credit to them.[26] That, and Charles' assistance to them in 1663, saved them from perishing. It became usual for the troops to be paid in sugar, the only form of payment the Portuguese could manage, and it was the merchants who sold the sugar on their behalf.[27] Indeed, the dower payments to Charles himself were sent to England in the form of sugar.[28]

Maynard's role in the pay negotiations earned him much odium from Castelo Melhor and Macedo, the former requesting Maynard's recall.[29] Schomberg and the officers, on the other hand, were full of praise for his work and clearly relied on him.[30] The animosity of Castelo Melhor and Macedo, as well as the amount of time Maynard spent on army affairs, did not help the merchants with their problems, and went far to undermine his authority and control as consul.[31]

The morale of the troops suffered because the Portuguese authorities – as reported in the Gazettes of the time – were grudging in their praise of their fighting qualities unless they were demanding reinforcements from England.[32] The fact that the Portuguese once donned red coats to frighten the Spaniards on the Beira front, however, shows that the

Portuguese army were aware of their capability.[33] The behaviour of the troops at the battles of Ameixial and Valença (1663 and 1664, respectively) was never given its due. For instance, to show his appreciation for the efforts of the English troops at Ameixial, Afonso VI sent three pounds of snuff to each company. The king had a monopoly of tobacco.[34] On receiving it, the men promptly threw it up in the air,[35] preferring more public recognition of their services. After Valença, the morale of the English brigade was particularly low. As a result of not having been given the support from the Portuguese and the French which they had a right to expect, the English casualties were extremely high. More than 450 were killed and wounded, whereas not more than 150 casualties were sustained by the other nationalities put together. As the English numbered about one in twenty of the armed forces of Portugal, that was a high proportion.[36] A chaplain present on the battle field told Colbatch that the steady English advance up a steep hill under enemy fire, without firing themselves, was considered by the Portuguese to have been so foolhardy, that they thought that the English were deserting to Spain. They were given no covering fire by the French and Portuguese. Vila Flor, the commanding officer of the Portuguese was reported to have said 'Aqueles herezes são melhor que os nossos santos'. ('Those heretics are better than our saints').[37] Maynard's endeavours to obtain thanks or public recognition of valour from the Portuguese government were quite fruitless.[38] His reports to England, together with reports sent back by officers, prompted Clarendon to write to Castelo Melhor in forceful terms. He said that the king was pained to hear that the troops were regarded by Portugal as a burden, when in fact they were being deprived not only of their pay, but also of the honour and glory due to them for performing particularly onerous and dangerous tasks with valour and success.[39] Schomberg was disgusted by the attitude of the ministers and told them that if the English were not wanted in Portugal, they should be sent home.[40] Secretary of state Macedo, writing to Russell in London the following December, was to blame what he called the 'confusion' of this battle on the fact that Schomberg had refused to let any Portuguese officer interfere in the management of the English Brigade, because of his commission to lead them.[41]

Thus in addition to problems of pay and proper recognition for the services rendered to the Portuguese crown by the auxiliary forces, there were problems of command. The English troops were happy to have the experienced Protestant general Schomberg as their commander.[42] Schomberg had been brought to Portugal in 1662 to reform and reorganize the Portuguese army, which had led to jealousy on the part of the Portuguese officers; gradually, official support for Schomberg was withdrawn. It seems that the furore over Valença prompted the

Portuguese to make changes in the command. Schomberg, who had been camp master general, was made *Governador das Armas*, under the Commander-in-Chief, the Marquês de Marialva. In that post, he had to give orders to all the forces through two Portuguese officers, the general of the cavalry and the camp master general.[43] This meant that the English and French troops (whom Schomberg also commanded) would have to take orders from Portuguese officers. The reasons why the English officers were against doing this were set out in a petition sent to Clarendon in August 1664.[44] Their argument was that if they came under Portuguese officers their promotion would depend on the recommendation of the latter, and no one got promotion in Portugal unless approved for it by the Jesuits and friars. Furthermore, they considered the Portuguese officers incompetent, and serving the king of Portugal under such conditions would dishonour England. Because Schomberg steadily refused to relinquish direct command of the English troops, unless so commanded by Charles II or Clarendon, Castlo Melhor was forced to submit and a new agreement was reached between the English troops and the Portuguese government, allowing Schomberg to remain in command.[45] On 10/20 November, however, the agreement was abrogated by the Portuguese, and Afonso VI wrote to Schomberg saying that the separate command had ceased to exist and that all foreign troops would have to take orders from Portuguese generals.[46] Maynard forecast that the English troops would obey orders from Charles II in the matter, but said that the French troops refused to submit and were sending representatives to France.[47] In December, Castelo Melhor wrote to Russell in the London embassy, telling him to explain to Clarendon that the change in command was necessary for the morale of the Portuguese troops. It was essential that they should think that their own king was in command of them through his own officers.[48] This argument was accepted in London and by May 1665 orders from Charles for the troops and Schomberg to submit had been received in Portugal.[49] Schomberg was not given direct command over the English troops again until February 1667.[50]

Altogether, including reinforcements sent out from time to time, a total of 5,000 English auxiliaries served in Portugal between 1662 and 1668. By 1668 there were only 1,000 men left, 80% had been lost.[51] John Colbatch considered that the English troops gradually won the respect of the common people among whom they were quartered, for the latter had begun to use the expression 'palavra de hum Ingrez', or 'word of an Englishman', as meaning a firm promise.[52] None the less, in 1665 several officers and soldiers were murdered in their quarters, and when Lt. Ashton and a soldier were assassinated in the street by Portuguese troopers, who in turn were apprehended by English soldiers, the Portuguese troopers were freed unpunished by the Portuguese authorities.[53]

The lot of the English troops was an unhappy one, and they had much to bear. Two men laboured constantly for their welfare – Schomberg and Maynard. Schomberg told Clarendon that the court in Portugal was ill-disposed to Maynard because he was so zealous in the affairs of the king (Charles II) and his subjects. The Portuguese hated all foreign troops, he said, but especially the English, because they were Protestants.[54] At the insistence of Castelo Melhor, Maynard was recalled to England in 1668. Early in that year Schomberg, Colonel Dempsey and Colonel Trelawny wrote to Arlington, saying that if the consul went to England great confusion would be caused, because the claims of the troops depended entirely on his daily solicitations at the court on their behalf.[55] It is fair to say that, in the circumstances in which the troops found themselves, no one could have conscientiously acted as their agent and still remained popular with the Portuguese authorities. Maynard's energy and zest for work must have been formidable. Between 13/23 August 1663 when Fanshaw left Lisbon, until the arrival of Southwell in January 1666, Maynard had an onerous number of responsibilities. In his capacity as agent for the troops, he had to negotiate at Court and make trips to the front; he had to act as agent or chargé d'affaires on top of his consular duties, and the latter were heavier than normal because England was at war with the Dutch. On the personal level, too, he had his troubles. His wife died, and his brother, Andrew, a captain in Henry Pearson's regiment of foot, was wounded at Valença.[56]

Their difficulties had welded the Cromwellians and royalists into a body of men whose behaviour in action was disciplined and exemplary. Southwell wrote to Arlington in September 1668, just before the departure from Portugal of the few men that remained, and said:

> I do not believe there is to be found againe in ye worlde a better body of men. Never any fought more bravely in ye field or lived more quietly in their quarters, and being as equal in discipline as in their valour, only their enemies complaine, and not the inhabitants, who as it hath been affirmed to me, did now with tears wave them from the frontiers.[57]

When they left, four hundred men were sent to Tangier under Lt.-Col. Rumsey; others joined the Spanish army or became merchants in Portugal, but five hundred men and thirty officers returned to England. Some of the latter joined guards regiments in England. Schomberg left Portugal in 1668, and he eventually died fighting for William III in Ireland in 1690, aged seventy-five.[58]

12

The English College and
Anglo-Portuguese Relations

The College of St Peter and St Paul in Lisbon was known locally as the *Inglesinhos*, and the dimunitive was an indication of the affection in which it was held in Portugal. However, Maynard and the members of this Catholic seminary were at odds from the time he arrived to take up his post as consul and agent in January 1657.

The establishment abroad of colleges for the education and training of priests who would devote their lives to the perpetuation of their faith in their own country began in the sixteenth century. The movement was largely due to the efforts and organizing ability of Dr William, later Cardinal, Allen. No English college had been established in Lisbon in that century, and it had been the responsibility of the Jesuits at São Roque to appoint a chaplain to cater for the needs of English Catholics there.[1] One such chaplain, Nicholas Ashton or Aston (Anthony Walwyn) conceived the idea of founding an English college in Portugal. He bought a house in Lisbon for the purpose and at his death bequeathed it to Father William Newman (Ralph Sliefield).[2] The latter became intimate with a Portuguese *fidalgo*, Dom Pedro Coutinho, who agreed to endow an English seminary college but only on condition that it was a secular foundation,[3] that is, a foundation for training parish priests. Besides leaving 1,500 *cruzados* to the college at his death to cover future rents, he gave 5,000 *cruzados* to cover the cost of the site. He offered the seminary to the See of England, and it was accepted by the Bishop of Chalcedon. The government of the college was vested in the Bishop of Chalcedon and his successors in the vicariate of England.[4] The Jesuits opposed the foundation, but on 3 December 1621 (N.S.) the king issued an *alvará* for the founding of the college and its endowment.[5] Pope Gregory XV conferred the usual privileges on the Lisbon college on 22 September 1622 (N.S.).[6] Pope Urban VIII issued the bull for its founding in 1627, and the college became operative when the Reverend Joseph Harvey (alias Haynes), Archdeacon of the English church, arrived with a party of ten students from Douai. The public opening of the college took place on 22 February 1629, but Harvey died on the same day. In 1630, Thomas White (alias Blacklow) was appointed the second president of the college, and he drew up its rules.[7] The college was to be a school for English Catholic boys, as well as a seminary.

The inquisitor general of Portugal was appointed the protector of the college, which gave it great prestige and influence. The protector was licensed to examine and ordain students. Between 1635 and 1646, he made no fewer than seven visitations, indicating his keen interest, an interest which was shown by succeeding inquisitors general.[8] Whereas the Jesuits had formerly performed the task of being visitors of foreign ships for the Inquisition, in 1640 the office was granted to the College at a fee of 25,000 *reis* per annum. The original deed is among the college records at Ushaw. It is also interesting to note that the college received 150,000 *reis* per annum from taxes received at the *portos secos*.[9]

The college annals show that some 164 men passed through it during the seventeenth century. Some of the wealthier students paid their own way, whilst others were paid for by members or former members of the college, often relatives. For instance, Richard Russell, when Bishop of Portalegre, gave 6,000 crowns to the college for the right to name his relatives to be maintained in it while he lived and after his death.[10] He supported at least eleven boys, including two Seymours, two Waldegraves and two Digbys.[11] One of his nieces was placed with Dona Joana Coutinho, to learn the language and manners and to be looked after.[12] Richard Russell himself had gone to the college in 1642 at the age of twelve and worked as a servant of Dr Daniel to pay for his education.[13]

During the seventeenth century, the college appears to have had three principal aims: to train missionaries, who returned to England to succour recusants and to convert English Protestants to Catholicism, both in England and in Portugal; to serve the Portuguese crown; and as opportunities presented themselves, to gain control of the English factory. By gaining that control, it obtained a good regular income from consulage and opportunities to influence the mercantile community in London, Bristol and other ports. These advantages ended with Maynard's appointment as consul in 1656, so it was inevitable that he and the college should clash.

When missionaries returned to England from their colleges, whether they were seculars or regulars, they did so under aliases and as laymen. Those from Portugal passed backwards and forwards with apparent ease.[14] In England they became a part of the large Catholic organization whose effectiveness is difficult to judge accurately, because of its secrecy and because of the jealousies and active animosity between regulars and seculars, which was the legacy of the Wisbech stirs.[15] The regulars and seculars were both well established in England by 1650. Of concern to the Lisbon college was the organization of the seculars, who had been granted a bishop by the pope in 1622, with a title from Greece or Asia, in order to avoid confusion of titles with Anglican incumbents in England. Dr William Bishop, elected Bishop of Chalcedon in 1623, died in 1624, and was succeeded by Dr Richard Smith. The latter left

England in 1631 due to difficulties caused by the ambiguous wording of the pope's brief. Thus the seculars in England were left with no real leadership, and were ruled by twenty-four canons with a dean. This chapter, or bishop's advisory council, lacking a bishop, became the source of much dissension. Dr Smith died in 1655, but it was not until 1685 that another bishop was appointed.[16]

Amidst this disorder, the second president of the Lisbon college, Thomas White, alias Blacklow, began to lead a movement in England whose followers denied the deposing power of Rome, and wanted a rapprochement with the government of the day in England.[17] They also believed in the validity of the chapter, insisting that it had the right to elect a new bishop at will, and they wanted to have the Jesuits expelled. This group obtained control of the chapter in 1650, though the effective leader of the party became John Sergeant, who was appointed secretary of the chapter in 1653.[18] John Sergeant (aliases Smith and Holland) was born in 1622, became a convert whilst working as a secretary to Thomas Morton, Bishop of Durham, and went to Lisbon in 1642 to perfect his studies at the *Inglesinhos*. He returned to England in 1652.[19] Sergeant remained a follower of Blacklow until his death in 1707, playing an extremely active role against the Jesuits at the time of the popish plot.[20] The fact that Blackloism never affected the *Inglesinhos* to any extent was because Sergeant did not return to Lisbon after 1652. There, the person whose influence was greatest was Richard Russell. His political work served the college very well, raising its prestige and influence. As far as is known, he never allowed himself to become involved in Blackloism, although he was elected a canon of the Chapter in 1661.[21] It is probable that he and Sergeant worked together harmoniously between 1657 and 1660, because Russell boasted on his return to Lisbon that he and Sergeant had converted above three thousand of His Majesty's subjects in three and a half years.[22] Large portraits of both men hang side by side in Ushaw College Library today, as they had done previously in the *Inglesinhos*.

It was Richard Russell who epitomized the way the college served the Portuguese crown. His role as secretary and amanuensis extraordinary to Francisco de Melo during the negotiations for the Treaty of Westminster and the Marriage Treaty have already been described (see above, pp. 82-88). His success as a diplomat followed a scholarly and administrative career. He left Lisbon in 1651 for further studies at Douai and Paris before ordination, and then returned to Lisbon in 1655, where he was appointed procurator at the college. Russell came from a Berkshire Catholic family, and one of his sisters married a Waldegrave.[23] He rapidly became *persona grata* with Charles II, his ministers and others of influence in Whitehall, and seems to have gained everyone's confidence. It has been shown how he became the only person other than Melo at the embassy who knew of the initial negotiations for the royal marriage; he acted as a go-between for Melo with Charles and his ministers, and he helped to regiment merchant support for the marriage and the 1661 treaty. Because he was entrusted by Melo with the distribution of the *mimos* or sweeteners, he must have been able to call on the recipients for personal support, if needed, at a later date. It is not known whether, as secretary to Melo, he was able to wear clerical garb again, but when he returned from Portugal in the autumn of 1661, with the ratification of the marriage treaty, he did so as bishop-elect of Cabo Verde. A contemporary at court said that he was greeted as bishop by everyone, including Clarendon, and that his manners had lately assumed *grandezza*. He boasted that Charles II had promised to receive Queen Catherine from his hands.[24] Charles had already done him the honour of having him placed behind the throne when he announced his marriage plans to Parliament, and Russell was indeed to be present at the wedding ceremony.[25] Russell always remained on good terms with Catherine, whom he taught to speak English. She much disliked Melo: the latter had to rely on Russell, as long as he remained ambassador in London, for communicating with her when needed.[26]

Russell succeeded in retaining the favour of successive administrations in Portugal. On his return to Lisbon in November 1660, with Melo, Queen Luisa gave him a present of 1,080 *cruzados*, and a pension of seventy-five golden guineas per month. He returned to England with Melo in 1661, and it was on Charles' recommendation, when he took back the treaty for ratification, that he was appointed bishop-elect of Cabo Verde, with a promise that he would be nominated to the first vacant see in Portugal.[27] Shortly after the marriage, Queen Luisa was forced to retire, but Russell remained in England at the embassy for most of the five years the Conde de Castelo Melhor was in power. The Russell papers at Ushaw are a witness to the intimacy and friendship which he maintained with Castelo Melhor, Maċedo and others. After the deposition of Afonso VI and the return of the former queen's faction, led by Prince Pedro, he returned to Portugal to find the only apparent opposition to his appointment as bishop of Portalegre came from the church itself. Letters of commendation from Charles II soon put the matter right and he took over his see in 1671.[28] He never returned to active diplomatic work, but he maintained close ties with the *Inglesinhos* and his influence there was great.

Even more remarkable was that in spite of the considerable friction which developed between England and Portugal between 1662 and 1668 – over the treatment meted out to the English troops in Portugal, and the difficulty of trying to prevent Portugal from making an alliance with France – Russell, an Englishman in the service of Portugal, was able to retain not only the trust and confidence of the Portuguese but also of the English. For instance, when Sir Peter Wyche and Mr Roper were sent out to congratulate Afonso VI on his marriage, all the business with the Portuguese court was entrusted not to them, but to Russell, who travelled with them.[29] Although Southwell judged that Russell was valued in Portugal only as he was useful to Portugal, and as a piece of Sande (Melo),[30] none the less, when Southwell returned to England in 1669, he was happy to do Russell favours in England, presumably because by doing so he thought to please people in power in England.[31] On his final return to Portugal in 1668, Russell negotiated the arrangements for the collection of the remainder of the dower. For that service he received 10,850 *cruzados* over two years.[32]

Despite Russell's many admirable qualities, Maynard – always a loyal Englishman and a staunch Anglican – never thought him a loyal Englishman. The English College was training Catholics to disrupt the Anglican supremacy in England: Russell was a product of that college, and Maynard knew from long experience the attitude and aims of English catholic exiles, many of whom put their religion before their country. On several occasions Maynard advised Arlington that he had been warned by friends against trusting Russell.[33] Perhaps he did not think Russell could serve two masters in connection with matters at issue between the two countries. If Russell were first and foremost a servant of Portugal, the extent to which he appeared to be in the trust of those in England was a matter of concern to all loyal Englishmen in Portugal, where English interests were being increasingly obstructed.

In one instance, indeed, Maynard's distrust was proved well-founded. In 1671, Maynard reported that the English merchants in Portugal were obtaining no redress concerning their complaints, because the Portuguese were hoping to increase their commerce and navigation as a result of a scheme planned by Jews to ingratiate themselves with the prince regent. It was planned to set up the manufacturing English and French cloths in Portugal itself. Ten French families had already been imported from France and the French ambassador was enraged at the threat to French trade with Portugal. Bishop Russell and Francis Holbech, an English Catholic merchant, had undertaken to assist the scheme by bringing over several cloth workers and baymakers from England. The Portuguese agent in London was to further the business.[34] At the end of twenty-eight years of war with Spain, Portugal's economy was in desperate straits, so a memorial written by Dr Duarte Ribeiro de Macedo, the Portuguese ambassador in Paris, recommending that Portugal should adopt Colbert's ideas and try to encourage local industries, was influential.[35] The envisaged scheme aimed at encouraging and improving local industries at the expense of imported manufactures, by bringing in foreign workers to train the

Portuguese. The improvement was to be effected by foreign workers brought to Portugal to teach their skills to the Portuguese. The encouragement was to come from a series of sumptuary laws (the chief of which were passed in 1677, 1686, 1688, 1690 and 1702)[36] and, of course by increasing the customs valuation on imported items, so that it would be impossible for those goods to be sold at a profit in Portugal.[37] This policy has come to be known as that of the Conde de Ericeira, but it was in fact supported by a strong group at court, including D. Luís de Meneses and Frei António das Chagas.[38]

Russell's involvement in the scheme assumes greater importance when it is remembered that, during the seventeenth century, the size of the economic cake was thought to be invariable and that it was only the sharing out of that cake that could vary, according to diligence or negligence of merchants and government policy.[39] As Maynard pointed out, if Portugal no longer took English manufactures, the king of England's customs would be greatly decreased and people in England would become unemployed for want of markets for their produce.[40] It is not surprising, therefore, that Russell's willingness to assist Portugal in the scheme should have caused his English contemporaries to doubt his loyalty. They believed the scheme would cause serious unemployment in England and break many of the English merchants in Portugal. By 1683, Fanshaw said that the factory was in a miserable condition on account of the factories set up in Portugal.[41]

If Russell and Holbech had not given their assistance to the scheme in the initial stages, other persons would have been brought in to accomplish the same ends. Nevertheless, Russell's assistance perhaps explains the distrust that Maynard felt for the man, and why there is no sign in the Russell Papers or the State Papers, Portugal, that after 1671 he was *persona grata* with men in power in England. He did much to damage English interests and became entirely Portuguese.

The idea of an English Catholic seminary overseas taking control of a consulship and a factory was not new. It had happened at San Lucar de Barrameda at the end of the sixteenth century, and had enabled the seminary to utilize consular fees to further its work.[42] It is not surprising, therefore, that when an opportunity offered itself for the college in Lisbon to accomplish something similar, it was taken.

Mention was made in Chapter 3 of a Father John Robinson[43] of the English College, who was appointed consul of the English nation in Lisbon on 13 July 1650 by decree of John IV. That decree states that he was nominated for the job by the king of England (Charles II, in exile).[44] The reason for Charles II's interest in Robinson was almost certainly because of the assistance which he gave to the murderer of Isaac Dorislaus, the Commonwealth representative at The Hague in 1649. Robinson was either the chaplain of, or attached to, the Portuguese embassy there. He may, perhaps, have just been housed there en route to missionary work in England. Colonel Whitford, who murdered Dorislaus,[45] was a Catholic and he went to Robinson to be resolved in point of conscience beforehand, whether or not he could lawfully kill Dorislaus. Robinson told the Portuguese ambassador what was intended and the latter ensured that the embassy doors were left open, so that Whitford was able to repair there for sanctuary, until he was able to make his escape to Brussels.[46]

It is not known what qualifications Robinson had for the job of consul and for dealing with merchant affairs. He was educated in philosophy and the humanities before he became a priest in 1638.[47] The decree of 1650 states that he was experienced in commercial matters, and given that the Jesuits and other priests frequently engaged in trade, it is possible that the college might also have done so. Nothing has been found in the college records to link John Robinson to any commercial experience, however, so it can only be assumed that his appointment was purely political. It is unlikely that the idea of appointing a priest to the Lisbon consulship would have emanated from Charles. If Charles, to express his gratitude, had asked Robinson to name a favour, it is certain that the latter would have consulted the college before asking for the consulship. Charles would have been delighted, in his poverty-ridden state, to do a favour at so little cost to himself.

A. R. Walford says that because there are no records of Robinson's consulship, his must have been a time of peace and appeasement.[48] This is too simplistic an assumption. It is true that there are no records of his period in office, but at the time he was appointed there were only seven merchants out of prison, and there were no ships or seamen for him to care for, because the men had all been imprisoned and ships impounded a month earlier, on 2/12 June 1650. Bearing in mind what we know of the factory's organization, and that the consul's house was the factory meeting place, the college automatically became the factory meeting place on Robinson's appointment. From 1650-6 when the 1654 treaty was ratified, therefore, the college *was* the centre of the factory and the English nation in Portugal, for Robinson was not a private individual and he was at all times subject to the discipline of the college and his superiors. Unfortunately for the college the confiscations and the war with England would have meant small consulage payments until 1652 when trade began to improve. Without the factory minute books, and without a full set of college account books, it is impossible to make an accurate assessment of the extent to which the college profited by the arrangement. Robinson would have brought to the college perhaps what it valued more highly than money; influence among the English community.

It is not surprising, therefore, that in 1656 Mettam told Thurloe that opposition to the 1654 treaty was being stirred up by an Irish Dominican in France, some English clergymen in Lisbon and others in the agent's office in London (missionaries being housed there), who hated the present English government and were doing all they could to disparage, if not disadvantage it. More specifically, he said that Russell and Robinson made use of ridiculous fictions and stories to render Thurloe odious and to foster the factions among the merchants.[49] Until the treaty was ratified, the merchants did not know whom to please or how to hedge their bets to stay in business. With the implementation of the treaty of 1654, what had been accomplished for the college would be ruined, because it provided for a Protestant consul. It would have been that to which the college was truly opposed. Once the treaty was ratified, there was little that the college could do except bide its time, hoping for another opportunity. At the Restoration, Russell was excellently placed to influence the selection of a new consul. It is no wonder that Maynard wished to return to England to make sure of keeping his place. Although he and Russell apparently worked together at the time of the marriage treaty negotiations, their relationship can have been, at best, an armed neutrality. To keep his post, Maynard had not only to be reappointed by Charles II, but, also, to keep the goodwill of the Portuguese government. That goes a long way to explaining his uncharacteristic decision to play down questions regarding the Inquisition, which nearly wrecked the negotiations.

After Maynard's return to Portugal in 1660, the college began a concerted attempt to dislodge Maynard from his post and to have a Catholic nominee put in his place: how they failed to do so will be seen in the following chapter. In 1669, with Maynard's reinstatement, attempts ceased in Lisbon to have a Catholic nominee appointed to the consulship. Under the presidency of Mathias Watkinson, from 1672-1710, the college made special efforts to obtain converts from among the English people in Portugal, and it was particularly successful in Oporto, as has been seen. One of the converts, Edward Murcott, was appointed vice-consul by his colleagues. Maynard had the satisfaction of seeing his objections to this appointment upheld by Charles II, but although Murcott resigned as ordered, the Oporto merchants insisted that Murcott continue to function in the office and they withheld the portion of his consulage which should have been paid over to Maynard. Maynard's only remedy was to sue, but that proved more costly than the amount of the consulage he might have received, as the Portuguese judges delayed judgement, the defendants having employed priests and friars as solicitors.[50] Forcing a merchant to sue or defend himself in court was expensive, and one of the surest ways of sapping his resources and breaking him. The college never allowed Maynard to live in peace.

13

The Life of a Consul

It is impossible to study Anglo-Portuguese relations in the second half of the seventeenth century without reference to the reports of Thomas Maynard, consul in Lisbon for four years and consul-general for a further thirty.

Maynard was born in 1622/23, a younger son of Thomas Maynard of Brixton, Devon, and Agnes Lambert of Plymouth.[1] The Maynards were of Norman descent and had held West Sherford from the time of Henry VIII. They also became bailiffs of East Sherford. The estate comprised two manors totalling 273 acres in the early seventeenth century.[2] Writing in 1675, Maynard said that his father's family and fortunes suffered grievously in the Royalist cause during the Civil War. The family was reduced to great want and misery because both his father and elder brother lost their lives in the king's service, and because his father's estate had been sequestered and all his moveables sold.[3] It is strange, therefore, how Maynard succeeded in making himself *persona grata* with the Commonwealth government. If, as Portuguese sources record, he married a first cousin of General George Monck, this may have helped.[4] He had other good Commonwealth connections. His second cousin, John Maynard (1620–90), Member of Parliament for Totnes in the Short and Long Parliaments, and in 1653–4 Serjeant-at-Law, became Protector's Serjeant in 1658.[5]

It is known that in 1639 Maynard was sixteen and was an apprentice at La Rochelle, learning the trade of merchandising and the French language.[6] After three years in France, he went to work in Aveiro, Portugal as a factor for Rowland Hill, an English merchant in Oporto, who was married to the sister of Cromwell's chaplain, Sterry.[7] Maynard returned to England sometime between 1648 and 1650, to assist his distressed family and to marry the lady to whom he had been betrothed.[8] According to Francis Parry, agent and later, resident (1670–80), Hill had a kindness for Maynard and, in order to repay an old debt, he obtained employment for Maynard with the Protectorate government in 1655 as courier and agent for Cromwell with John IV.[9] Even by the autumn of 1654, Maynard was recommended for the post of consul in Portugal by the merchants of Exeter, Dartmouth, Plymouth and London. The London recommendation bears forty-six signatures. In these documents, Maynard is described as being a merchant of Plymouth. It is stressed that he knew Portugal and the language well; was of 'good life and conversation'; of known integrity and ability, and 'well affected' to the Commonwealth.[10] In spite of this, it appears that his real sympathies remained royalist, for Clarendon was later to tell Sir Richard Fanshaw, who was being sent to Portugal as ambassador, that Mr Maynard deserved well of the king and had been sent to Portugal in Cromwell's time by his Majesty's leave and direction.[11]

It is interesting that no petitions against Maynard or criticisms of his methods of working have been found during the Protectorate, when Maynard's authority appears to have been upheld by the government in England, and the merchants in Portugal knew where they stood, politically and religiously. Queen Luisa and Melo were both anxious to see that the terms of the treaty were observed, and Maynard had an excellent relationship with the queen and her ministers. Even the affair of Margaret Throckmorton does not seem to have destroyed that relationship. Had it done so, the queen would never have sent him to England in 1660, an acknowledgement that she knew him to be a good friend to Portugal, whom she could trust. Maynard's standing in Portugal is illustrated by the fact that he was the only person, other than grandees and ambassadors, allowed without permission in the queen's antechamber.[12]

This picture changed completely when Charles II ascended the throne. The Catholic and royalist factions among the merchants united in an effort to oust him because, on the one hand, political divisions in England were repeated in Portugal, and, on the other, the English College's ascendancy among the English nation in Portugal had been ended with Maynard's patent of 1656 which had superseded that of their own man, Father John Robinson. The college never ceased to make things difficult for Maynard. Thus, on his return, Maynard was accused of unbridled passion; 'intolerable nature to oppress'; prejudicing the merchants by imprudence and partiality, and 'discovering' the secrets of their trade to the Portuguese. Clarendon's assurance that he had been a king's man throughout, and the queen's letter to Charles II stating her approval of Maynard, calmed the spate of petitions.[13] The Conde de Castelo Melhor took over the government and Sousa de Macedo became secretary of state on the queen's forced retirement in 1662, and for the next five years Maynard's relations with the Portuguese government were to be tempestuous. Castelo Melhor was deeply suspicious of Maynard because of his favour and standing with the queen and her government; Southwell later confirmed that this was the principal reason for the hostility to the consul.[14] Macedo saw Maynard as an appointee of the despised usurper, Cromwell. Further, the auxiliary forces sent out under the terms of the 1661 treaty had arrived in Portugal in the summer of 1662, and as mentioned above (p.

137), Maynard was appointed agent for them.[15] His efforts on their behalf and in keeping English sailors on English ships, and redressing the grievances of the merchants because of the non-observance by Portugal of the terms of the 1654 treaty, did nothing to endear him to Portugal's rulers at the time. Castelo Melhor asked Clarendon to remove the consul.[16] He told Maynard to his face that he was pro-Spanish and a creature of Secretary Bennet's:[17] an allegation he was later forced to withdraw.[18] In October 1665, Castelo Melhor asked Sande to negotiate for Maynard's removal because of his 'aspero modo' (abrasiveness).[19] Shortly afterwards he again wrote to Sande, saying '. . . it is impossible to accomplish any business with this consul, God damn it, my lord marquis, and I will not have anything more to do with him.'[20]

The situation was clearly very serious. In Maynard's favour, it must be remembered that Fanshaw left Portugal in August 1663, leaving him with a workload likely to make anyone impatient and abrasive. Many a man in Maynard's circumstances might have devoted himself to ingratiating himself with Castelo Melhor and Macedo, but Maynard's sense of responsibility was too strong, and he was anyway tainted by his success with the former regime. Not only were the interests of Englishmen in Portugal diametrically opposed to those of the government in Portugal at the time, but they were often of an urgent nature. There was no time for the slow diplomacy of seventeenth century Portugal, which Southwell likened to a pilgrimage.[21] It is significant that after the fall of Castelo Melhor in 1667, Southwell reported that Maynard was again *persona grata* at court. Both the Duke of Cadaval and Ruy Moura Telles spoke well of him, the duke 'not without singular commendation', and those who did not speak well of him did not speak ill.[22]

None the less, the pressure brought to bear in London for Maynard's removal in 1665 had reluctantly forced Charles II to act, so that when Southwell arrived in Portugal in 1666, he had brought with him a gently worded letter of recall from the king for questioning by the Council. In this letter Charles said that he was persuaded that Maynard had behaved himself well in his service.[23] Unfortunately none of these events was secret and Maynard's departure was delayed for lack of shipping due to the Dutch war and a court case.[24] Many people assumed that Maynard would lose his office. This led to others seeking the job and offering bribes to agents.[25] Maynard's efforts to keep the troops from starving were assisted by the majority of English merchants, who extended credit to them.[26] However, some merchants began to complain. They averred that because of the quarrel at court and Maynard's recall, he could not act on their behalf as he should and they made this an excuse not to pay him consulage. Maynard did not want to sue them, as he did not want the Portuguese ministers to know.[27] The situation was ripe for the English College to try again to instal a Catholic consul. These endeavours were aided by Richard Russell of the college, at that time secretary in the Portuguese embassy in London. When the 1661 treaty was being negotiated, Russell had dispensed the sweeteners, so his favour was high among those who mattered in the government in England.[28] Thus, on 27 March 1668 (O.S.), Maynard's patent was cancelled and one Francis Holbech, a Catholic merchant in Portugal and a good friend of Russell's, was appointed in his stead.[29] Holbech never seems to have worked as consul and, at the time of the patent being issued, Maynard had not even been back to England to be examined by the Council, for he only departed four months later.[30] It is interesting to note that the patent of Holbech, who was a Catholic, provided for him as consul to house and pay half the salary of a Protestant chaplain. The implementation of such a proviso would have been inconceivable in Portugal at that time. In the spring of 1669, Charles wrote to the prince regent and to the factory, advising them of Maynard's reinstatement.[31]

On his return to Portugal after being cleared of the charges laid against him at the Council meeting in London on 8 March 1668/9,[32] Maynard could have hoped for a more trouble-free existence, in view of the change of government. This was not to be, however, because of the animosity of Southwell and Parry, who did all they could to break him. Although there is documentation to identify the animosity, its cause can only be conjectured. Unlike Maynard, who had been apprenticed in his teens and had had to earn his living as a merchant, Southwell had been early destined for a diplomatic career and had graduated from the Queen's College, Oxford, and entered Lincoln's Inn before completing his education by continental travel.[33] Parry had first gone to Lisbon as Southwell's secretary. He had, according to Maynard, a calling in the church.[34] It is clear that Southwell was an ambitious opportunist, always anxious to be well thought of by people in positions of power. For example, he wrote to Mr Floyd in March 1667:

I am glad by your letter to understand the probability of your friendship with Mr Williamson which will work good effects not onely as to your engraciating [*sic*] with my Ld. Arlington, but in good offices and information from him unto me, which while I am absent from Court is as indispensable as the Aire I am to breath.[35]

Mr Floyd seems to have carried out his instructions well. Southwell became so intimate with Williamson that by the time he left England, after his visit there in 1668, he was addressing Williamson as 'dear brother'.[36]

In the light of what Southwell did later, the letter he wrote to Arlington as early as February 1667 is significant. He told Arlington that Maynard was a man of pretty parts, but officious and liberal when making his court though, being passionate and imperious, he would never live in quiet. He recommended that Arlington should not struggle on Maynard's behalf in case he became entangled in Maynard's embroilments. He then went on to say that because of his troubles with the merchants, the consul was really lacking in funds, though he would not admit it. Southwell wished that Maynard could have some quiet place in England which would keep him out of want and contention.[37] It was a letter full of destructive innuendo. Again, Southwell was in London when the Holbech patent was prepared in March 1668. No documentary proof has been found, but it is more than probable that he was consulted in the matter. Southwell returned to Portugal with instructions to investigate the complaints of the merchants, and it may well be that had the latter been more polite and subservient to him, he would not have written to Arlington in favour of Maynard before his examination by the Council. Even then, his reason for doing so, he said, was not that Maynard was the ablest of consuls (as he privately told Mr Floyd) but only that if the consul were turned out, the merchants would say that bribery had given them the victory.[38]

Southwell left Portugal in June 1669. It is clear from the State Papers that, although Parry had officially been left in Lisbon to deal with the collection of dower payments, he in fact began to assume the mantle of government representative, and reported regularly to both Williamson and Arlington, until he was appointed agent for the collection of the dower in May 1670.[39] As an apprentice, Maynard had not had a formal education, and so his reports are noticeably less well-constructed than Parry's. Parry also began to concern himself with merchant matters, in particular the negotiations for a new treaty. Between February 1673 and February 1675, the State Papers contain no letters from Maynard to anyone in London.[40] On 8/18 February 1674/5, Maynard wrote to Williamson, saying that he had been hugely unhappy in being deprived of Williamson's letters for some years, and that now he understood it was Mr Parry's intention to dispossess him of the consulship.[41] Although the State Papers contain nothing more on the subject, it is possible to piece together what happened from correspondence in the Southwell papers. In 1674, Southwell purchased from the crown a reversionary grant of the patent for the consulship of Lisbon for Parry. It was exactly like Maynard's patent of 27 June 1660.[42] Unfortunately, the actual patent is not among Southwell's papers; all that is extant is the original of the Articles of Agreement between Southwell and Parry.[43] By this agreement, Parry was to pay Southwell one third of the profits of the post half yearly, at the usual rates of exchange and render him an annual account. Parry agreed not to part with the office in farm without Southwell's knowledge. The grant to Parry was to be operative on the death or other determination of Maynard's patent. The words 'other determination' were an open invitation to Maynard's enemies. For Southwell, the money spent on the purchase of this grant was doubtless regarded as an investment. For Parry, it was an opportunity to make more money and to build up an estate. Parry promised to keep the matter secret, so it would seem that the whole proceedings were irregular.[44] Naturally, the matter was soon public knowledge. Whether the news was leaked in England and conveyed to Portugal via the Portugal merchants in London to their factors in Lisbon, as Parry maintained, or whether Parry spread the news in Lisbon, as Maynard averred, it is impossible to judge.[45] Maynard and Parry shared the services of one Tom, a copying clerk, so Maynard and everyone else would have been aware that secretary of state Coventry addressed his letter of 21 December 1674 (O.S.) to 'Mr Parry, Consull at Lisbone', whilst his letter of 25 January 1674/5 O.S. was addressed to 'Mr Maynard, at Lisbone'.[46] In the latter letter, he assured Maynard that he knew of no attempt to take Maynard's place, by Parry or anyone else.

The correspondence in the Southwell papers, to which these events gave rise, has been the source of many of the details we have concerning Maynard's life, and has also demonstrated the extent of the animosity Southwell felt for Maynard.[47] Maynard reacted by sending his wife to England with a letter to Arlington.[48] We only have Southwell's version of events in London, but we do know that Arlington considered Southwell to have been at fault for the wording of the articles of agreement between himself and Parry, which were prejudicial to Maynard.[49] In any event, the end of the matter, much to Southwell and Parry's chagrin, was reported by Parry to be that the king had assured Maynard of his post for life with a proviso. We do not know what that proviso was.[50] Still, the damage done in Portugal by these two men could not be eradicated so easily. For five years Parry had been slowly eroding Maynard's position in Lisbon, by acting as the merchants' intermediary with the English government. Maynard was made to lose face and, above all, his authority. The merchants must have increasingly refused to pay Maynard his consulage without his recourse to costly court cases. That, in turn, would be seen as a sign of weakness in England, and lead to the eventual withdrawal of his patent, which was probably how Southwell and Parry planned the affair; hence the phrase 'other determination' in the Articles of Agreement between them, to which Arlington objected. Maynard was right to be shocked, suspicious and angry. As he confessed to Arlington in the letter taken to England by his wife: 'My Lord, I was ever hugely loath to discover to you how I came to be so low in the world'.[51] In May 1675, Parry said that Maynard had neither a good shirt to his back nor a shoe to his feet.[52] The strain of poverty and uncertainty for the future must have been severe. The following month he gave a sober master of a ship a box on the ear in the open street for telling him (Maynard) that he would report him if he would not give him his despatches, which Maynard had withheld until he had been paid consulage.[53]

Although Maynard was supported by the king and remained at his post, Parry was not relieved of his appointment. He continued to be a divisive force in the English community in Lisbon, and Maynard had to endure his presence until the end of 1680. Even in departing, Parry caused division in the factory. Some of his friends among the merchants arranged for four hundred *milreis* to be taken from the Fund for Distressed Seamen in order to buy a farewell present of plate for him.[54] Maynard said it was a bad business, creating a precedent for the treasurer to dispose as he pleased of the monies. In that instance, Maynard said, less than half of the factory had given their consent for the gift, so Maynard had a solicitor draw up a petition to the king in council to compel the treasurer to refund the money.[55]

That the king and Arlington supported Maynard over the consulship affair, shows that both men appreciated his work. We know that, eleven years earlier, Charles II had told Afonso VI that Maynard was honest, hard-working, benevolent, an argumentative diplomat, but very good for shipping.[56] Maynard also had other support in England. James Houblon, the wealthy Huguenot banker and London merchant thought highly of him. Houblon told Pepys, in reply to an enquiry, that when he next saw him he would tell Pepys how useful the consul was to the trade, and how well he deserved the money he drew out of it; what esteem he had at court and in the capital city and what honour he gave to the character he bore for the nation.[57]

Why Southwell nursed such animus against Maynard is not known for certain, but two letters among the Southwell papers give a pointer.[58] It appears that when Maynard returned to England in 1668, a man named Biggleston (chosen by Southwell) was given a procuration (to act as a procurer) and was to receive consulage on Maynard's behalf during his absence. Maynard also gave a procuration to Nicholas Pollexfen, another merchant in Lisbon, and brother of John Pollexfen, a prominent London merchant, but we do not know why. This latter procuration was drawn up before a public notary, authorizing Nicholas to recover all debts, consulage and other dues. When the merchants found that two men had procurations, they refused to pay either. Maynard took Biggleston to court for recovery of the consulage and asked Southwell to assist him in recovering the 3,000 crowns involved. Biggleston died and the claim was made on his partners. Judgement was given in Maynard's favour in 200 crowns, but the case went to the

Relação on appeal, and in the end no money changed hands.

On the face of it, the question of whether consulage was or was not paid to Maynard was really not Southwell's affair, because he left Portugal shortly after Maynard's return in 1669. Why then, was Southwell so very sensitive on the subject?[59] Why did he not just dismiss the matter by saying that Maynard had brought all the trouble on his own head by giving two procurations? Whilst he was in Portugal, Southwell had accumulated large debts.[60] As a merchant himself, Maynard would have been aware of Southwell's financial difficulties. In 1668, perhaps, Maynard had suspected some form of collusion between Biggleston and Southwell. Perhaps, like all merchants at the time, Maynard preferred to keep financial matters in the family, and the Pollexfens and Maynards had intermarried.[61]

In view of the foregoing, it is impossible to accept as unbiased the criticisms of Maynard which were made by Southwell and Parry. Equally, Castelo Melhor and Macedo were unable to judge Maynard dispassionately. This explains why many harsh criticisms of Maynard are to be found in the State Papers between 1662–75. In addition, there were many difficulties among the English merchant community in both Lisbon and Oporto which were deliberately fomented by Richard Russell and the English College in order to oust Maynard in favour of a Catholic consul. It is necessary, therefore, to assess Maynard's work as a consul by drawing on other factors and other people's comments.

Rowland Hill, the merchant who had employed Maynard in Aveiro, would not have recommended Maynard to Cromwell as a special agent in regard to the treaty if he had not been certain that Maynard was able, reliable and honest. Maynard must have carried out his duties satisfactorily, otherwise the recommendations which had been made in 1654 by the merchants of Exeter, Dartmouth, Plymouth and London that he be made consul in Lisbon, would not have been heeded. Those documents spoke of Maynard as being of good life and conversation and of known ability and integrity.

After Maynard had been in Lisbon as consul for six months, Mettam wrote to Thurloe saying that the consul was 'a stirring man in his nation's behalf'.[62] That is the key description of Maynard. Active, energetic, and with a strong sense of responsibility, Maynard cared greatly about his country and his charges. Thus, even though his family had been royalists, and he himself had royalist sympathies, he was prepared to work energetically in Portugal for the Protectorate government.

In the affair of Margaret Throckmorton, Maynard showed considerable qualities of leadership, by sending Zachary Cradock, the chaplain, back to England speedily, and by organizing the other merchants in his own support. His refusal to hand over Margaret to the Inquisition was courageous. The whole affair showed an appreciation of diplomatic possibilities and powers of negotiation on Maynard's part, because throughout the tricky and dangerous proceedings he seems to have retained the respect of the Portuguese ministers and the queen. The factory, too, were grateful, for they allowed him an extra quarter per cent consulage in recognition of his efforts.[63]

Maynard made the most of the opportunity offered by Monck's part in the Restoration in order to obtain a new patent. However, he fully repaid Queen Luisa's trust in him. Melo reported that Maynard arranged for him to see Monck and Morice and was involved in negotiations with Clarendon and other important men.[64] When negotiations were in progress for the 1661 treaty, he may well have been behind the English insistence that unless agreement could be reached regarding commercial matters, England would make an alliance with Spain.[65] Maynard returned to Portugal in September 1660, and Melo wrote to the queen and confirmed that Maynard had served her well and faithfully, having helped Melo willingly and with great care. He deserved, Melo said, to be rewarded.[66] Thus Maynard's part in bringing about the 1661 treaty was not inconsiderable. His behaviour would not have surprised the Portuguese in Lisbon, where it had become apparent that though Maynard constantly criticized Portuguese people and institutions for their dilatory ways, and pressed the rights of his countrymen under the 1654 treaty, he was daily putting down roots in the country and becoming emotionally involved in Portugal's fortunes. His obvious joy at the news of the victory of Elvas is an example of this.[67] These lusophile tendencies in Maynard continued to be apparent. He rejoiced in their joys and felt for their sorrows,[68] and there is no doubt that he was generally liked and respected by the Portuguese.

The picture of the man painted by these authorities and events is the reverse of the passionate quarrelsome individual painted by fractious merchants, Castelo Melhor and Macedo, Southwell and Parry. That Maynard survived the concerted attacks made upon him during the difficult years says much for his resilience and endurance. The orchestrated animosity of the English College; the difficulties regarding the auxiliary forces; the animosity and distrust of Castelo Melhor and Macedo, do not seem to have dimmed Maynard's old verve and ebullience as evinced in his reports. None the less, the years between 1670 and 1680 (particularly after 1672, when he must have realized that something was very wrong) did have an effect on him. Southwell and Parry sapped much of his self-confidence, which he never quite regained, even after he had Charles II's promise that he would hold his post as consul general for life. Maynard still retained supporters in London, however, for Parry's successor, Charles Fanshaw, who arrived in Lisbon in November 1680, was instructed to cultivate

Maynard more in future.[69] A good working relationship was established between the two men.[70] In 1683, Maynard told Jenkins that since Parry's departure he had had no more court cases.[71] Charles Scarburgh replaced Fanshaw in 1686 and again, he and Maynard appear to have worked harmoniously together.

If a reason for Maynard's survival as consul-general against such odds as he experienced between 1662 and 1680 is needed, it is very simply that he was efficient. He actively cared for Englishmen and English interests in Portugal, with very little support from London (after the Restoration) as far as treaty matters were concerned. To have remained *en poste* for so long, he must surely have had the support of the majority of Portugal merchants in London and the more important members of the factory in Lisbon. If the factory Minute Books had not been lost in 1807, it would have been possible to say who had supported Maynard and why they did so. As it is, we do not know.

Perhaps Maynard's greatest contribution to English interests in Portugal was the part he played over the years in setting up the Lisbon and Oporto chaplaincies, in spite of the Inquisition and the influence of the English College in Portugal. Maynard was a deeply convinced Anglican, and it is ironical, therefore, that he was dismissed from his office at the end of 1689 on the grounds that he was a Catholic sympathiser and had supplied a ship-load of guns to James II for his expedition to Ireland. A Lisbon factor, named Robert Gislingham, who had been involved with a number of other English merchants and factors in alleged bullion smuggling in 1683, was the person who laid the charges against Maynard in England.[72] In December 1689, Maynard asked Shrewsbury to allow him to defend himself at the Council Board in England. He explained to Shrewsbury that he had always done what he could to prevent conversion of Englishmen to Catholicism in Portugal during James II's reign. He himself, he said, had lived for fifty years where only the religion of Rome was tolerated, besides three years in France, and he had never heard a mass since he was born, so Gislingham might just as well have called him a Turk or a Jew as a Catholic.[73] It was to no avail. Almost before his letter could reach Shrewsbury, Maynard received his letter of dismissal. Maynard replied on the same day (9/19 January 1689/90), saying that he would return to England to appeal to the Council Board.[74] In October 1690, Maynard wrote to Nottingham, declaring his successor to be a person whom the king of Portugal refused to confirm.[75] He may have been right, because there are no reports from Portugal in the State Papers between October 1690 and February 1692. In 1692 Maynard wrote to Nottingham and explained that he had not returned to England because the only proofs of his innocence of charges brought against him were to be found in Portugal. In England he would be in danger of being proceeded against as a malefactor and dyed as a criminal, notwithstanding his innocence.[76]

That is the last communication known to have been written by Maynard. It is sad to think of a man who had done so much for so long for England's interests in Portugal passing into oblivion. There is a note on the back of *Add.Ms.* 19399, f.146, to the effect that Maynard lived in Lisbon until the age of eighty without any molestation from the Inquisition. As the first part of that note states that Maynard was imprisoned by the Inquisition during the time that Meadows was envoy in Portugal, however, not very much credence can be put on the second part of the statement.

It would be interesting to know for certain what happened to Maynard in the end. When John Colbatch, who went to Lisbon as chaplain with John Methuen in 1693, wrote to Bishop Burnet in 1696, he spoke of the 'late consul'. Did he mean that as 'former' or 'dead'?[77] As the letter in question partly concerned the facilities for communal worship among the English residents in Lisbon, it would have been incredible if he had not discussed the matter with a still present former consul-general. Maynard's handwriting was extremely feeble in 1692. Because Colbatch did not mention him by name, the probability is that he was dead by 1696. He may have died before Colbatch arrived in Portugal. Certainly, an active man like Maynard would have had little incentive to live without the stimulus of his job. He was probably consigned to the deep in a sugar box, off the south shore of the River Tagus, as were all Englishmen who died Protestants in Portugal at that time.

14

Conclusion

It has been said that before 1580, Portugal was England's political equal and her commercial superior.[1] By the eighteenth century, Britain had gained colonies in America and trading posts in India. Britain also controlled the major part of Portugal's trade, becoming Portugal's commercial and political superior. A Frenchman, writing in 1730, estimated that English commerce at Lisbon was greater than that of all other nations put together. He stated that English merchants in Portugal did not confine themselves to trade with their own country, but that they had business dealings with all parts of Europe, whilst English shipping fetched and carried for all nations.[2]

S. Sideri is representative of many modern historians who say that the treaties with Britain of 1654, 1661 and 1703 (the latter being outside the scope of this book) were largely responsible for Portugal's economic decline.[3] In a study of Anglo-Portuguese trade relations from the seventeenth to the twentieth centuries, he even goes so far as to say that Portugal was forced by Britain into the same type of commercial system as were Britain's North American colonies, so that Portugal in fact became commercially and financially dependent on Great Britain, to such an extent that Britain controlled her foreign policy too. He calls it a system of informal colonialism.[4] It is arguable, however, that this dependence of Portugal on Britain need never have happened, in spite of the drain on the Portuguese economy of the twenty-eight-year war with Spain. Portugal had been a trading nation for centuries, so why did the Portuguese merchants not play a greater role in the economy? By giving foreign merchants privileges in order to encourage trade, John IV's forebears had not decreased the importance and influence of their own merchants in the economy of the country, as is evident until the reign of John III, when the Inquisition was established in Portugal. The privileges given to foreign merchants in Portugal never preferred strangers to natives, as was the case with the Hansards in England after 1474. In the seventeenth century, natives and strangers all paid 23% customs duty. The fact that Portugal could not produce enough for its own needs was not a bar to a strong economy. The wealth and power of the Dutch at the time is proof of that fact. The Dutch created their nation whilst fighting an even longer war against Spain. Whereas Dutch merchants increased in numbers and prospered, the Portuguese merchants played a decreasing role in their country's economy. It was not that they had lost their expertise. Portuguese merchants were chiefly New Christians and of the Jewish race, given the prejudice of the *fidalgos* and their families against engaging in trade. New Christians smuggled their capital out of Portugal whenever possible. Had they been able to remain in Portugal without fear for their lives and property, they could have invested their capital there and in the Portuguese dominions (to which they had easier access than English merchants). There would then have been nothing to stop them from acting as factors in trade between England and Portugal. Portugal's economy was based on trade and commerce, and by destroying the men who were the pillars of the economy, the Inquisition forced Portugal into economic dependence on other countries. That was the view, or the thrust, of a number of seventeenth-century writers, diplomats and observers, Portuguese and French, as well as English.

The principal among them was Padre António Vieira (1608–97), the Jesuit adviser of John IV, who went to Lisbon in 1641 and soon became influential at court. As early as 1643, Vieira said that commerce was essential for the survival of Portugal, and he recommended a general pardon for the Portuguese Jews, on the grounds that they would then return to Portugal with their capital. His ideas were openly bruited from the pulpit. In 1646, John IV sent him to France and Holland to persuade men to return to Portugal if their capital were made immune from the Inquisition. All Jews were anxious that their property should be safe until sentence was passed.[5] In a *paracer* to John IV, Vieira said that Portugal could not be saved without money, and the best method of obtaining it was by commerce. For successful commerce there was no surer way than to rely on the Jews (New Christians), who were men of industry and capital. He said, also, that if Jews were re-admitted to Portugal, it would be possible to sustain the war against Spain for many years. It was lack of commerce which had reduced the greatness and wealth of Portugal.[6] John IV agreed with Vieira, and that is why he published the *alvará* of 6 February 1649 which made the Brazil Company possible. Inevitably, Vieira was imprisoned by the Inquisition (1665). He was released and sentenced to perpetual silence in 1667, but the pope stepped in and Vieira lived in Rome between 1669–75, when he went to Brazil.[7]

Vieira's contemporaries considered that he may have been the author of a book entitled *Noticias Reconditas y posthumas del procedimiento de las Inquisiciones de España y Portugal con sus presos.*[8] The book is in two parts, the first in Portuguese and the second in Spanish. It was probably written in the seventh decade of the seventeenth century, because the last date mentioned in it is 1673. It is not known for certain who wrote the book, but it is known that a Portuguese Jew called David Netto was responsible for publishing it in 1722 in Villa Franca (that is London, land of the free), and that it had been much copied and widely disseminated before that. There is, for example, a manuscript copy of the first part among the Tenison collection of manuscripts in the Lambeth Palace Libary.[9] Lúcio de Azevedo thinks it is possible that a former tribunal notary, Pedro Lupino Freire, who had been sacked by the Inquisition and sent to Brazil for five years for giving away the secrets of the Inquisition, but who went to Rome in 1673, may have written the book, and that Vieira polished his language.[10] Certainly both men had the knowledge and experience to write it, and Azevedo, whose opinion must carry considerable weight, says that every single fact written in the work concerning the Inquisition prisons and the sufferings of the prisoners is the absolute truth.[11] The Lambeth Palace manuscript, (pages 94–103), sets out the reasons why the writer considers that the Inquisition and its methods were responsible for the economic decline of Portugal, and the passing of commerce into the hands of foreign merchants. Flocks of sheep formerly kept for wool had been consumed, and because of the Inquisition, there was no one left with sufficient capital to subsidize cottage industries. In 1619, the Portuguese merchants could have raised fifty-four million *cruzados* as well as being able to call on foreign funds. At the time of writing they could only raise half a million. Most of the merchants in Portugal and Goa had been imprisoned and all their capital confiscated. This had encouraged a flight of capital abroad. Since the *edital* of 1657, which cancelled the *alvará* of John IV in 1649, fourteen million *cruzados* had been confiscated, but not even 500,000 *reis* was paid over by the *fisco* to the crown. These events led to an increase in the numbers of foreign merchants, with Portugal becoming the Indies for other nations (*vem a ser as Indias dos Estrangeiros*). The same decline was visible in India.

Another contemporary writer of some note, also critical of the Inquisition as a factor in Portuguese economic decline, was D. Luis da Cunha (1662–1740), sometime ambassador in London (1696–1712), and Portugal's envoy extraordinary at the coronation of George I. Da Cunha wrote to D. Marco Antonio de Azevedo Coutinho (1688–1750), who in 1736 became Portugal's first foreign minister, giving him his views on the Inquisition.[12] He said that by persecuting New Christians, who were those most able to sustain industry and commerce, the Inquisition had caused the Portuguese economy to decline. He suggested that Jews should be given liberty of conscience: as Jews, they would not then come under the power of the Inquisition. Foreign merchants were reluctant to use New Christians as factors because of the money they would lose if the latter were imprisoned. They knew that claims on the *fisco* would involve court cases in spite of any treaties and conservators. As a result, foreign merchants themselves became more firmly entrenched in the Portuguese economy. Da Cunha seemingly envisaged Jews as citizens apart, rather comparable to worker bees, for he suggested that they should not be allowed to serve in civil or military employment, but only to work in trade and commerce. They were not to be allowed to invest in land or keep *specie* in coffers, but had to invest in public works or on the exchange. It seems that other contemporary diplomats also considered that Portugal should give liberty of conscience to the Jews, for after the Peace of Ryswick (1697), M. d'Argon and M. d'Arbanz, two French delegates who went to London to agree tariffs between France and England, told da Cunha so when they discussed the matter with him. They said that the remedy for Portugal's economic ills was in her own hands.

Criticism of the effect which the Portuguese Inquisition was having on the Portuguese economy was not confined to laymen. The Jesuits had long understood the problem, and that is why they helped the New Christians in their last great fight to obtain a general pardon between 1673–81.[13] It is notable, however, that none of these critics of the Inquisition wanted to do away with it, but only to reform the ways in which it was being used, so that the Portuguese economy would not be ruined.

English merchants also realized the importance of New Christians for Portugal's economic survival. A sacrilege committed in a church at Odivelas in May 1671[14] unleashed a series of decrees for the extirpation, banishment and degradation of Jews, and these caused both Maynard and Parry to express the view that the Inquisition was damaging Portuguese, and therefore English, commerce. Maynard did not particularly like Jews,[15] but he said that if the Jews were extirpated, it would destroy all the merchants in Portugal and be the ruin of commerce.[16] Parry considered that even the Inquisition was not really in favour of the banishment of Jews.[17] After all, without Jews their most profitable source of income would be gone.· Parry explained to Arlington that if the Jews were banished, it would cost the English nation in Portugal about 200,000 crowns in unpaid debts.[18] He further explained to Williamson that the Jews in Portugal never kept more than a quarter of their capital in that country because of the difficulties they experienced, not from the witch hunt then in progress, but from the everyday attitude of the people and the Inquisition towards them. The English merchants did not want to sell goods to the Jews at that time, though they dared not sell them to others, because that would be to show distrust of the Jews, who would then refuse to pay anything for the goods they had already received on credit. Most of the Jews could only satisfy old debts by new sales.[19] In October 1671 Parry wrote to the prince regent telling him of the calculated losses to the English nation in Portugal if the decrees against the New Christians were to be enforced, and saying that by virtue of the 1661 treaty, these debts would be payable by the Crown Fiscal. The uncertainty in this regard was harmful to trade and he asked that a speedy decision might be reached.[20] The trade of other nations in Portugal would have suffered equally.

In 1672, the Inquisition itself stepped in and gave a general pardon to those New Christians returning to trade. All those who had been punished for Judaism after judgement by the Inquisition, however, were to be further degraded by being prohibited from riding in coaches, litters or on horses; they were not to use silk or objects of precious metal and they were not to be allowed to perform public office or honorary duties or to be tax gatherers.[21] In publishing his own decree, the inquisitor general had once more shown that the Inquisition considered itself to be the chief authority in matters of faith. He had also ensured the continuance of the Inquisition's most profitable source of income, at Portugal's expense. Maynard blamed the Inquisition for Portugal's economic decline. Reporting that an *auto da fé* had been arranged for August 1683, he told Secretary Jenkins that it would destroy whatever trade and shipping had been left to the Portuguese.[22]

Ostensibly, the Inquisition had been established to maintain the moral standards of the nation, but the vast majority of people imprisoned by the Inquisition were accused of holding the Jewish faith. Lúcio de Azevedo says that in round figures, twenty thousand people were imprisoned for this between 1536 and 1732, compared with three thousand for other offences.[23] The damage done to the economy becomes clearer from a list compiled by António Joaquim Moreira in *História dos Principais Actos e Procedimentos da Inquisição em Portugal*, which showed that between 1682-91, 1,329 New Christians were judged (659 men and 670 women). Of these, 57% were upper-middle-class merchants, lawyers, officials and doctors, and 30% were artisans.[24] It should be noted that this was the period when the Conde de Ericeira and his friends were doing all that they possibly could to re-establish Portuguese industries. A similar proportion may be observed in a list of those imprisoned for the Jewish faith in Bragança, compiled by Francisco Manuel Alves. This included 343 merchants and business men, 241 silk workers, 111 leather workers, 89 cobblers and a few doctors, advocates and clerks.[25]

Portugal's population in the seventeenth century was only three million at most, and it must be remembered that all prisoners' estates were sequestered by the Inquisition on arrest, and not on sentence. The property was paid into the *fisco* and from there it was used to sustain the Inquisition. It was never returned to prisoners if or when they were released. The Inquisition was maintaining itself and growing in power and wealth on the capital of those classes of people who are normally relied upon to be the mainspring of the nation's prosperity. In order to survive, these unfortunate New Christians, mostly of mixed race by the seventeenth century, resorted to becoming informers for the Inquisition. A quick glance in the *Livro das Habilitações I*, for instance, shows that one in nine of all informers were merchants.[26] Doubtless these informers hoped that they would thus themselves escape being imprisoned by the Inquisition. The majority of Portuguese merchants must have lived in fear and suspicion. It was not an atmosphere in which commerce could flourish. Prisoners of the Inquisition never knew who had accused them or of what they were supposed to be guilty. Their families were left destitute and they lost all property and funds in Portugal.

Portugal's cottage industries could not have hoped to meet the needs of Portugal's colonies, nor, indeed, the demands of Portugal itself. The increasing number of privileges given in Portugal to encourage foreign merchants to trade there, even before the advent of the Inquisition, is proof of this. Portugal's merchants, however, could have been far more active in seventeenth century commercial affairs if they had had the capital. They certainly had the expertise. As da Cunha pointed out, nowhere in Europe could one cash a Bill of Exchange on a Saturday, because all the exchanges were controlled by Jews.[27] It was the ignominy, injustice and degradation to which Jews were subjected in Portugal by the Inquisition which strangled their abilities in that country and forced them to send their capital abroad. The Inquisition may have been thought to be a social necessity at the time, but it was an extravagance which Portugal could not afford. Portugal had to wait until the Marquês de Pombal came to power in the mid-eighteenth century before anyone was found with enough courage to take action in the matter. The Inquisition was not abolished until 1820.

In sapping the economy, the Inquisition created a situation where a foreign nation was bound to fill the vacuum. Thus when gold was discovered in Brazil at the very end of the seventeenth century, Portuguese merchants were not in a position to take advantage of the miraculous boost to the economy which it brought to Portugal. That Britain did fill the vacuum was not due to commercial treaties, because equal privileges were given by Portugal to the French, Dutch and even Spaniards. Indeed, English merchants were frequently less favoured in practice that the French and Dutch. H.E.S. Fisher has suggested that, apart from the effects on trade of the War of the Spanish Succession, the eighteenth-century supremacy of England in the Portugal trade was due to the success of her maritime policy and to the ability of her merchants to extend long credit.[28] English supremacy was also due in great measure to those merchants who, in the seventeenth century, kept up the pattern of trade by remaining in Portugal in spite of the continuous difficulties they experienced there. Eighteenth-century England owed much to the leadership, toughness, determination and patriotism of men like Thomas Maynard.

Notes

Abbreviations

American Historical Review	A.H.R.
Anais da Academia Portuguesa de História	Anais.
Arquivo Histórico Portugues	A.H.P.
Arquivo Histórico Ultramarino	A.H.U.
Arquivos dos Condes da Ponte, Cartas de Francisco de Melo a Afonso VI (Queen Luisa) 1657–1661	A.C.P.1.
British Library	B.L.
The British Historical Society of Portugal	B.H.S.P.
Calendar of State Papers, Domestic Series	C.S.P.Dom.
Calendar of Treasury Books	C.B.
Commons Journal	C.J.
Dictionary of National Biography	D.N.B.
Economic History Review	Ec.H.R.
English College Papers	E.C.P.
The Genealogists Magazine	G.M.
Hispanic American Historical Review	H.A.H.R.
The Historical Association (Lisbon Branch)	H.A.L.B.
Historical Manuscripts Commission	H.M.C.
History Today	H.T.
Journal of Modern History	J.Mod.H.
Journal of the Society for Army Historical Research	J.S.A.H.R.
Lords Journal	L.J.
The Mariners' Mirror	M.M.
Transactions of the Royal Historical Society	T.R.H.S.
State Papers	S.P.

1   A.C.P.1. will have two sets of folio numbers. The numbers in brackets represent the numbers of the folios of the copied letters at present held in the archives of the Condes da Ponte.

2   All Additional Manuscripts (*Add.Ms.*) are from the British Library.

3   All Rawlinson Manuscripts are from the Bodleian, Oxford.

4   The English College Papers are from Ushaw College, Co. Durham.

5   The Russell Papers are from Ushaw College, Co. Durham.

1   *Rivalries in Europe and Overseas*

1   David Ogg, *Europe in the Seventeenth Century*, p.498.
2   See, for example, *C.S.P.Dom.* 1658–9, Council Meeting of 6 July 1658.
3   P.R.O., *S.P.108*/1 Parts I and II; *S.P.108*/2 Part III and *S.P. 108*/1 Part III.
4   S. H. Steinberg, *The 'Thirty Years War' and the Conflict for European Hegemony 1600–1660*, p. 14.
5   Ibid., pp. 15–16.
6   Ralph Davis, *The Rise of the English Shipping Industry in the Seventeenth and Eighteenth Centuries*, p. 19.
7   Steinberg, p. 16.
8   Ibid., pp. 23–4.
9   Ibid., p. 6.
10   Ogg, p. 231.
11   J. H. Parry, *The Age of Reconnaissance*, p. 168.
12   Ibid., p. 178.
13   *Encyclopaedia Britannica*, 11th edn (USA, 1910), vol. 7–8, p. 409.
14   Parry, pp. 170–01.
15   C. R. Boxer, *The Portuguese Seaborne Empire, 1415-1825*, pp. 110–13.
16   Ibid., pp. 114–15.
17   H. V. Livermore, *A New History of Portugal*, p. 170.
18   J. H. Elliott, *Richelieu and Olivares*, pp. 144–5.
19   *Add.Ms. 25277, f. 51*, 'A relation from Lisbone touching the Inauguration of Don John Duke of Braganza to ye kingdome of Portugal', 22 December 1640; Livermore, pp. 171, 173; Quirino da Fonseca, *Os portugueses no mar: Memórias históricas e arquelógicas das naus de Portugal*, p. 460.
20   *Add.Ms.* 25277, f. 51v.
21   Frédéric Mauro, *Le Portugal et l'Atlantique au XVIIe siècle. 1570–1670*, p. 460.
22   C. Roma du Bocage, *Subsidios para o estudo das relações exteriores de Portugal em seguida a Restauração (1640–1649)*, p. 50.
23   E. Prestage and K. F. L. Mellander, *The Diplomatic and Commercial Relations of Sweden and Portugal, 1641–1670*, pp. 31–2; *S.P.89*/15, f. 298, translation of Article 13 of the 5th Book of the Ordinances of Portugal.
24   E. Prestage, *The Diplomatic Relations of Portugal with France, England and Holland from 1640–1668*, p. 175.
25   M. J. Dumont, Baron de Carels Croon, *Corps Universal Diplomatique du Droit des Gens . . .*, IV (i), pp. 215–18, Article 2; E. Prestage, *A Embaixada de Tristão de Mendonça Furtado a Holanda em*

1641, p. 72.
26 V. Rau, 'A Embaixada de Tristão de Mendonça Furtado e os Arquivos Notariais Holandeses', pp. 96, 122.
27 Prestage, *A Embaixada*, p. 72.
28 E. Prestage, 'The Treaties of 1642, 1654 and 1661', *Chapters in Anglo-Portuguese Relations*, ed. E. Prestage, p. 134.
29 Evidence for this is to be found among the uncollated treaty papers, Portugal (*S.P.103*/57), see papers headed 'The merchants propound in favour of the Portugal ambassador's paper' and 'A Remonstrance for the Continuance of trade from England to Portugal'.
30 G. Chalmers, *A Collection of Treaties Between Great Britain and Other Powers*, II, pp. 258–67.
31 Prestage, *Chapters . . .*, pp. 135–7.
32 *C. J.* II, 495–6, 775; *C.S.P. Dom.*, 1641/3, 343.
33 *C.S.P. Dom.*, 1644/5, 605.

2 *The Commercial and Social Background to Anglo-Portuguese Relations*

1 Rose Macaulay, *They went to Portugal*, p. 15.
2 *Rot. Litt. Pat.*, 1201–16, ed. Hardy, p. 20, quoted by V. M. Shillington and A. B. Wallis Chapman, *The Commercial Relations of England and Portugal*, p. 24.
3 B. W. Diffie, *Prelude to Empire, Portugal Overseas before Henry the Navigator.* p. 45.
4 H. V. Livermore, 'The Privileges of an Englishman in the Kingdom and Dominions of Portugal', *Atlante*, ii (1954), p. 64.
5 A. A. Ruddock, *Italian Merchants and Shipping in Southampton, 1270–1600*, pp. 12–19.
6 Shillington and Chapman, pp. 47–8.
7 Livermore, 'Privileges of an Englishman', pp. 64–5.
8 M. J. Dumont, Baron de Carels Croon, *Corps Universel Diplomatique du Droit des Gens . . .* I (ii), p. 286.
9 Livermore, 'Privileges of an Englishman', 64, n. 3; also *A New History of Portugal*, p. 69.
10 Lending money at interest, or usury, had long been an offence under canon law. In England it also became an offence under secular law in 1487 and 1495. Similar laws were made in other countries at various times, but the principle was universal.
11 Many studies have been made of medieval trade. See, for instance: E. M. Carus-Wilson, *Medieval Merchant Venturers, Collected Studies* (London, 1954); *Studies in English Trade in the 15th Century*, eds E. E. Power, and M. M. Postan, (London, 1933); *The Cely Papers*, ed. H. E. Malden, Camden Society, 3rd Ser. I (London, 1900).

12   *Add.Ms.* 27344, f. 20 (index under Afonso V) List of privileges collected by Consul General Abraham Castres, Lisbon, 1746. See also: Livermore, 'Privileges of an Englishman', p. 66, n.l.
13   Livermore, 'Privileges of an Englishman', p. 66, n. 2.
14   Livermore, *History*, p. 97.
15   José de Almada, *Para a história da aliança luso-britanica*, pp. 7–8.
16   Livermore, 'Privileges of an Englishman', p. 67, n.l.
17   Schanz, *Englische Handelspolitik*, II, p. 498, p. 522.
18   *Add.Ms.* 27344 and Livermore, 'Privileges of an Englishman', p. 67.
19   Quoted by Shillington and Chapman, p. 105.
20   Livermore, 'Privileges of an Englishman', pp. 73–4, p. 74, n.l.
21   Ibid., p. 59, n.l.
22   J. V. Serrão, *História de Portugal*, III, pp. 281, 332.
23   *Tudor Economic Documents*, eds. R. H. Tawney and E. Power, II, pp. 28-31; Croft, Pauline, *The Spanish Company*, p. viii.
24   Croft, pp. ix-x.
25   C. Read, 'Queen Elizabeth's seizure of the Duke of Alva's payships', *J. Mod. H.*, v (1933), pp. 443–6, narrates the incident.
26   Croft, p. ix.
27   Shillington and Chapman, p. 140.
28   Croft, p. xii.
29   Ibid., p. xiii.
30   Ibid., p.l. (fifty).
31   Livermore, 'Privileges of an Englishman', p. 74.
32   Shillington and Chapman, p. 141.
33   Ibid.
34   *S.P.103/57*, Treaty papers, Portugal, 'A Remonstrance for the continuance of trade', p. 4.
35   *Tudor Economic Documents*, III, pp. 149–73, Guicciardini's Description of Antwerp; S. T. Bindoff, 'The Greatness of Antwerp'. *New Cambridge Modern History*, II, 50–69.
36   H.M.C. 71, *Finch*, i, p. vii; T. S. Willan, *The Early History of the Russia Company, 1553–1603*, p. 190.
37   S. B. Chrimes, *Henry VII*, p. 238. For a detailed history of the Hanseatic League, see; P. Dollinger, *The German Hansa*.
38   W. E. Lingelbach, 'The Merchant Adventurers in Hamburg', *A.H.R.*, ix (1903–4), pp. 265–73.
39   A tax farmer entered into an agreement with the king or ruler to pay him a given sum at regular intervals for the privilege of collecting taxes. It was then his business to administer the collection of those taxes according to rates set down by the sovereign. The tax farmer had to be able to gauge the possibilities of trade and make a profit for himself, within those specified intervals.

40   Serrão, p. 326, quotes source as M. V. Cotta do Amaral, *Priviligios de Mercadores Estrangeiros no Reinado de D. João III* (Lisbon, 1965), pp. 79–116.

41   *Add.Ms.* 34329, ff. 11–6, copy of 'Carta de Privilegios e Foral dos Ingleses confirmado por el Rey D. João IV'. The petition made in 1645 was ordered to be observed in 1647.

42   Mary Brearley, *Hugo Gurgeny, Prisoner of the Lisbon Inquisition*, p. 23.

43   *The Advocate*, London, 1652. A copy is printed in R. W. K. Hinton, *The Eastland Trade and the Common Weal*, pp. 212–3.

44   M. Ashley, *Financial and Commercial Policy under the Cromwellian Protectorate*, p. 2, pp. 8–11; G. E. Aylmer, *The States Servants, The Civil Service of the English Republic, 1649–1660*, pp. 214–16, 247–50.

45   Ashley, p. 148.

46   First published 1664, but written *c.* 1630. Arguments used were accepted and current long before 1660.

47   P. J. Bowden, *The Wool Trade in Tudor and Stuart England*, p. 44.

48   R. Davis, 'English Foreign Trade 1660–1700', *Ec.H.R.*, 2nd Ser. vi (1954), pp. 165–6.

49   F. J. Fisher, 'London's Export Trade in the Early Seventeenth Century', *Ec.H.R.*, 2nd Ser. iii (1950), p. 154.

50   Sir Thomas Gresham (1519?–1579), royal Agent in Antwerp in 1551. Writing to William Cecil on 1 March 1559 about the queen's debts, he advised that merchants should be used by her to pay her debts and keep up the exchange rate. *Tudor Economic Documents* II, p. 150.

51   R. H. Tawney, *Business and Politics under James I. Lionel Cranfield as Merchant and Minister*, describes Cranfield's career.

52   R. Grassby, 'Social Mobility and Business Enterprise in 17th century England', in *Puritans and Revolutionaries . . .*, eds. D. Pennington, and K. Thomas, p. 356.

53   Grassby, pp. 358–9.

54   C. M. Andrews, *British Committees, Commissions and Councils of Trade and Plantations, 1622–1675.* pp. 12–4, pp. 21, 23.

55   B. Worden, *The Rump Parliament, 1648–1653*, p. 32, pp. 166–8; *Acts and Ordinances of the Interregnum, 1642–1660*, II, pp. 4–14, 18, 168–91;
Bulstrode Whitelocke, *Memorials of the English Affairs*, II, p. 519, III, pp. 66–7.

56   A. H. de Oliveira Marques, *History of Portugal*, p. 265.

57   Grassby, p. 360.

58   de Oliveira Marques, p. 265

59   Livermore, *History*, pp. 146–7; Serrão, III, pp. 37–8, p. 169; J. Lúcio de Azevedo, *Épocas de Portugal Económico*, pp. 89–119.

60   de Oliveira Marques, p. 272; Serrão, III, pp. 283–4, 299 and map, 323.

3   *The Religious Factor in Anglo-Portuguese Relations*

1   *Add.Ms.* 23726, f. 82v, A description of Portugal of Willoughby Swift, whose name appears on a petition from the merchants in Lisbon to the Bishop of London, 7/17 September 1686 (*Add.Ms.* 19399, f. 142). *Add.Ms.* 23726 is a collection of handwritten recollections of Portugal, but it is unfortunately not always possible to marry the recollection to a name among the list of contributors.
2   C. R. Boxer, *The Golden Age of Brazil*, p. 133.
3   *Add.Ms.* 23726, f. 82v.
4   C. R. Boxer, *The Portuguese Seaborne Empire, 1415–1825*, pp. 78–9, 330.
5   *Add.Ms.* 23726, f. 83.
6   Ibid., f. 26^v
7   Ibid., ff. 83^v–85.
8   Ibid., ff. 87^v–91.
9   *Rawlinson Ms.* D. 60, f. 87, Hinde to Turner, Oporto, 6 November 1685 N.S.; f. 91, Hinde to Turner, Oporto, 10 May 1685 N.S.; f. 99, Hinde to Turner date obliterated, but probably Autumn 1686; f. 102, Hinde to Turner, Oporto, 24 June 1686 N.S.; f. 103, Hinde to Turner, Oporto, 30 January 1686 N.S.
10   *Rawlinson Ms.* D.60, f. 103, Hinde to Turner, Oporto, 30 January 1686 N.S.
11   *Rawlinson Ms.* D.60, f. 102, Hinde to Turner, Oporto, 24 June 1686 N.S.
12   *Rawlinson Ms.* D.60, f. 91, Hinde to Turner, Oporto, 10 May 1685 N.S.
13   The papal bull establishing the Inquisition was published in Portugal on 22 October 1536, see J. Lúcio de Azevedo, *História dos Christãos Novos Portugueses*, p. 89.
14   Ajuda *49–IV–20*, ff. 184–208.
15   Mary Brearley, *Hugo Gurgeny, Prisoner of the Lisbon Inquisition*, p. 68. The Inquisition accused Gurgeny of being a cleric because he spoke no Portuguese and conducted his defence in Latin.
16   Ajuda *49–iv–20*, ff. 199–203.
17   Ibid., ff. 206–7.
18   V. Rau, 'Subsidios para o estudo do movimento dos portos de Faro e Lisboa durante o Século XVII', *Anais*, viii (1957), p. 211.
19   The instructions laid down by the inquisitor general.
20   H.M.C. *5th Rep.*, i, p. 22; *L.J.* v, 57.
21   List of consuls appointed to Lisbon, 1583-1943, *H.A.L.B.* (1942) xx, 484–5.
22   *Blenheim Palace* C.2 1 (or 7?), now in British Library, 'An account of the proceedings of the Court of the Inquisition against Elizabeth

Vasconcellos in 1706'. It is not known what happened to her. See also: *S.P. 103/57*, List of merchants' complaints, Complaint 28.
23 *Add.Ms.* 23726, f. 25.
24 G. F. Johnstone, Canon of Gibraltar and British Chaplain, Oporto, 'Notes on the Ecclesiastical Registers of the Anglican Chaplaincy, Oporto', *G.M.*, xii (March 1955), p. 17.
25 M. G. Hutchinson, *The English Cemetery at Malaga*.
26 *S.P. 103/57*, 'Merchants' Complaints', Complaint 29. C. Sellers, *Oporto Old and New*, pp. 47, 51.
27 C. Roth, *A History of the Marranos*, p. 33.
28 See, for example, *S.P. 89/15*, ff. 9–9^v, Maynard to Jenkins, Lisbon, 7/17 October 1682.
29 R. Hakluyt, *Principal Navigations, Voyages; Traffiques and Discoveries of the English Nation*, ed. W. Raleigh, XII, pp. 33–4.
30 A. McFadyan, 'Anglo-Spanish Relations, 1630–1660' (ph.D. thesis), pp. 19–20.
31 W. R. Trimble, 'The Embassy Chapels question', *J.Mod.H.*, xvii (1946), p. 107.
32 *C.S.P. Venetian*, xxx, 167, Sagredo to Doge and Senate, London, 21 January 1656 (N.S.?).
33 Trimble, p. 104.
34 Trimble, p. 104; E. R. Adair, *The Extraterritoriality of Ambassadors in the 16th and 17th Centuries*, p. 180.
35 Trimble, p. 102.
36 John Bossy, *The English Catholic Community, 1570–1850* p. 140.
37 McFadyen, pp. 59–61.
38 Roth, pp. 40–1.
39 Lúcio de Azevedo, pp. 82, 84, 133. Michael Geddes, *Miscellaneous Tracts*, I. p. 424.
40 Lúcio de Azevedo, p. 97. The mesas originally established at Porto, Lamego and Tomar soon ceased to function.
41 Geddes, I, pp. 423–8.
42 Rau, p. 211.
43 Mendes dos Remedios, *Os Judeus em Portugal*, pp. 258–9. An authenticated version of all privileges to officials and familiars was printed in Lisbon in 1785.
44 Geddes, I, p. 426.
45 António Baião, *Episódios Dramaticos da Inquisição Portuguesa*, III, pp. 240–7, is a case illustrating this. See also: A. J. Saraíva, *A Inquisição Portuguesa*, p. 106.
46 Saraíva, pp. 48–9.
47 A. Baião, 'El-Rei D. João IV e a Inquisição', *Anais*, vi (1942), p. 25.

48   Lúcio de Azevedo, p. 242; Saraíva, pp. 45–6.
49   Baião, 'El-Rei D. João IV e a Inquisição', pp. 24–6.
50   Lúcio de Azevedo, p. 129.
51   Ibid., p. 130.
52   Ibid., p. 258; A. J. Saraíva, *Inquisição e Cristãos Novos*, p. 253.
53   Lúcio de Azevedo, p. 249.
54   C. R. Boxer. 'Padre António Vieira, S. J., and the Institution of the Brazil Company in 1649' *H.A.H.R.*, xxix (1949), 474.
55   Lúcio de Azevedo, pp. 251, 255; for copy of *alvará* see ibid., pp. 477–83; Saraíva, *Inquisição e Cristãos Novos*, p. 262.
56   Lúcio de Azevedo, p. 257.
57   Ibid., p. 258.
58   H. Kamen, 'Confiscations in the Economy of the Spanish Inquisition', *Ec.H.R.*, 2nd Ser., xviii (1965), p. 519.
59   Lúcio de Azevedo, pp. 269–70; Boxer, 'Padre António Vieira', p. 481.
60   Baião, *Episódios Dramaticos*, II, p. 299.
61   Boxer, 'Padre António Vieira', p. 481, n. 5, infers this; Roth, p. 307, states that da Silva was allowed to come out as a penitent because of court intervention. Duarte da Silva was to accompany Catherine of Braganza to England in 1662 as the Portuguese king's agent for the dowry.
62   Lúcio de Azevedo, pp. 264, 269–70.
63   Ibid., p. 263.
64   Ibid., p. 258.
65   Ibid., p. 263.
66   E. Prestage, 'O Conselho do Estado. D. João IV e D. Luisa de Gusmão', separata of *A.H.P.*, xi (1919). The consulta is transcribed in this booklet.
67   Prestage, 'O Conselho do Estado', p. 15; Baião, 'El-Rei D. João IV', p. 27.
68   John IV, *Cartas de El Rei D. João IV para diversas autoridades do Reino*, ed. P. M. Laranjo Coelho, examples can be seen on pp. 19, 22, 188.
69   Carlos Roma du Bocage, *Subsidios para o estudo das relações exteriores de Portugal em seguida a Restauração (1640–1649)*, I. p. 50. (Only one volume was published.)
70   G. Chalmers, *A Collection of Treaties* II . . . pp. 258–67.
71   E. Prestage and K. F. L. Mellander, *The Diplomatic and Commercial Relations of Sweden and Portugal 1641–1670*, p. 29; see Articles 23 and 28 of the treaty, p. 37.
72   Saraíva, *Inquisição e Cristãos Novos*, pp. 27–31.
73   Roth, p. 54.
74   H. V. Livermore, *New History*, p. 134; Lúcio de Azevedo, p. 25.

75 Lúcio de Azevedo, p. 70.
76 Saraíva, *Inquisição Portuguesa*, p. 39.
77 Ibid.
78 For these details see: Geddes, pp. 428–36; Brearley, pp. 65–8; Roth, pp. 109–18; Lúcio de Azevedo, pp. 139–40. Michael Geddes' account of the Inquisition's proceedings has been used because he was present at the *auto da fé* held in Lisbon in August 1683.
79 Geddes, pp. 441–48; Roth, pp. 118–21, 127–35.
80 Geddes, pp. 447–49; Saraíva, *Inquisição Portuguesa*, pp. 77–8.
81 Geddes, pp. 441–42; Roth, pp. 121–23, 141–42.
82 Saraíva, *Inquisição Portuguesa*, p. 60.

4 The War of 1650 and the Six Articles

1 R. C. Anderson, 'The Royalists at Sea in 1648', *M.M.*, ix (1923), pp. 35–8. This article was followed by a series which appeared in vols. xiv, xvii and xxi of the same on the subject of Rupert and the Royalist fleet. See also: R. Blake, *The Letters of Robert Blake*, ed. J. R. Powell, pp. 8–96; J. R. Powell, *The Navy in the English Civil War*; John Thurloe, *A Collection of the State Papers of John Thurloe, Esq. . . .* ed. Thomas Birch, I, pp. 134–6, Instructions dated 17/27 January 1649/50.
2 Ajuda, *50-V-36*, Documents 203, 204 and 205.
3 *Add. Ms.* 35251, ff. 30 and 30^v, John IV to Rupert, Alcântara, 18 May 1649 N.S. John IV, *Cartas de El Rei D. Joao IV para Diversas Autoridades do Reino*, ed. P. M. Laranjo Coelho, pp. 304–5, John IV to authorities named above, Alcântara, 20 May 1649 N.S.
4 *Thurloe*, I, pp. 131–2, Vieira da Silva to Rupert, Lisbon, 23 December 1649.
5 *Thurloe*, I, pp. 138–9, Vieira da Silva to Rupert, Lisbon, 18 March 1650 N.S.
6 *C. S. P. Dom.* 1649/50, 496–7.
7 T. Bentley Duncan, 'Uneasy Allies, Anglo-Portuguese Commercial, Diplomatic and Maritime Relations, 1642–1662' (Ph.D. thesis) p. 130, cites papers attached to Consulto Ultramarino, 21 January 1651, *A.H.U.* Bahia, Caixa V. See also: *Thurloe*, I, p. 141, Vane to John IV, Lisbon, 15 April 1650.
8 *Thurloe*, I, pp. 141–2, Vane to John IV, Lisbon, 15 April 1650.
9 *Thurloe*, I, pp. 145–6, Vane to John IV, Lisbon, 25 April 1650. See also: Blake, pp. 11–5.
10 *Add.Ms.* 20902, f. 153, 'Relação das Naos, e Armadas da India', being a detailed account of the Portuguese fleets sent to India. 1500–1653.
11 Blake, p. 13; *S.P.89/4*, ff. 72–3 and 88.

12 H.M.C. 51, *Leyborne-Popham*, p. 65, Diary Narrative of Popham's voyage.
13 John IV, *Cartas*, p. 356, John IV to Francisco de Melo, Lisbon, 24 March 1650 N.S.
14 Ibid., pp. 372–3, John IV to governors named, Lisbon, 8 June 1650 N.S.
15 *Leyborne-Popham*, pp. 65–6, Diary Narrative of Popham's voyage.
16 *Collecção Chronologica da Legislaçao Portuguesa*, ed. J. Justino de Andrade e Silva, vol. 1648–56, p. 62.
17 G. Chalmers, *A Collection of Treaties* . . . II, p. 278.
18 C. R. Boxer, 'Blake and the Brazil Fleet in 1650', *M.M.*, xxxvi (1950), 220.
19 *S.P.89/4*, ff. 83–96 and 100. Court of Admiralty Enquiry, 8 October 1651; Blake, p. 13.
20 *C.S.P.Dom.* 1650, 405, and J. G. Whitebrook, *Edward and John Bushell, Puritans and Merchants*, p. 7.
21 Blake, p. 15.
22 John IV, *Cartas*, pp. 372–6.
23 C. R. Boxer, 'Padre Antonio Vieira', p. 477.
24 John IV, *Cartas*, pp. 382–3, 433–4, 436, 439 and 445, John IV to various authorities between 24 June 1650 and 28 March 1651 N.S.
25 Ibid., pp. 380–1, John IV to the Conde de Ericeira, the Juiz da Alfandega, Oporto and the Chanceler do Porto, Lisbon, 20 June 1650 N.S.
26 Duncan, p. 162 cites *A.H.U.*, Bahia, Caixa V.
27 Boxer, 'Blake and the Brazil Fleets in 1650', recounts this action, but Duncan explains (p. 167, n.i), that Boxer did not know of the Peniche caravel which crowded sail for Madeira, vide Torre do Tombo, *Arquivo da Fazenda de Funchal*, Codex 396, f.5.
28 *S.P.89/4*, f. 115–115^v. Details of the sugars taken on the ships captured and taken to England.
29 Blake, pp. 56–63.
30 John IV, *Cartas* p. 424, John IV to D. Roderigo de Menezes, Lisbon, 4 November 1650 N.S.; E. Prestage and K. Mellander, *The Diplomatic and Commercial Relations of Sweden and Portugal, 1641–1670*, p. 40.
31 John IV, *Cartas* pp. 425–6, John IV to Collegiada de Guimarães, Lisbon, 13 November 1650 N.S.
32 Ibid., pp. 430–2, John IV to governors of Madeira and Terceira, Lisbon, 22 November and 5 December 1650 N.S.
33 E. Prestage, *The Diplomatic Relations of Portugal with France, England and Holland from 1640 to 1668*, p. 125; H.M.C., 29, *Portland*, I, p. 546, John IV to Parliament, Lisbon, 9 November 1650 N.S.
34 *Portland*, I, p. 546, Guimarães to Parliament, Southampton, 15/25

December 1650.
35   *C.S.P.Dom.* 1650, 468.
36   *Portland*, I, p. 546, Parliament to Guimãraes, London, 16/26 December 1650.
37   *Thurloe*, I, p. 168, Council of State to Blake, London, 24 December/3 January 1650/1.
38   *Portland*, II, pp. 71, 82.
39   *C.S.P.Dom.* 1651, 138–40. Council Meeting 10/20 February 1650/1.
40   *Portland*, I, pp. 571–2, Guimarães to Council of State, London, 30 April/10 May 1651; *C.J.*, VI, p. 585.
41   *C.J.*, VI, pp. 573, 575; *C.S.P.Dom.* 1651, 202–3; *Portland*, I, pp. 573–5, Guimarães to Council, London, 15/25 May and 23 May/2 June 1651.
42   *Portland*, I, p. 567, and *C.S.P.Dom.* 1651, 234.
43   Prestage, *Diplomatic Relations with France, England and Holland*, p. 27, cites his source as Tôrre do Tombo, Colecção S. Vicente, t.22, ff. 222–4.
44   For Beare, see Decree of 27 June 1650 in *Collecção Chronologica, 1648–1656*, p. 64. For Lane, see *The Deposition Books of Bristol, (1650–1654)*, eds. H. E. Nott and E. Ralph, II, p. 97.
45   Details of the contribution fund will be found in Chapter 9.
46   *S.P.89/4*, ff. 93 and 93^{v}, Admiralty Report.
47   Duncan, pp. 179–80.
48   Whitebrook, p. 5.
49   *The Deposition Books of Bristol*, II, pp. 18–23, 97–100.
50   It has been suggested that a multiple of 300 might help to obtain an approximate comparable figure today, but it would be more realistic to estimate the cost of the loss of the same number of present-day ships and their cargoes, together with the stocks of the merchants.
51   Ajuda, *51-V-16*, Document 16, copy of letter John IV to D. Roderigo de Menezes, Lisbon, 22 June 1652 N.S.
52   Tôrre do Tombo, *Arquivo do Funchal, Codex* 396, ff. 4–5.
53   John IV, *Cartas* pp. 453, 458, John IV to governor of Oporto, Alcântara, 15 May and 10 June 1651, respectively.
54   Ajuda, *50-V-36*, document 203.
55   *Lists of Men of War, 1650–1700*, ed. R. C. Anderson, I, pp. 7–17. The Commonwealth had one of the strongest fleets the world had seen.
56   B. L., *Lansdowne Ms.* 190, f. 78, Cartas dos Privilegios da Naçam Britanica em Portugal.
57   Prestage, *Diplomatic Relations with France, England and Holland*, p. 128; *Portland*, i, p. 655; *C.J.*, vii, 188.
58   *Portland*, i, p. 656; *C.J.*, vii, 165; *C.S.P.Dom.* 1651/2, 368.
59   *C.J.*, vii, 188.

60   *C.J.*, vii, 243 and 245.
61   *Lansdowne Ms.* 190, ff. 78–9ᵛ.
62   F. Bernardi and U. Fiesco. *Oliviero Cromwell dalla battaglia di Worcester alla sua morte: Corrispondenza dei rappresentanti genovesi a Londra*, ed. C. Prayer p. xvi, 67.
63   McFadyen, 'Anglo-Spanish Relations, 1630–1660' p. 57. Source quoted is Secret Accounts of Cárdenas, Consulta of Council of State 2532.

5   *The Making and Ratification of the 1654 Treaty*

  1   C. R. Boxer, 'Blake and the Brazil Fleet in 1650', *M.M.*, xxxvi (1950), pp. 213–4.
  2   C. R. Boxer, 'English Shipping in the Brazil Trade, 1640–1665', *M.M.*, xxxvii (1951), p. 203.
  3   *Add.Ms.* 4192, 'State Papers, Treaties, etc.,' ff. 43–6. The document is headed 'A particular of the Articles of Peace desired by ye English merchants to be granted them by his Majesty of Portugall'.
  4   This matter will be dealt with at greater length in Chapter 10.
  5   See Chapter 9, pp. 122–6.
  6   *S.P.89/4*, f. 68, Note on trade between England and Portugal; C. R. Boxer, 'English Shipping in the Brazil Trade', pp. 200–1.
  7   *Add.Ms.* 4192, f. 139.
  8   Ibid., ff. 139–42 and 17–41. N.B. Penaguião did have the right to make concessions in spite of Cortes or the Brazil Company, *vide* his credentials copied in Portuguese in the Latin copy of the 1654 treaty, *S.P.* 108, 386.
  9   L. M. E. Shaw, 'The English Merchants and Portugal 1650–1690 – Consul Thomas Maynard' (London Univ. Ph.D. thesis 1986), pp. 257–77 gives a detailed explanation of how customs duties were operated at the time.
10   *Add.Ms.* 4192, ff. 141ᵛ–42.
11   Ibid., f. 281, Penaguião to Council of State, 6 June 1653 O.S.
12   Ibid., f. 169, 'Translation of Portuguese Ambassador's answer to some of the articles'.
13   *C.S.P.Dom.*, 1952/3, 382 and 389.
14   Ibid., 389.
15   *C.S.P.Dom.*, 1653/4, 23 and 483.
16   *Add.Ms.* 4192, ff. 248–50.
17   Oliver Cromwell, *The Writings and Speeches of Oliver Cromwell . . .*, III, pp. 32–3; A. H. Taylor, 'Galleon into Ship of the Line', *M.M.*, xliv (1958), pp. 279–81.
18   J. Thurloe, *A Collection of the State Papers of John Thurloe,*

Esq., I, pp. 316–17.
19   *C.S.P.Dom.*, 1653/4, 427. Warrant dated 2/12 July 1653.
20   Ibid., 432, 437, 439, 444 and 446.
21   Noël Deerr, *The History of Sugar*, II, p. 528.
22   *C.S.P.Dom.*, 1654, 250–1; *Thurloe*, II, p. 517.
23   *Add.Ms.* 4192, ff. 210–3; Penaguião to Council of State, London, 29(?) March 1653 O.S.
24   Ibid., ff. 244–5.
25   The legal and diplomatic aspects of the trial are analysed in E. R. Adair. *The Extraterritoriality of Ambassadors in the 16th and 17th centuries*, pp. 147–53. See also: *C.S.P.Dom.*, 1653/4, 269, 276–7; *The Nicholas Papers*, II, pp. 83–8; Bulstrode Whitelock, *Memorials of the English Affairs*, p. 595; D. Pantaleão de Sá e Menezes, *A Narration of the Late Accident in the New Exchange*; F. Clarke, *A Briefe Reply to the Narration of Don Pantaleon Sa;* contemporary news journals.
26   Francesco Bernardi and Ugi Fiesco, *Oliviero Cromwell dalla battaglia di Worcester alla sua morte . . .* p. xvi, Bernardi to Doge, London, 1 December 1653 N.S.(?)
27   *Add.Ms.* 4192, f. 75; *Thurloe*, II, p. 439, La Bastide de la Croix to de Baas, London, 10/20 July 1654.
28   *Cromwell*, III, p. 375.
29   Newberry Library, Chicago, *Greenlees Ms.* 158, Cárdenas to Cromwell, London, 9/19 July 1654. Quoted by Bentley T. Duncan, 'Uneasy Allies, Anglo-Portuguese Commercial, Diplomatic and Maritime Relations, 1642–62', p. 267.
30   G. Chalmers, *A Collection of Treaties between Great Britain and other Powers*, II, pp. 267–8.
31   *Thurloe*, I, p. 759 and III, pp. 59–61.
32   C. P. Korr, *Cromwell and the New Model Foreign Policy*, Berkley, pp. 100–01.
33   A. McFadyan, 'Anglo-Spanish Relations, 1630–1666', pp. 210–11.
34   Ibid., pp. 86–149.
35   *Thurloe*, III, pp. 200–01.
36   *C.S.P.Dom.*, 1655, 512. Captain Hatsell to Admiralty Commissioners, Plymouth, 31 July 1655 O.S.
37   *Cromwell*, IV, p. 154, Cromwell to Blake and Montague, 6 May 1656 O.S.
38   *C.S.P.Dom.*, 1655, 531, Blake on board *Hampshire*, Plymouth, to Admiralty Commissioners, 10 September 1655 O.S.; Ibid., 329.
39   *Cromwell*, III, pp. 275–6; *Thurloe*, III, p. 718, Blake to Cromwell on board *George*, Cascais Road, August 1655; R. Blake, *The Letters of Robert Blake . . .* p. 309.
40   *C.S.P.Dom.*, 1655, 608.

41 *Thurloe*, IV, p. 24, Maynard to Thurloe, Plymouth, 30 November 1655 O.S.

42 Blake, p. 322; *A Collection of Original Letters and Papers concerning the Affairs of England from the Year 1641–1660* (found among the Duke of Ormonde's papers by Thomas Carte, M.A.), 2 vols. (London, 1739), II, pp. 80–82. Letter from London to Ormonde, 28 February 1655/56.

43 *C.S.P.Dom.*, 1655, 392.

44 *C.S.P.Dom.*, 1655/56, 56 and 190.

45 *Thurloe*, IV, p. 546.

46 Blake, p. 324.

47 *Thurloe*, IV, p. 681, Meadows to Cromwell, 6/16 April 1656.

48 *Add.Ms.* 4192, f. 285.

49 Ajuda, *49-IV-20*, ff. 208–49v.

50 *Thurloe*, II, pp. 247–8; Conde de Canteneiro to Thurloe, London, 22 April 1654 O.S. Conde de Canteneiro was really the Marquês de Niza, one of Portugal's most senior diplomats, who had been ambassador in France from 1642–46 and 1647–49, see *Thurloe*, V, p. 113, Mettam to Thurloe, Lisbon 12/22 June 1656.

51 *S.P.108*/386, copy of 1654 treaty signed by John IV. The credentials are written into the treaty in Portuguese.

52 *Thurloe*, IV, p. 682, Meadows to Blake and Montague, Lisbon, 8 April 1656 N.S.

53 Ajuda *50-V-36*, doc. 188 and *49-IV-20*, doc. 95; *Add.Ms.* 20951, ff. 179–179v. Bishop of Targa to John IV, Elvas, 12 April 1656 N.S.

54 *Thurloe*, IV, p. 682, Meadows to Blake and Montague, Lisbon, 6/16 April 1656.

55 Ibid., pp. 758–9. Meadows to Blake and Montague, Lisbon, 3/13 May 1656.

56 *Thurloe*, IV, pp. 758–9, Meadows to Blake and Montague, Lisbon, 3/13 May 1656. An unsuccessful attempt had been made by Portugal in June 1654 to raise the 23% figure in the secret article to 26%, but England had refused to accept this, see *C.S.P.Dom.*, 1654, 218–9.

57 *Thurloe*, IV, pp. 758–9, Meadows to Blake and Montague, Lisbon, 3/13 May 1656.

58 *Thurloe*, V, p. 28, John IV to Cromwell, Alcântara, 26 May 1656 N.S.; Ajuda, *44-XIII-32*, doc. 110 F.

59 *Thurloe*, V, p. 14, Meadows to Generals-at-sea, Lisbon, 13/23 May 1656.

60 Ibid., p. 59, Meadows to Generals-at-sea, Lisbon, 25 May/4 June 1656.

61 *Cromwell*, IV, pp. 154–5, Cromwell to Blake and Montague, Lisbon, 6 May 1656, O.S.

62 *Thurloe*, V, pp. 97–8, Meadows to Blake and Montague, Lisbon,

31 May/10 June 1656.
63 Ibid., p. 125, Montague to Thurloe, on board *Naseby*, Cascais Road, 17 June 1656 (N.S.?).
64 Ibid., pp. 112–3, Meadows to Blake and Montague, Lisbon, 12/22 June 1656; Blake, p. 363.
65 Francisco de Brito Freire, *Relação que Fez ao Estado do Brasil a Armada da Companhia Anno 1655* (Lisbon 1657), pp. 178–80.
66 *Thurloe*, V, p. 113, Mettam to Thurloe, Lisbon 12/22 June 1656.
67 Ajuda, *50-V-36*, Doc. 188, ff. 509–510v, undated *parecer* (opinion), Father Fernandes to John IV.
68 There are at least eleven ms. copies of the treaty in the British Library, in Latin, English or Portuguese. Among them are: *Lansdowne Mss.* 140, ff. 81–90; 192, ff. 3–20, 22–34, 36–61; *Add.Ms.* 4192, ff. 8–12, 64–75; *Add.Ms.* 34329, ff. 18–34, 38–46; *Stowe Ms.* 192, f.6 is an example of tampering with Article 6.
69 *S.P.89/11*, f. 34, Parry to Arlington, Lisbon, 6/16 December 1670.
70 *Thurloe*, V, pp. 118–9, John IV to Cromwell, 24 June 1656; *Add.Ms.* 4192, f. 78 and *Add.Ms.* 4157, f. 64 (original letter in Latin). The same arguments had been advanced by the Marquês de Niza (Conde de Canteneiro), see *Thurloe*, II, p. 248.
71 *Cromwell*, IV, p. 241, Cromwell to John IV, August 1656.
72 *Thurloe*, V, p. 56, Mettam to Thurloe, Lisbon, 3/13 June 1656.
73 *Thurloe*, VI, p. 47, William Bird to Thurloe, Lisbon, 9/19 February 1656/7.
74 Ibid., pp. 49–50, Maynard to Thurloe, Lisbon, 16/26 February 1656/7.
75 Ibid., pp. 118–9, Maynard to Thurloe, Lisbon, 16/26 March 1657 and pp. 152–4, Maynard to Thurloe, 9/19 April 1657.
76 T. M. Schedel de Castello Branco, *Vida do Marquês de Sande*, p. 292, n.1.
77 Sir Richard Lodge, 'The Treaties of 1703', in *Chapters in Anglo-Portuguese Relations*, ed. E. Prestage, 170.

6 *Portugal and England 1656–1660*

1 *Rawlinson Ms.* A.42, f. 41. See also, Oliver Cromwell, *The Writings and Speeches of Oliver Cromwell . . .* IV, p. 239.
2 Ibid., IV, p. 322.
3 John Thurloe, *A Collection of the State Papers of John Thurloe, Esq.*, VI, p. 3, Maynard to Thurloe, Lisbon, 29 January 1657 N.S.
4 It was said to be worth *c*.£1,000 per annum in good years. See Violet Barbour, 'Consular Service in the Reign of Charles II', *A.H.R.*,

xxxiii (1927–1928), 564.

5 *Thurloe*, VI, p. 4, Maynard to Thurloe, Lisbon, 29 January 1657 N.S.

6 Ibid., pp. 48–50, 16 and 20 February 1657 N.S.

7 Ibid., p. 4, 29 January 1657 N.S.

8 C. R. Boxer, *Portuguese Seaborne Empire*, p. 122.

9 *Thurloe*, VI, p. 4, Maynard to Thurloe, Lisbon, 29 January 1657 N.S.

10 Ibid., 118–19, Maynard to Thurloe, Lisbon, 16/26 March 1657.

11 Ibid., pp. 312–3, Maynard to Thurloe, Lisbon, 6 June 1657 N.S.

12 Ibid., pp. 118–19, Maynard to Thurloe, Lisbon, 16/26 March 1657. Francisco de Melo is referred to as 'Dom' by Maynard and others. This is incorrect. The title was rarely conceded to *fidalgos* in Portugal, and the ambassador did not have it. See Schedel de Castello Branco, *Vida do Marquês de Sande*, p. 385, n.i.

13 *Thurloe*, VI, p. 401, Maynard to Thurloe, Lisbon, 14/24 July 1657. Schedel de Castello Branco, p. 210.

14 *Mss. do Convento da Graça*, Caixa 2, Vol. 2-C, 10 July 1657.

15 Frei Domingos do Rosario (Father Daniel O'Daly), was the queen's confessor, and rector of Corpo Santo Monastery.

16 For details of French policy concerning Portugal, see: V. Saint-Amour, *Receuil des Instructions donnees aux Ambassadeurs et ministres de France depuis le Traité de Westphalie jusqu'à la Révolution Française* (Portugal and Paris, 1886).

17 Schedel de Castello Branco, pp. 205–6. (The original of the queen's letter is to be found in the *Ms. de Vila Viçosa*, Livro 1^0 da Embaixada, f. 4.)

18 Ibid., pp. 206–7, 235–6; *Thurloe*, VI, pp. 386–8, Maynard to Thurloe, 8/18 July 1657.

19 As for n. 17 above.

20 Schedel de Castello Branco, p. 220. ·

21 Ibid., p. 224.

22 *A.P.C.*1, f. 59 (f. 164 et seq.) Melo to Queen Luisa, London, 9 May 1658 (N.S.): '. . . mas que o nosso tratado estivesse certo não se faria em forma alguma, sem que vossa magestade os ajudasse, porque eles não tinham com que sustenbar a armada de Espanha e que a liga sem algum bom fim não lhes servia . . . tudo será baldado sem este rquísito.'

23 *Thurloe*, VI, pp. 519–20, Maynard to Thurloe, Lisbon, 17/27 September 1657.

24 Schedel de Castello Branco, p. 300.

25 *Thurloe*, VII, pp. 284–5, Montagu to Thurloe, on board *Naseby* in the Downs, 21 July 1658 O.S.

26 *Thurloe*, VII, pp. 596–7, Maynard to Thurloe, Lisbon, 21/31

January 1658/9.
27   *A.P.C.*1, f. 77 (211v–13), Melo to Luisa, London, 3 July 1658 N.S., with copy letter from Downing to the States General; *Thurloe*, VII, p. 18, Luisa to Downing, Lisbon, 2 April 1658 N.S.
28   *A.P.C.*1, ff. 83v (230), Melo to Luisa, London, 6 September 1658 (N.S.)
29   *Thurloe*, VI, pp. 312–13, 386–8, Maynard to Thurloe, Lisbon, 6 June 1657 N.S., 8/18. July 1657.
30   Schedel de Castello Branco, p. 261. This news became known on 1 June 1659.
31   *A.P.C.*1, f. 19v (62–3), Melo to Luisa, London, 24 February 1657 N.S.
32   Schedel de Castello Branco, p. 272. No date for the letter is given, but it was probably written in 1659, because it mentions the victory at Elvas.
33   *Ms. de Vila Viçosa*, Livro 1° da Embaixada, f. 101, Luisa to Melo, Lisbon, 28 October 1659.
34   *Thurloe*, VI, pp. 398–400, Mettam to Thurloe, Lisbon, 13/23 July 1657.
35   *Thurloe*, VI, p. 5, Maynard to Thurloe, Lisbon, 29 January 1657 N.S.
36   *Thurloe*, VI, pp. 152–4, Maynard to Thurloe, Lisbon, 9 April 1657 N.S.
37   Schedel de Castello Branco, p. 206.
38   *Thurloe*, VI, pp. 476–7, Maynard to Thurloe, Lisbon, 21/31 August 1657.
39   *A.P.C.*1, f. 19v (62–3), Melo to Luisa, London, 24 December 1657 N.S.
40   Ibid., f. 134 (371–71v), Melo to Luisa, 21 May 1659 N.S.
41   *A.P.C.*1, f. 303 (784–784ᵛ), Melo to Luisa, London, 13 May 1660 N.S.
42   Ibid., f. 303ᵛ (785) Melo to Luisa.
43   Schedel de Castello Branco, p. 255. Beere obtained important favours for himself and his wife's family through Melo. See: *A.P.C.*1, f. 299ᵛ (773), Melo to Luisa, London, 20 April 1660 N.S.
44   An excellent summary of the economic arguments of the pro-Spanish lobby is to be found in *The Merchants' Humble Petition and Remonstrance to his Late Highness. With an Account of the Losses of their Shipping and Estates since the War with Spain*, with a Preface by Richard Baker (London, 1659).
45   Schedel de Castello Branco, p. 278.
46   *Add.Ms.* 20722, 'Some Remarks on Cardinall Mazareene's Negotiation of the Pyrenean Peace in 1659', written by Southwell at Kingsweston, October 1698, f. 18ᵛ. His informant was said to be

Richard Russell, Secretary to Melo and a member of the English College.

47 Maurice Ashley, *General Monck*, gives a detailed account of events leading up to the Restoration. Monck's meeting with Grenville is recorded on p. 207.
48 Schedel de Castello Branco, p. 278.
49 Ibid., pp. 563–4, Document 6.
50 Ibid., p. 284. Full text of the treaty is printed in *Quadro Elementar*, xvii, 118 et seq., note date given is incorrect.
51 *A.P.C.*1, f. 303^v (788^v), Melo to Luisa, London, 3/13 May 1660 N.S.
52 Ibid., f. 303^v (788).
53 Ibid., f. 303^v (787^v–8).

7 *The Affair of the Consul*

1 M. S. Jayne, 'British Prisoners of the Lisbon Inquisition', *H.A.L.B.* (1937), pp. 24–34, comments on both Process 7522 and the queen's letter in *Ms. S. Vicente*, xxiii, f. 211; A. Baião, *Episódios Dramaticos da Inquisição Portuguesa*, pp. 43–9 gives the complete text of the queen's letter.
2 Margaret Throckmorton may have been a member of the Warwickshire family. See J. Bossy, *The English Catholic Community*, p. 177.
3 See Chapter 9, p. 109.
4 Unlike other processes, this one is incomplete, but there is a note on the outside cover to the effect that Margaret Throckmorton was deported. Her eventual fate is not known.
5 See Chapter 5, n. 70, p. 183.
6 T. M. Schedel de Castello Branco, *Vida do Marquês de Sande*, p. 216. (The embassy was in Weld Place, Lincoln's Inn Fields, near Thurloe's house.)
7 Ibid., p. 255. Richard Bradshaigh, or Bradshaw, alias Barton (1601/2-69), Provincial in England from 1656–60, see Henry Foley, *Records of the English Province of the Society of Jesus*, I, pp. 227–32.
8 *A.P.C.*1, f. 282^v (725–6), Melo to Luisa, London, 16/26 March 1660.
9 Ibid.
10 Schedel de Castello Branco, p. 254. Arthur Annesley, (1614–86), later became the 1st Earl of Anglesey.
11 *A.P.C.*1, f. 288^v (768–70), Memorandum from Council of State to Melo, dated 17/27 March 1660.
12 There is no doubt that the consul's house was broken into by the Inquisition. On 12/22 February, the queen wrote to Melo confirming

this, though saying the door broken was of a lodging adjoining the consul's house, but in his courtyard. She also said that at her request the Inquisition had freed Maynard the day before, and had also freed Margaret. *Ms. de Vila Viçosa*, Livro 1º da Embaixada, f. 143, Luisa to Melo, Lisbon, 22 February 1660 N.S.

13 *A.P.C.*1, f. 296 (760–760ᵛ), Melo to Luisa, London, 20/30 March 1660.
14 Ibid., f. 296 (761–761ᵛ), Melo to Luisa, London, 21/31 March 1660.
15 Ibid., f. 297ᵛ (764–765ᵛ), same to same, 27 March/6 April 1660.
16 Ibid., and Schedel de Castello Branco, p. 258.
17 There was such a rule regarding Portuguese government appointments, but so far as it is known, it did not apply to consuls who were foreigners.
18 An example of this can be found in Schedel de Castello Branco, p. 363.
19 *A.P.C.*1, f. 297ᵛ (764–765ᵛ), Melo to Luisa, London, 27 March/6 April 1660.
20 Ibid., f. 298 (766–7), Melo to Luisa, London, 31 March/10 April 1660.
21 Ibid., f. 299 (721), same to same, London, 31 March/10 April 1660.
22 No record has been found of the alleged petition or new patent.
23 There is no record of attendance by people of other nations.
24 The Inquisition was not two hundred years old in Portugal, and an Englishman, Hugo Gurgeny, was a prisoner of the Inquisition, for example: see M. Brearley, *Hugo Gurgeny* . . .
25 *A.P.C.*1, f. 300 (724–78), Melo to Luisa, London, 15/25 April 1660, enclosing memorandum of 13 April 1660.
26 See Chapter 3, n. 60, p. 176.
27 Henrique de Sousa Tavares, 3rd Conde de Miranda do Covo, later 1st Marquês de Arronches.
28 *Ms. Convento da Graça*, Caixa 4, Tomo III, f. 2. Miranda to Melo, The Hague, 2 April 1660 N.S.
29 Ushaw College, Russell papers. Memo signed by Melo (Marquês de Sande) and dated 7 January 1662 O.S.
30 *S.P.89*/10, f. 220, Parry to Williamson, Lisbon, 16/26 May 1670.
31 Ibid., f. 282, Parry to Arlington, Lisbon, 23 August/2 September 1670.
32 Ibid., f. 311, same to same, Lisbon, 20/30 September 1670.
33 Ashley, *General Monck*, p. 202.
34 *Ms. de Vila Viçosa*, Livro 1º da Embaixada, f. 154. Luisa to Melo, Lisbon, 25 April 1660 N.S. This letter was deciphered by Senhora Castello Branco, who very kindly lent me her notebooks.

35   *S.P.89*/15, f. 181, Maynard to Jenkins, Lisbon, 5/15 May 1683.
36   *A.P.C.*1, f. 322 (840–840ᵛ), Melo to Luisa, London, 1/11 June 1660.

8   The Treaty of 1661

1   T. M. Schedel de Castello Branco, *Vida do Marquês de Sande*, p. 360.
2   *A.P.C.*1, f. 331 (866–866ᵛ), Melo to Luisa, London, 13 June 1660 N.S.
3   Ibid., f. 333 (873–77), at (876–7), Melo to Luisa, London, 10 July 1660 N.S.
4   Ushaw, English College Papers, Annals, p. 35.
5   John Thurloe, *A Collection of the State Papers of John Thurloe, Esq.*, VI, p. 399, Mettam to Thurloe, Lisbon, 3/13 July 1657.
6   Schedel de Castello Branco, p. 215.
7   *English College, Lisbon*, (n.d.)., illustrated with original pencil drawings by W. Haeburn-Little.
8   Ibid., see p. 9, where Russell is said to have assisted ambassadors Melo and Macedo.
9   E.C.P., Annals, p. 55. Castello Branco did not, as far as is known, consult the College annals.
10   *A.P.C.*1, f. 303ᵛ (789ᵛ), Melo to Luisa, London, 14 May 1660 N.S.
11   Ibid., f. 359ᵛ (962), Melo to Luisa, London, 2 September 1660 N.S.
12   Maurice Ashley, *General Monck*, pp. 210–1.
13   *A.P.C.*1, f. 338 (890), Melo to Luisa, London, 27 July 1660 N.S.
14   Ibid., f. 338ᵛ (892), Melo to Luisa, London, 27 July 1660 N.S.
15   Ibid., f. 338ᵛ (890–1), part of the same letter as above.
16   Schedel de Castello Branco, p. 363.
17   Ibid., p. 373.
18   Ibid., p. 362.
19   *A.P.C.*1, f. 322ᵛ (841), Melo to Luisa, London, 10 June 1660 N.S.; Ibid., f. 333 (873–877ᵛ at 874–5), Melo to Luisa, London, 10 July 1660 N.S.
20   Ibid., f. 335 (879), Melo to Luisa, London, 13 July 1660 N.S.; Schedel de Castello Branco, p. 363 and Document 7, pp. 564–6.
21   *A.P.C.*1, f. 345 (909–909ᵛ), Melo to Luisa, London, 2 August 1660 N.S.
22   Ibid., f. 350 (926–927ᵛ), Melo to Luisa. 10 August 1660 N.S.
23   Ibid., f. 358ᵛ (956–7), Melo to Luisa. 30 August 1660 N.S.
24   Ibid., ff. 358ᵛ, 359ᵛ (956, 962), Melo to Luisa, London, 30 August

1660 N.S. and 2 September 1660 N.S.
25   Ibid., ff. 358^v, 368^v (956–7, 983^v), Melo to Luisa, London, 30 August 1660 N.S. and 30 September 1660 N.S.
26   Ibid., ff. 358, 359^v (956–7, 961–961^v), Melo to Luisa, London, 30 August 1660 N.S. and 2 September 1660 N.S.
27   Ibid., f. 358 (957), Melo to Luisa, London, 30 August 1660 N.S.
28   Ibid., f. 361 (967–972^v), Melo to Luisa, London, 2 September 1660 N.S.
29   Schedel de Castello Branco, pp. 369–70.
30   *Ms. Vila Viçosa*, Livro 1⁰ da Embaixada, Document 54 (cypher) Luisa to Melo, Lisbon, 12 July 1660 N.S.; Schedel de Castello Branco, p. 370.
31   Schedel de Castello Branco, p. 363.
32   Ibid., p. 377.
33   Ibid., p. 378.
34   Ibid., p. 381.
35   *S.P.89*/16, f. 258, Draft of proclamation.
36   G. Chalmers, *A Collection of treaties* . . . II, pp. 286–96.
37   The *cruzado* was valued at roughly 5.66 to the £ in 1662; see *C.T.B.*, I, pp. 407, 435; F. Mauro, *Le Portugal et l'Atlantique au XVIIe siècle, 1570–1670*, pp. 395–432 states that the value of the dower in London at the time was a maximum of £365,000.
38   See, for example, F. A. de Castro e Mendonça, *Memória Histórica acerca da Perfida e Traiçoeira Amizade Inglesa*, p. 26; J. V. Claro, *A Aliança Inglesa, História e fim dum Mito*, p. 102; F. P. da Cunha Leal, *Portugal e Inglaterra*, p. 178; E. Freire de Oliveira, *Elementos para a História do Municipio de Lisboa*, IV, p. 273.
39   *Ms. do Convento da Graça*, Caixa 2, Vol. 2-C, Documents 2, 3 and 4, instructions dated 8 January 1661.
40   Schedel de Castello Branco, p. 390.
41   *C.T.B.*, I, p. 496; II, pp. 573–4.
42   *S.P.89*/10, f. 188, Southwell's calculation of the Queen of England's portion, with Parry's adjustments to the same, Lisbon, 12 March 1669 N.S.
43   *C.T.B.*, III, p. 152; VIII, 1596.
44   C. D. Chandaman, *The English Public Revenue, 1660–1688*, p. 130.
45   *S.P.89*/11, f. 85, Parry to Williamson, Lisbon, 17 March 1671 N.S.
46   *S.P.89*/5, f. 5, Maynard to Nicholas, Lisbon, 12/22 February 1660/1.
47   Schedel de Castello Branco, pp. 303–4; C. R. Boxer, *Salvador de Sá and the Struggle for Brazil and Angola, 1602–1686*, pp. 338–9.
48   *S.P.89*/4, f. 189, Maynard to Nicholas?, Lisbon, 3/13 November

1660.

49   Schedel de Castello Branco, p. 404.

50   José de Almada, *A aliança inglesa* . . . I, p. 43.

51   Facts obtained from Walter B. T. Abbey, *Tangier under British Rule, 1661–84* (Jersey 1940); *Grande Enciclopedia Portuguesa e Brasileira*, vol. 30, pp. 658–62. See also H. V. Livermore, *New History*, pp. 112–13.

52   Ahmad Khan Shafaat, ed., *Anglo-Portuguese Negotiations Relating to Bombay 1660–1667*, (Oxford University Press 1922). Letter from Bombay 3/13 March 1665 and letter from India 26 September/6 October 1662. Quoted by Duncan T. Bentley, 'Uneasy Allies, Anglo-Portuguese Commercial, Diplomatic and Maritime Relations, 1642–1662' p. 417.

53   Duncan, pp. 417–18, quotes source as *A.H.U.* India, Caixas xxv, xxvi.

54   Ibid., p. 418.

55   *H.M.C.*, 50, Heathcote, pp. 87–8, Bennet to Fanshaw, Whitehall, 14 May 1663 O.S.

56   *S.P.89/6*, f. 185ᵛ, Maynard to Bennet, Lisbon, 5 November 1663 N.S.

57   Virginia Rau, *D. Catarina de Bragança, Rainha de Inglaterra*, p. 56.

58   *S.P.89/7*, f. 145, D. Francisco de Melo Manuel da Camara to Charles II, London, 24 February 1666 O.S.

59   *S.P.89/10*, ff. 41–2, Southwell to Arlington, Lisbon, 7/17 March 1669. Only permission to repair ships in distress was granted, see Ibid., ff. 10–11, Prince Regent to Viceroy of India, Lisbon, 3 February 1669 N.S.

60   Schedel de Castello Branco, p. 409.

61   *S.P.89/5*, f. 95, Charles II to Portuguese ambassador, London, Hampton Court, 4/14 June 1662.

62   *The Privileges of an Englishman in the Kingdoms and Dominions of Portugal Contain'd in the Treaty of Peace Concluded by Oliver Cromwell*, (London, 1736), p. xi.

63   *S.P.89/6*, f. 104, Maynard to Bennet, Lisbon, 1 May 1663 N.S.

64   *S.P.89/6*, f. 233, Francisco Fereira Rebelo to Charles II, London, 6/16 May 1664.

65   Chandaman, pp. 205–06. Charles began his reign with a debt of £925,000 and subsequent annual revenue was £100,000 short.

66   Charles sent Sir Richard Fanshaw, his envoy in Portugal, to Spain at the request of Afonso VI. Fanshaw mediated a peace there from 1664–6.

67   Boxer, *Salvador de Sá* . . ., p. 339.

68   *S.P.89/6*, f. 104, Maynard to Bennet, Lisbon, 1 May 1663 N.S.

69 Details will be given in Chapter 11 below.
70 V. Rau, *D. Catarina de Bragança* . . ., p. 8.
71 *S.P.89/5*, ff. 24 and 28ᵛ, Maynard to Nicholas, Lisbon, 9/19 June
and 20/30 March 1661, respectively.
72 Schedel de Castelo Branco, see Chapter 7, pp. 385–414.
73 Ushaw College, Russell pps., Melo to Russell, Paris. 3 March
1666 N.S.
74 *D.N.B.*, III, p. 1223. *The Diary of John Evelyn* IV, p. 318; III, p.
320.
75 *The Diary of Samuel Pepys*, VIII, p. 70.
76 Ajuda, 51-VI-20, ff. 179–207.
77 B. L. *Egerton Ms.* 1534.
78 *D.N.B.* III, p. 1227.
79 Rau, *D. Catarina de Bragança* . . ., p. 335.

9 Trading in Portugal

1 C. W. Previté Orton, 'The Italian Cities till c.1200', *Cambridge
Medieval History*, V, p. 236.
2 E. R. Adair, *The Extraterritoriality of Ambassadors in the 16th and
17th Centuries*, pp. 62–3, 244–5.
3 *C.S.P.Dom.*, 1649/50, p. 34.
4 *Rawlinson Ms.*, A. 42, f. 41; *Thurloe*, V, pp. 374–5, agreement
between Maynard and the merchants in Lisbon.
5 V. Barbour, 'Consular Service in the Reign of Charles II', pp. 556,
561; *C.J.*, VIII, p. 468.
6 *S.P.89/4*, ff. 161–7, Patent of 27 June 1660.
7 This change was clearly because of the unsatisfactory method of
payment to the minister laid down under the Protectorate patent. See
n. 4 above.
8 Wyndham Beawes, *Lex Mercatoria Rediviva, or the Merchants'
Directory*, p. 260. Maynard is known to have been involved in mercantile ventures.
9 *Register of the Privy Council, Car. II*, 2/64, p. 479, 28 July/7
August 1675. Quoted by Barbour, p. 562.
10 Alfred C. Wood, *A History of the Levant Company*, p. 218.
11 V. Barbour, 'Consular Service', pp. 564–5.
12 This was a lengthy contest. See, e.g. *S.P.89/15*, ff. 76, 84, 123,
139, 170, 173, 178, 200 and 269.
13 *The Case of the British Merchants Trading to Portugal*, London,
1695?; A. H. Norris, 'Records of the English Factory at Lisbon. A
Unique Survival', *B.H.S.P.*, iii (1976), p. 34.
14 *S.P.89/16*, f. 241. Complaint by members of the factory, addres-

see unknown. The present was for Francis Parry, who left Portugal in 1680.

15   Barbour, 'Consular Service', pp. 567–8.
16   *Thurloe*, VI, pp. 48–50, Maynard to Thurloe, Lisbon, 20 February 1657 N.S.
17   Ibid., pp. 631–2, Maynard to Thurloe, Lisbon, 4 December 1657 N.S.
18   *Hospital Committee Book*, held by the British Historical Society of Portugal, f. 59.
19   Norris, 'Records of the English Factory', p. 35.
20   Ibid., 36.
21   A. R. Walford, *The British Factory in Lisbon*, pp. 34–5.
22   S. George West, 'Members of the Lisbon Factory in the late Seventeenth Century', *H.A.L.B.* (1954), p. 708.
23   Ibid., pp. 705–8.
24   *Add.Ms.* 19399, ff. 142–4. Petition dated 17 September 1686 N.S. This petition was published by Dr Geddes in *Several Tracts against Popery*, London, 1715, pp. 376–7.
25   West, 'Members . . .', p. 708.
26   R. G. Jayne, 'The Murder of William Colston', *H.A.L.B.* (1946–50), p. 620.
27   West, 'Members . . .', p. 706.
28   *S.P.89/4*, ff. 161^v–2.
29   C. Sellers, *Oporto Old and New*, p. 49. No date is given.
30   Mary Brearley, *Hugo Gurgeny . . .*, p. 60.
31   Sir Godfrey Fisher, 'The Brotherhood of St. George at San Lucar de Barrameda', *Atlante*, i (1953), p. 32.
32   *Add.Ms.* 34331, f. 137, Maynard to Southwell, Lisbon, 28 May 1670 N.S.
33   *Merchants and Merchandise in 17th Century Bristol*, p. xiv.
34   The Bushell brothers, who operated in Lisbon, London, Bahia and Jamaica, are an example of such a house. See: J. C. Whitebrook, *Edward and John Bushell, Puritans and Merchants*. There was no law of limited liability until 1855, see C. A. Cooke, *Corporation Trust and Company*, p. 156.
35   For a detailed exposition of factors and their duties, see: T. S. Willan, *Studies in Elizabethan Foreign Trade*, pp. 1–33, and John Browne, *The Marchants Avizo*.
36   Barbour, 'Consular Service', p. 554.
37   *S.P.89/11*, f. 107, Maynard to Arlington, Lisbon, 28 April 1671 N.S.
38   *The Case of the British Merchants Trading to Portugal*, see note 13, above.
39   Ibid.

40   Barbour, 'Consular Service', p. 554.
41   *S.P.89/9*, ff. 138–9^v, Southwell to Arlington, Lisbon, 10 November 1668 N.S.
42   *Add.Ms.* 34338, f. 15, Southwell to Lord Keeper of the Seal, undated.
43   *Add.Ms.* 34331, f. 94, Southwell to Floyd, Lisbon, 29 November 1668 N.S.
44   Sir Richard Lodge, 'The English Factory at Lisbon', *T.R.H.S.* (1933), p. 226.
45   Walford, *The British Factory*, pp. 41-3.
46   *Add.Ms.* 34331, f. 94, Southwell to Floyd, Lisbon, 29 November 1668 N.S.
47   Walford, *The British Factory*, p. 43.
48   Queen Luisa, John IV's wife, who was regent for her largely incapacitated son, Afonso VI, was ousted in 1662 at the instigation of the Conde de Castelo Melhor, who ruled Portugal in Afonso VI's name until 1667. In that year, a palace revolution took place; Castelo Melhor was banished, and Prince Pedro, Afonso VI's brother, took control. Afonso was also banished and only on his death in 1683 did Pedro assume the crown.
49   *S.P.89/13*, ff. 20–1, Parry to Williamson, Lisbon, 29 September/9 October 1674.
50   *S.P.89/14*, f. 40, Parry to Coventry, Lisbon, 12 April 1678 N.S.
51   *Add.Ms.* 35101, ff. 159^v–60, Parry to Coventry, Lisbon, 26 March/5 April 1678.
52   H.M.C.50, *Heathcote*, p. 81, Fanshaw to Bishop of London, Lisbon, 21 April/1 May 1663.
53   See n. 34, above. Whitebrook, *Edward and John Bushell*, p. 7.
54   *Add.Ms.* 23726, f. 25.
55   Notes in the Record Box of St George's church, Lisbon, a copy of which is held by the British Historical Society of Portugal.
56   *S.P.89/5*, ff. 6, 25 and 65, Maynard to Nicholas, Lisbon, 12/22 February 1661, 9/19 June 1661 and 4 November 1661 N.S.
57   *Heathcote*, pp. 81-2, Fanshaw to bishop of London, Lisbon, 21 April/1 May 1663.
58   Ibid., pp. 176–7, Marsden to Fanshaw, Lisbon, 3/13 February 1665.
59   *Lisbon Inquisition Process* No. 17633, and *Add.Ms.* 19399, f. 142, the Factory to the bishop of London, Lisbon, 7/17 September 1686.
60   See n. 7 above.
61   *S.P.89/15*, f. 296, Certificate signed by Nicholas Trevanion and John Pongsley, London, 29 December 1683 O.S.
62   Sellers, *Oporto*, p. 39.
63   A. R. Walford, 'List of British in Lisbon, 1755', *H.A.L.B.* (1946–

50), pp. 639–52 and Colecção Pombalina, Vol. 692, ff. 223–7. The list was compiled for the Marques de Pombal by an anonymous person.

64   *Lisbon Inquisition Process* 7522.

65   In fact, Catherine's Lord Chamberlain was Philip Stanhope, 2nd Earl of Chesterfield, who was only Hutchinson's step-grandmother's great-nephew. Allen Hutchinson murdered William Colston, a long-established and well-liked English Catholic merchant in 1675. By means of bribes and a *carta de seguro* (a kind of bail bond), he remained free of prison in Portugal. Colston's friends persuaded Secretary of State, Joseph Williamson, to order an enquiry under a statute of Henry VIII's for the trial of murders committed beyond the seas (*S.P.Dom.* 1677/8, 212–3). This was held on 20 June 1677. Hutchinson's lawyer had to fall back on the plea that the statute of Henry VIII did not apply in this case, as it only related to crimes committed in the king's own dominions overseas, and that if he were triable in England, it must be before the constable and marshal by the Civil Law. Nonetheless, Hutchinson was imprisoned in Newgate and was to have come before the king at Westminster on Saturday next after the octave of Trinity (P.R.O., *KB.29*/335, m.i.). There is no record of this having happened, so he must have escaped or obtained his release by bribery, because he returned to Portugal and obtained his pension. See also, Jayne, 'William Colston', pp. 620–33.

66   E. Rosenthal, 'Notes on Catherine of Braganza, Queen Consort of Charles II of England', *H.A.L.B.* (1937), pp. 16–17. Copies of Catherine's will are to be found in B.L. *Stowe Ms.* 576.

67   G. J. Aungier, *History and Antiquities of Syon Monastery*, pp. 100–12.

68   Ibid., p. 101.

69   Rosenthal, 'Notes', p. 17.

70   E. Prestage, *Frei Domingos do Rosario, Diplomata e Politico (1595–1662)*, pp. 2, 3, 51.

71   *Thurloe*, VI, p. 809, Maynard to Thurloe, Lisbon, 17/27 February 1657/58.

72   *S.P.89*/12, ff. 37^v–9, Parry to Arlington, Lisbon, 5/15 March 1671/2; *Add.Ms.* 35101, ff. 153–4, Parry to Coventry, 27 February/9 March 1677/8; *S.P.89*/11, f. 96^v, Parry to Arlington, Lisbon, 4/14 April 1671.

73   *S.P.89*/16, f. 43^v, Fanshaw to Jenkins, Lisbon, 28 February 1684 N.S.

74   *Add.Ms.* 35101, f. 141–141^v, Parry to Oporto merchants, Lisbon, 12 February 1678 N.S.; *Add.Ms.* 34333, f. 117, Parry to Coventry, Lisbon, 25 February/7 March 1678/9.

75   *Thurloe*, VI, pp. 4–5, Maynard to Thurloe, Lisbon, 29 February 1657 N.S.

76 *S.P.89*/7, f. 5, Maynard to Bennet, Lisbon, 4/14 February 1664/5.
77 *S.P.89*/7, f. 222, Southwell to Williamson, Lisbon, 13/23 August 1666; *Add.Ms.* 34329, ff. 37–46, copy of treaty in Latin, ff. 18–34, in English.
78 *S.P.89*/9, ff. 69–69ᵛ, Royal Instructions to Southwell, Whitehall, 31 May 1668.
79 Ibid., f. 131, Southwell to Arlington, Lisbon, 28 October/7 November 1668.
80 *S.P.89*/10, f. 297, Maynard to Arlington, Lisbon, 6/16 September 1670.
81 *Add.Ms.* 34332, f. 17ᵛ, Parry to Arlington, Lisbon, 12/22 October 1671. See p. 113.
82 Ibid., f. 3, Parry to Arlington, Lisbon, 12/22 October 1671.
83 *Add.Ms.* 27344, f. 208.
84 *Add.Ms.* 34332, f. 22, Parry to Arlington, Lisbon, 12/22 October 1671.
85 *S.P.89*/11, ff. 17–17ᵛ, Parry to Williamson, Lisbon, 15/25 November 1670.
86 Ibid., ff. 23–4, Parry to Arlington, 15/25 November 1670.
87 Ibid., f. 34, Parry to Arlington, 6/16 December 1670.
88 Ibid., f. 71, Parry to Williamson, Lisbon, 21/31 March 1670/1.
89 Ibid., f. 43ᵛ, Maynard to Arlington, Lisbon, 17/27 December 1670.
90 Ibid., ff. 227–227ᵛ, same to same, Lisbon, 15/25 October 1671.
91 Ibid., f. 259, Maynard to Arlington, Lisbon, 5 January 1672 N.S.
92 *S.P.89*/12, ff. 9–10, Parry to Arlington, Lisbon, 23 January/2 February 1671/2.
93 Ibid., ff. 35–6, Maynard to Arlington, Lisbon, 15/25 March 1671½.
94 Ibid., ff. 69–70, Parry to Arlington, Lisbon, 4/14 May 1672; Ibid., ff. 186ᵛ–7, Parry to Arlington, Lisbon, 16/26 November 1672; Ibid., f. 81, Parry to Arlington, Lisbon, 28 May/7 June 1672.
95 *Add.Ms.* 25120, Coventry to Parry, Whitehall, 18 January 1674 O.S.
96 *S.P.89*/14, f. 35, Parry to Coventry, Lisbon, 19 February/1 March 1677/8.
97 Ibid., f. 34, Parry to Williamson, Lisbon, 19 February/1 March 1677/8.
98 *Add.Ms.* 35101, ff. 225ᵛ–6, Parry to Coventry, Lisbon, 15/25 July 1679.
99 Ibid., f. 224, Parry to Thynne, Lisbon, 17/27 June 1679.
100 Ibid., ff. 217ᵛ–8, Parry to Sunderland, Lisbon, 8/18 April 1679.
101 *Add.Ms.* 25120, f. 32, Coventry to Parry, Whitehall, 9 June 1679.
102 *S.P.89*/14, f. 74, Parry to Jenkins, Lisbon, 1/11 June 1680.

103 Ibid., f. 86, Parry to Sunderland, Lisbon, 5/15 October 1680.
104 Ibid., f. 137, Fanshaw to Jenkins, Lisbon, 29 September 1681 N.S.
105 *S.P.89*/15, f. 34, Fanshaw to Jenkins, Lisbon, 8 December 1682 N.S.

10 *Religious Tensions and the 1654 Treaty*

1 H. Kamen, 'Confiscations in the economy of the Spanish Inquisition', *Ec.Hist.R.*, xviii (1965), 512.
2 A. J. Saraíva, *A Inquisição e os Christãos Novos*, pp. 265–6.
3 Michael Geddes, *Miscellaneous Tracts*, I, pp. 542–3, and H. Kamen, 'Confiscations', pp. 521–2.
4 *S.P.89*/5, f. 170, Undated Grievances of English Merchants in Portugal.
5 *S.P.89*/6, f. 242, Grievances of English Merchants in Portugal, 8 June 1664 N.S.
6 *Add.Ms.* 34332, f. 28, Parry to Arlington, Lisbon, 12/22 October 1671.
7 Saraíva, *A Inquisição Portuguesa*, pp. 118–9.
8 *S.P.89*/15, ff. 191–191^v, Maynard to Jenkins, Lisbon, 15/25 May 1683.
9 *S.P.89*/6, ff. 215 and 218^v–9, Maynard to Bennet, Lisbon, 7/17 February and 11/21 March 1663/4 and Ibid., ff. 303–5, an account by Maynard of the affair of the *Advise* (Latin).
10 Ibid., ff. 231–231^v, Afonso VI to Charles II, April 1664. There is a Portuguese version of the protest among the Russell Papers, written in the hand of Secretary of State, Sousa de Macedo.
11 R. G. Marsden, ed., *The Law and Customs of the Sea*, Publications of the Navy. Records Society, XLIX, vol. I, p. 513.
12 Ibid.
13 *S.P.89*/6, f. 285, Maynard to Bennet, Lisbon, 2/12 November 1664.
14 Ibid., f. 293, same to the same, Lisbon, 19/29 November 1664.
15 *Add.Ms.* 34332, f. 45^v, Undated comments of Portugal's Merchants on a possible new treaty, among the Southwell papers, c. 1673.
16 *Add.Ms.* 34331, f. 137, Maynard to Southwell, Lisbon, 18/28 May 1670.
17 *S.P.89*/10, f. 195^v, Parry to Williamson, Lisbon, 28 March/7 April 1670. Ibid., f. 204, Maynard to Arlington, 13/23 April 1670.
18 Ibid., f. 256, Gaspar d'Abreu to Charles II, London, June 1670.
19 *S.P.89*/11, f. 146, London, 3 July 1671 O.S.
20 *S.P.89*/14, ff. 173^v–4, Fanshaw to Jenkins, Lisbon, 16 March

1682 N.S.
21   Ibid., ff. 201–201ᵛ, Maynard to Jenkins, Lisbon, 2/12 May 1682.
22   When a Dutch seaman turned papist in 1670, secular judges refused to try him as he 'belonged' to the Inquisition. See: *S.P.89*/10, f. 195, Parry to Williamson, Lisbon, 28 March/7 April 1670.
23   *S.P.89*/14, ff. 201–201ᵛ, Maynard to Jenkins, Lisbon, 2/12 May 1682.
24   Ibid., f. 216, Maynard to Jenkins, Lisbon, 9 July 1682 N.S.
25   Ibid., f. 204, Fanshaw to Jenkins, Lisbon, 26 May 1682 N.S.
26   Ibid., f. 205, Fanshaw to Regent, Lisbon, 30 May 1682 N.S.
27   Ibid., f. 206, Fanshaw to Jenkins, Lisbon, 9 June 1682 N.S.; Ibid., f. 212, being an abstract of Maynard's letters on the subject.
28   *S.P.89*/10, ff. 205ᵛ–6, Maynard to Arlington, Lisbon, 13/23 April 1670.
29   *S.P.89*/11, ff. 220–220ᵛ, Maynard to Whom it May Concern, Lisbon, 5/15 October 1671.
30   *S.P.89*/13, f. 150ᵛ, Undated Memorial of Grievances of the English nation in Portugal; *S.P.89*/13, f. 200, Grievances of the English Nation in the Port of Belem, signed Thomas Cornish, Belem, 7 September 1676.
31   *S.P.89*/15, f. 211, Maynard to Jenkins, Lisbon, 1/11 August 1683.
32   *S.P.89*/11, ff. 227–227ᵛ, Maynard to Arlington 15/25 October 1671.
33   *Add.Ms.* 34332, f. 28, Parry to Arlington, Lisbon, 12/22 October, 1671.
34   E. Prestage, *The Diplomatic Relations of Portugal with France, England and Holland from 1640 to 1668*, pp. 109–10.
35   Ajuda *49-IV-20*, Doc. 84, f. 211.
36   Information taken from notes made by H. F. Fulford Williams, Chaplain, St George's church, Lisbon, 1937–45, held by the British Historical Society of Portugal.
37   Canon G. F. Johnston, Chaplain, Oporto, 'Notes on the Ecclesiastical Register of the Anglican Chaplaincy, Oporto', *G. M.*, xii (1955–8), p. 17.
38   *Lisbon Inquisition Process*, 7522, evidence given by Pedro d'Oliveira to the Inquisition, 10 January 1660 N.S.
39   *S.P.89*/15, f. 180ᵛ, Maynard to Jenkins, Lisbon, 5/15 May 1683.
40   *Add.Ms.* 22908, f. 23, Colbatch to Burnet, Lisbon, 27 October 1696 N.S.
41   *S.P.89*/9, f. 153, Southwell to Williamson, Lisbon, 19/29 November 1668.
42   *Add.Ms.* 22908, f. 23, Colbatch to Burnet, Lisbon, 27 October 1696 N.S.
43   Ibid.

44   *S.P.89*/16, f. 141, Fanshaw to Sunderland, Lisbon, 18 December 1684 N.S.; *C.S.P.Dom.*, 1686/7, 290.

45   *Add.Ms.* 19399, ff. 146–7ᵛ, Maynard to Bishop of London, Lisbon, 7/17 September 1686. It is interesting to note that Maynard told the Inquisition that Englishmen were entitled, under Article 14, to exercise their religion in their houses and with their families *being of the same nation and religion*. This clause is not in Article 14, but John IV had asked Cromwell to have it included in Article 14, in his letter to the Protector of 24 June 1656, see *Thurloe*, pp. 118–19, John IV to Cromwell, and Chapter 5 above.

46   On the death of Afonso VI in 1683, Pedro, the Prince Regent, assumed the crown under the name of Pedro II.

47   *S.P.89*/16, f. 309, Maynard to Pedro II, Lisbon, September 1686; Ibid., f. 307, Maynard to Sunderland, Lisbon, October 1686.

48   Ibid., f. 301, Maynard to Sunderland, Lisbon, 7/17 September 1686.

49   Ibid., ff. 299–300, Maynard and leading merchants to their principals in London, Lisbon, 7/17 September 1686. The date shown for this letter and that of n. 48 above in the *Descriptive List of State Papers Portugal*, compiled by C. R. Boxer, i, is incorrect.

50   *Add.Ms.* 19399, ff. 142–3, English merchants' petition to Bishop of London, Lisbon, 7/17 September 1686.

51   J. Heringa, *De eer en hoogheid van de staat*, (Groningen, 1961), pp. 82, 634. The resident's name was Johan Wolfsen.

52   *D.N.B.*, xi (1887), pp. 443–7.

53   *S.P.89*/16, f. 303, Scarburgh to Sunderland, Lisbon, 16/26 November 1686.

54   Ibid., f. 317, Scarburgh to Sunderland, Lisbon, 1/11 March 1686/7.

55   Ibid., f. 365, Scarburgh to Shrewsbury, Lisbon, 6 August 1689 N.S.

56   Ibid., f. 377, Smallwood to Shrewsbury, Lisbon, 4/14 January 1689/90.

57   *S.P.89*/15, ff. 101–101ᵛ, Fanshaw to Jenkins, Lisbon, 15 February 1683 N.S.; Ibid., f. 120, Maynard to Jenkins, Lisbon, 8 March 1683 N.S.; Ibid., f. 181ᵛ, same to same, Lisbon, 5/15, May 1683.

58   Ibid., f. 296, Affidavit of Nicholas Trevanion and John Pongsley, concerning Protestant chaplain in Oporto, 1671–5, London, 29 December 1683. There is a discrepancy in dates between this affidavit and n. 57 above.

59   Ibid., f. 115, Samuel Barton to (?) narrating tenure as chaplain, London, 8 March 1682/3; Ibid., f. 190, Maynard to Jenkins, Lisbon, 15/25 May 1683.

60   Ibid., f. 84, Maynard to Jenkins, Lisbon, 6/16 February 1682/3.

61   Ibid., f. 37ᵛ, Maynard to Jenkins, Lisbon, 12/22 December 1682;

Ibid., ff. 74–5, Fanshaw to Jenkins, Lisbon, 2 February 1683 N.S.
62 Ibid., f. 40, Fanshaw to Jenkins, Lisbon, 29 December 1682 N.S.; Ibid., f. 63, Barton to Rev. T. Turner, Aveiro, 12/22 January 1682/3; Ibid., f. 101, Fanshaw to Jenkins, Lisbon, 15 February 1683 N.S.
63 Ibid., f. 63 and ff. 28–28ᵛ, Barton to Rev. Turner, Aveiro, 12/22 January 1682/3 and 7/17 December 1682 respectively.
64 Ibid., f. 86ᵛ, Maynard to Jenkins, Lisbon, 6/16 February 1682/3.
65 Ibid., f. 271, Fanshaw to Jenkins, Lisbon, 26 November 1683.
66 Ibid., f. 36, Maynard to Jenkins, Lisbon, 12/22 December 1682.
67 Ibid., ff. 40–40ᵛ, Fanshaw to Jenkins, Lisbon, 29 December 1682 N.S.; Ibid., ff. 193–193ᵛ, Fanshaw to Jenkins, Lisbon, 25 June 1683.
68 Ibid., f. 197ᵛ, Fanshaw to Jenkins, Lisbon, 5 July 1683 N.S.
69 Ibid., f. 101, Fanshaw to Jenkins, Lisbon, 15 February 1683 N.S.
70 *S.P.89*/14, f. 199, Maynard to Jenkins, Lisbon, 11 May 1682 N.S.
71 *S.P.89*/15, f. 40, Fanshaw to Jenkins, Lisbon, 29 December 1682 N.S.
72 Ibid., ff. 73 and 74, Fanshaw to Jenkins Lisbon, 31 January and 2 February 1683 N.S.
73 *S.P.89*/16, ff. 127–127ᵛ, Fanshaw to Sunderland, Lisbon, 11 September 1684 N.S.
74 *Rawlinson Ms.*, D.60.99, Hyde to Turner, date obliterated.
75 *S.P.89*/16, ff. 317–8, Scarburgh to Sunderland, Lisbon, 1/11 March 1686/7.
76 Ibid., f. 323, Scarburgh to Sunderland, Lisbon, 11/21 April 1687.
77 Ajuda, *51-X-17* contains a vast correspondence on the subject.
78 *Publications of the Catholic Record Society*, xxxviii (1941), Introduction, pp. 8–13, xxix–xxxi.
79 J. Miller, *Popery and Politics*, p. 21.
80 Ibid., p. 25 and J. Kenyon. *The Popish Plot*, pp. 28, 32.
81 *C.S.P. Venetian*, 1673/5, 375 and 443. See also: Miller, p. 25.
82 Kenyon, p. 42.
83 *Add.Ms.* 34334, f. 1, Parry to Coventry, Lisbon, 11/21 March 1678/9; *Add.Ms.* 35101, ff. 203–4, Parry to Coventry, Lisbon, 4/14 February 1678/9, and ff. 213–4, Parry to Wrothersley, Lisbon, 18 March 1679 N.S.; *Add.Ms.* 25120, f. 30, Coventry to Parry, Whitehall, 24 March/3 April 1678/9.
84 Kenyon, p. 56.
85 *Correspondence of the Family of Hatton*, I, p. 137, C. Hatton to his brother, London, 3 August 1676. The editor incorrectly states that the ambassador concerned was Francisco de Melo, Conde da Ponte. In 1676, the ambassador was Dom Francisco de Melo Manuel da Camara.

11   *The Auxiliary Forces*

1   J. Childs, 'The English Brigade in Portugal, 1662–68', *J.S.A.H.R.*, iii (1975), at 135.
2   See Chapter 8.
3   C. R. Boxer, 'Marshal Schomberg in Portugal, 1660–1668', *History Today* (October 1976), p. 655.
4   T. M. Schedel de Castello Branco, *Vida do Marquês de Sande*, p. 348; J. Childs, *The Army of Charles II*, pp. 163–4.
5   Childs, 'The English Brigade', p. 136.
6   *S.P.*89/6, f. 23, Record of the Court Martial of Col. Molesworth at Moura, 21 February 1663 N.S.
7   *Calendar of Clarendon State Papers*, V, pp. 242–3, Maynard to Clarendon, Lisbon, 28 July/7 August 1662.
8   Childs, 'The English Brigade', pp. 136–7.
9   *S.P.*89/5, f. 107^v, Abstract made by Fanshaw, 10/20 October 1662.
10 Ibid., f. 121, Fanshaw to Afonso VI, Lisbon, 8 October 1662 N.S.
11 Ibid., f. 129, archbishop of Lisbon to Fanshaw, Lisbon, 17 October 1662 N.S. See verso for summary of contents.
12 *S.P.*89/6, ff. 27–8, Fanshaw to Clarendon, Lisbon, 12 March 1663 N.S.; Boxer, 'Marshal Schomberg', p. 655.
13 The Declaration of Breda, 4/14 April 1660, guaranteed that Commonwealth soldiers would be received into royal service upon as good pay and conditions as they then enjoyed. See *English Historical Documents*, VIII (1660–1713), pp. 118–22.
14 Bodl., *Clarendon Ms.*, 77, ff. 31–2, Inchiquin to Clarendon, Lisbon, 30 June/10 July 1662, and *S.P.Dom.* 1661/2, 440.
15 *S.P.*89/6, ff. 142–142^v, Fanshaw to Bennet, Lisbon, 3/13 July 1663.
16 Ibid., f. 267, Maynard to Bennet, Lisbon, 8 August 1664 N.S.
17 *Clarendon*, V, p. 424, English Officers to Clarendon, 28 September/8 October 1664. The crown for 6/3d. is an oblique reference to Charles II's unkept promise made in the Declaration of Breda, see n. 13 above.
18 *S.P.*89/4, f. 168, undated appointment.
19 *S.P.*89/6, f. 165, Viana, 7 September 1663 N.S.
20 Ibid., f. 196, Warrant, London, 15 December 1663 O.S.
21 *H.M.C.*, 50, *Heathcote*, p. 67, Cocke to Fanshaw, Lisbon, 15 March 1663 N.S.
22 *S.P.*89/6, f. 21, Maynard to Secretary of State, Lisbon, 1/11 February 1662/3.
23 *Heathcote*, p. 66, Bennet to Fanshaw, London, 6 March 1662/3 O.S.

24   *S.P.89/7*, f. 298^v, Southwell to Arlington, Lisbon, 6 November 1666 N.S.; *S.P.89/8*, f. 189^v, Maynard to Arlington, Lisbon, 20/30 August 1667.

25   *S.P.89/8*, ff. 229^v–30, Southwell to Williamson, Lisbon, 31 October 1667 N.S.

26   *S.P.89/9*, f. 49^v, Maynard to Arlington, Lisbon, 7 April 1668 N.S.

27   *S.P.89/8*, f. 189, Maynard to Arlington, Lisbon, 20/30 August 1667.

28   *Heathcote*, p. 40, Fanshaw to Captain Allin, Lisbon, 29 October/8 November 1662.

29   *S.P.89/6*, f. 254, Castelo Melhor to Clarendon, Lisbon, 11 June 1664 N.S.

30   *S.P.89/9*, f. 15, Schomberg, and Cols. Dempsey and Trelawny to Arlington, Lisbon, Undated (1668?), but see also many letters in *Clarendon*, V, from Schomberg and the officers of the troops in Portugal.

31   This subject will be dealt with in Chapter 13.

32   *S.P.89/6*, f. 188, Sande to Charles II, London, 15/25 November 1663.

33   Ibid., f. 286, Maynard to Bennet, Lisbon, 2/12 November 1664.

34   J. Colbatch, *An Account of the Court of Portugal under the Reign of the present King, Dom Pedro II*, p. 23.

35   Ibid., p. 147.

36   *S.P.89/6*, ff. 248–248^v and 259, Maynard to Bennet, Lisbon, 3 July N.S. and 5/15 July 1664, respectively; *S.P.89/16*, f. 177, Description of the army in Portugal, undated.

37   Colbatch, p. 140, pp. 145–50.

38   *S.P.89/6*, ff. 259–259^v, Maynard to Bennet, Lisbon, 5/15 July 1664.

39   *Clarendon*, V, pp. 414–15, Clarendon to Castelo Melhor, Draft letter, 18 August 1664 O.S.

40   Ibid., p. 419, Schomberg to Clarendon, By hand of officer, 29 August 1664 N.S.

41   Russell papers, Macedo to Russell, Lisbon, 16 December 1664 N.S.

42   *S.P.89/6*, f. 104, Maynard to Bennet, Lisbon, 1 May 1663 N.S.

43   Russell papers, Castelo Melhor to Schomberg, Lisbon, 2 October 1664 N.S.

44   *Clarendon*, V, p. 410, Petition of 27 July/6 August 1664.

45   *S.P.89/6*, f. 271, Maynard to Bennet, Lisbon, 8 September 1664 N.S.

46   *Clarendon*, V, p. 443, Afonso VI to Schomberg, Lisbon, 10/20 November 1664.

47   *S.P.89/6*, f. 291, Maynard to Bennet, Lisbon, 19/29 November

1664.
48   Russell papers, Castelo Melhor to Russell, Lisbon, 16 December 1664 N.S.
49   *S.P.89/7*, f. 41, Maynard to Bennet, Lisbon, 10 May 1665.
50   *S.P.89/8*, f. 46, Maynard to Arlington, Lisbon, 7 February 1667 N.S.
51   Childs, 'The English Brigade', p. 141; *C.S.P.Dom.*, 1667/8, 540.
52   Colbatch, p. 170.
53   *S.P.89/7*, f. 26, Maynard to Arlington, Lisbon, 9/19 March 1664/5.
54   *S.P.89/16*, f. 177, gives a description of the army in Portugal. There were English, French and German auxiliaries there; *Clarendon* V, p. 443, Schomberg to Clarendon, 10/20 November 1664.
55   *S.P.89/9*, f. 15, Schomberg, Dempsey and Trelawny to Arlington, Lisbon, undated.
56   *Heathcote*, p. 171, Maynard to Fanshaw, Lisbon, 12/22 December 1664; *S.P.89/6*, f. 248, Maynard to Bennet, Lisbon, 3 July 1664 N.S.; Childs, *The Army of Charles II*, p. 238.
57   *Add.Ms.* 34331, f. 68, Southwell to Arlington, Lisbon, 18 September 1668 N.S.
58   Childs, 'The English Brigade', p. 141; Boxer, 'Marshal Schomberg', p. 663.

12   *The English College and Anglo-Portuguese Relations*

1   W. Croft, *Historical Account of Lisbon College*, pp. 1–2.
2   E.C.P. Document dated 1 September 1629 N.S., copied in the hand of Father Bernard, stating reasons for the founding of the college.
3   W. Croft, p. 3.
4   Ibid., p. 8; E.C.P., copy of document stating why licence was granted to the college, endorsed 1 September 1629. When the pope gave English Catholics a bishop in 1622, he stipulated that a title should be chosen from Greece or Asia, so as not to provoke bishops of the Church of England or prejudice the right of the king to nominate bishops.
5   E.C.P., copy of *Alvará* dated 3 December 1621 N.S.
6   Ibid., copy of a report of the Desembargo do Paço, about decision taken in 1622.
7   W. Croft, p. 6.
8   E.C.P., record written up by Father Bernard.
9   Ibid., Account Book No. 68, p. 119. Authority quoted is an *alvará* of 1622.
10   Russell papers, Russell to Watkinson, Portalegre, 20 November

1673 N.S.

11 E.C.P., Account Book No. 68, pp. 20, 50, 51.

12 Russell papers, Russell to Watkinson, Portalegre, 5 April 1673 N.S.

13 E.C.P., Annals, p. 35.

14 *S.P.89/5*, f. 5ᵛ, Maynard to Nicholas, Lisbon, 12/22 February 1660/61.

15 At the end of the sixteenth century many distinguished Catholics were imprisoned in Wisbech Castle, Cambridgeshire, where severe quarrels developed between regulars and secular priests.

16 J. Miller, *Popery and Politics*, pp. 37–9; Sergeant, J., *An Account of the Chapter erected by William, titular Bishop of Chalcedon . . .*, pp. 30–1, 40.

17 Ibid., (both). Miller, p. 42; Sergeant, pp. 42–3.

18 J. Bossy, *The English Catholic Community, 1570–1850*, p. 62.

19 Sergeant, p. ix.

20 M. V. Hay, *The Jesuits and the Popish Plot*, pp. 162–3.

21 Sergeant, p. 86.

22 *S.P.89/4*, f. 198, Maynard to Nicholas, Lisbon, 20/30 November 1660.

23 E.C.P., Annals, pp. 35, 55.

24 H.M.C., 71, *Finch*, I, pp. 158–9, Anthony Beckenham to Winchelsea, London, 7 October 1661 O.S.

25 Schedel de Castello Branco, pp. 402, 426; E.C.P., Annals, p. 55. Russell's presence at the wedding ceremony is not confirmed elsewhere. The marriage was private and conducted by the Abbé d'Aubigny.

26 V. Rau, *D. Catarina de Bragança*, pp. 62, 102; Schedel de Castello Branco, p. 420; Russell papers, Sande (Melo) to Russell, Paris, 3 March 1666, N.S.

27 E.C.P., Annals, p. 55.

28 *S.P.89/9*, f. 106, Southwell to Williamson, Lisbon, 5/15 September 1668; *S.P.89/11*, f. 217, Russell to Arlington, Lisbon, 6 October 1671 N.S.

29 *Add.Ms.* 34338, f. 70, Arlington to Southwell, Whitehall, 6 November 1666, by hand of Peter Wyche.

30 *S.P.89/8*, f. 21, Southwell to Arlington, Lisbon, 3 February 1667 N.S. These are Southwell's own words. He inferred that Russell was Sande's henchman.

31 *S.P.89/11*, f. 217, Russell to Arlington, Lisbon, 6 October 1671 N.S.

32 Ibid., f. 58, Instructions to Alderman Backwell for receipt of the residue of the Queen's portion, undated. See also: *S.P.89/10*, ff. 215–6ᵛ, Commission and heads of instructions re dower, London, March

1670.

33 *S.P.89/6*, f. 238, and *S.P.89/8*, f. 87, Maynard to Bennet (Arlington), Lisbon, 8 June 1664 N.S. and 5/15 March 1667, are examples.
34 *S.P.89/11*, ff. 113–113^v, Maynard to Arlington, Lisbon, 4 May 1671 N.S.
35 D. Ribeiro de Macedo, *Discurso sobre a Introducão das artes em Portugal*, pp. 1–2.
36 J. Borges de Macedo, *Problemas de Historia da Industria Portuguesa no Seculo XVIII*, pp. 38, 41. Dates of sumptuary laws are to be found at p. 25.
37 *S.P.89/11*, ff. 115–115^v, Parry to Arlington, Lisbon, 29 April/9 May 1671.
38 Borges de Macedo, p. 27.
39 See, for instance, 'Scheme of Trade', printed in Somers Tracts, VIII, p. 32.
40 *S.P.89/14*, f. 15, Maynard to (Coventry ?), Lisbon, 2/12 August 1677.
41 *S.P.89/15*, f. 54^v, Fanshaw to Jenkins, Lisbon, 16 January 1683 N.S.
42 Sir Godfrey Fisher, 'The Brotherhood of St George at San Lucar de Barrameda', pp. 37–8.
43 E.C.P. Annals show that Robinson entered the college in 1635 as a convictor.
44 *Collecção Chronologica da Legislacão Portuguesa*, p. 65.
45 *D.N.B.*, XV (1888), under Dorislaus. Whitford obtained a pension after the Restoration.
46 H.M.C. 29, *Portland*, I, pp. 599–200.
47 E.C.P., Annals
48 A. R. Walford, *The British Factory in Lisbon*, p. 26.
49 J. Thurloe, *A Collection of the State Papers of John Thurloe, Esq.*, VI, p. 114, Mettam to Thurloe, Lisbon, 12/22 June 1656.
50 This struggle took place between December 1682 and November 1683, and details can be found in *S.P.89/15*, ff. 37, 76, 84, 111, 123, 125, 178, 207 and 269.

13   *The Life of a Consul*

1 There are two published Visitations of the County of Devon: *The Visitation of the County of Devon in the Year 1620*, ed. T. Colby, vi, and *The Visitation of the County of Devon, comprising the Heralds' Visitations of 1631, 1564 and 1620*, with additions by Lt. Col. J. L. Vivian. That edited by Colby does not show Thomas at all (p. 182–3), but includes a brother, Nicholas, not shown in Vivian's family tree (p. 561), in

which Thomas is shown as being the third son. Proof of Maynard's ancestry is to be found in the records of the Inquisition. See: A. Baião, *Episódios Dramaticos da Inquisição Portuguesa*, III, p. 240. The Goalter Mainard (Walter Maynard) mentioned there was one of Thomas Maynard's younger brothers, who was vice-consul in Oporto for many years. There does not seem to be any record of the exact dates of his vice-consulship, but it was probably from *c.*1670–1680.

2 C. Demain Saunders, 'The early Maynards of Devon and St Albans', *G.M.* VI (1932–4), No. 12, p. 627.

3 *Add.Ms.* 34332, f. 71, Maynard to Arlington, Lisbon, 8/18 February 1674/5.

4 Schedel de Castello Branco, *Vida do Marquês de Sande*, p. 360. Author's source was *Ms. de Vila Viçosa*, Livro Primeiro da Embaixada, f. 154, a letter in cypher which was decoded by her. Unfortunately it has proved impossible to confirm this information from records available in this country, owing to the bomb damage suffered by the Plymouth and Exeter areas during the Second World War. Parish records sent to Exeter for safe keeping were destroyed. Currently held records at Sherford (the Maynards' parish) only go back to the mid-eighteenth century.

5 *Visitation of Devon* (Vivian), II, p. 561; *D.N.B.* xxxvii (1894), pp. 155–7.

6 H.M.C., 77, *de l'Isle and Dudley*, VI, pp. 646–9, Petition to the Earl of Leicester from the merchants in La Rochelle, following the French Decree of 26 January 1639 N.S.

7 *Add.Ms.* 35099, f. 165, Parry to Southwell, Lisbon, 8/18 June 1675; *S.P.89*/16, f. 371, Maynard to Shrewsbury, Lisbon, 3/13 December 1689.

8 *Add.Ms.* 35099, f. 165, Parry to Southwell, Lisbon, 8/18 June 1675; *Add.Ms.* 34332, f. 71, Maynard to Arlington, Lisbon, 8/18 February 1674/5.

9 Add.Ms. 35009, f. 165, Parry to Southwell, Lisbon, 8/18 June 1675.

10 *Rawlinson Ms.* A.61, ff. 411, 413, 415, 419, dated 28–31 October 1654.

11 H.M.C., 50, *Heathcote*, p. 24, Clarendon to Fanshaw, Worcester House, 6 December 1661 O.S.; *Calendar of Clarendon State Papers*, III, p. 222, Rumbold to Ormonde, 22 December 1656, and 263, Rumbold to Ormonde, 16 March 1657 O.S.

12 Schedel de Castello Branco, p. 283.

13 See, for example, merchant petitions *S.P.89*/4, f. 213, *S.P.89*/5, f. 83; and *S.P.89*/5, f. 42, Afonso VI to Charles II, Lisbon, 3 September 1661 N.S. signed by Queen Luisa.

14 *S.P.89*/6, f. 223, Southwell to Arlington, Lisbon, 24 August 1666

N.S.
15 *S.P.89*/4, f. 168, and *S.P.89*/6, ff. 165 and 197.
16 *S.P.89*/6, f. 254, Castelo Melhor to Clarendon, Lisbon, 11 June 1664 N.S.
17 Henry Bennet became Lord Arlington in the autumn of 1664.
18 *S.P.89*/6, ff. 260–1, Maynard to Bennet, Lisbon, 5/15 July 1664. Ibid., f. 267, Maynard to Bennet, Lisbon, 8 August 1664 N.S.
19 Copy letter of 9 October 1665 among uncollated Russell papers, Ushaw.
20 *Add.Ms.* 38038, f. 35, Castelo Melhor to Sande, Lisbon, 28 October 1665.
21 *S.P.89*/9, Southwell to Arlington, Lisbon, 14/24 December 1668.
22 *Add.Ms.* 34331, ff. 75–6ᵛ, Southwell to Arlington, Lisbon, 8/18 September 1668.
23 *S.P.89*/7, f. 98, Charles II to Maynard, n.d.
24 Ibid., ff. 200 and 218, Maynard to Arlington, Lisbon, 16/26 July 1666 and 13/23 August 1666.
25 *S.P.89*/8, f. 86, Maynard to Arlington, Lisbon, 5/15 March 1666/7.
26 *S.P.89*/9, f. 49, Maynard to Arlington, Lisbon, 7 April 1668 N.S.
27 *S.P.89*/8, f. 45, Maynard to Arlington, Lisbon, 7 February 1667 N.S.
28 Schedel de Castello Branco, pp. 359–84.
29 *S.P.89*/5, f. 155 and *C.S.P.Dom.* 1667/8, 310.
30 *S.P.89*/9, f. 85, Maynard to Arlington, Lisbon, 20/30 July 1668.
31 *S.P.89*/10, ff. 43 and 45, Charles II to Prince Regent, Westminster, 8 March 1669 and to the factory in Lisbon.
32 *S.P.44*/31, Draft letter in hand of Arlington from Charles II to the factory at Lisbon, dated 8 March 1668/9.
33 *D.N.B.*, liii, (1898), pp. 299–303.
34 *Add.Ms.* 34332, f. 71ᵛ, Maynard to Arlington, Lisbon, 18 February 1674/5.
35 *Add.Ms.* 34330, f. 1, Southwell to Floyd, Lisbon, 22 March 1667 N.S.
36 *Add.Ms.* 34331, f. 40, Southwell to Williamson, 25 July/4 August 1668.
37 *S.P.89*/8, ff. 20ᵛ–1, Southwell to Arlington, Lisbon, 3 February 1667 N.S.
38 *S.P.89*/9, f. 139ᵛ, Southwell to Arlington, Lisbon, 31 October/10 November 1668; *Add.Ms.* 34331, f. 92, Southwell to Floyd, Lisbon, on the same date.
39 *S.P.89*/10, f. 219, instructions to Parry, London, May 1670.
40 Between *S.P.89*/12, f. 218, Maynard to Arlington, Lisbon, 5/15 February 1672/3 and *S.P.89*/13, f. 58, Maynard to Williamson, Lisbon, 8/18. February 1674/5.

41 *S.P.89*/13, f. 58, Maynard to Williamson, Lisbon, 8/18 February 1674/5.
42 *Add.Ms.* 35099, f. 150, Parry to Southwell, Lisbon, 24 September/ 4 October 1674.
43 *Add.Ms.* 34332, f. 58, Articles of Agreement between Sir Robert Southwell, Clarke of H.M.'s most Hon. Privy Council and Francis Parry, Esq., Resident for H.M. in the Court of Portugall.
44 *Add.Ms.* 35099, f. 150, Parry to Southwell, Lisbon, 24 September/ 4 October 1674.
45 Ibid., f. 150^v, Parry to Southwell, Lisbon, 24 September/4 October 1674; *Add.Ms.* 34332, f. 74, Maynard to Southwell, Lisbon, 8/18 February 1674/5.
46 *Add.Ms.* 35099, f. 150, Parry to Southwell, Lisbon, 24 September/ 4 October 1674; *Add.Ms.* 25120, ff. 1 and 6, Coventry to Parry, 24 December 1674 O.S. and Coventry to Maynard, 25 January 1674/5, both letters from Whitehall.
47 See for example, *Add.Ms.* 34332, f. 75, Southwell to Parry, Spring Gardens, 4/14 March 1674/5.
48 *Add.Ms.* 34332, ff. 71–2, Maynard to Arlington, Lisbon, 8/18 February 1674/5.
49 Ibid., f. 82, Southwell to Parry, Spring Gardens, 24 April 1675 O.S.
50 *Add.Ms.* 35099, f. 180, Parry to Southwell, Lisbon, 17/27 August 1675; Ibid., f. 182, Parry to Southwell, Lisbon, 31 August/10 September 1675. The unknown proviso may explain why Maynard returned to England in 1685 after the death of Charles II. Maynard obtained a new patent on 31 July 1685, on the same terms as his patent of 27 June 1660, see *C.S.P.Dom.*, 1685, 289.
51 *Add.Ms.* 34332, ff. 71–2, Maynard to Arlington, Lisbon, 8/18 February 1674/5.
52 *Add.Ms.* 35099, f. 163, Parry to Southwell, Lisbon, 12/22 May 1675.
53 Ibid., f. 164, Parry to Southwell, Lisbon, 25 June/4 July 1675.
54 *S.P.89*/16, f. 241, Unidentified members of the factory to ?, n.d.
55 *S.P.89*/14, ff. 150–150^v, Maynard to Jenkins, Lisbon, 20/30 December 1681.
56 *S.P.89*/6, f. 228, Charles II to Afonso VI, Westminster, 28 April 1664 O.S.
57 *Rawlinson Ms.* A. 179, f. 102, Houblon to Pepys, 12 February 1686 O.S. This letter is only initialled by the writer, but according to *Catalogi Codicum Manuscriptorum Bibliothecae Bodleianae* (5), I, p. 182, the writer is Houblon.
58 *Add.Ms.* 34332, f. 73, Maynard to Southwell, Lisbon, 8/18 February 1674/5; Ibid., ff. 79–80, John Pollexfen to Southwell, London, 7

April 1675 O.S., enclosing (at f.81) a statement of Nicholas Pollexfen of what happened as a result of the two procurations given in 1668.

59 *Add.Ms.* 34332, f. 77, Undated draft letter Southwell to Maynard.

60 *C.S.P.Dom.*, 1670, 130 and 192; *C.S.P.Dom.*, 1671, 499.

61 *Visitations of the County of Devon, comprising the Heralds' visitations of 1631, 1564 and 1620*, with additions by Lt. Col. Vivian.

62 J. Thurloe, *A Collection of the State Papers of John Thurloe, Esq.*, VI, p. 398, Mettam to Thurloe, Lisbon, 13/23 July 1657.

63 *S.P.89/5*, f. 30^v (postscript to letter), Maynard to Nicholas, Lisbon, 3 August 1661 N.S.

64 *A.C.P.1*, f. 338^v (889–98^v), Melo to Luisa, London, 27 July 1660 N.S.

65 Ibid., f. 350 (926–7^v), Melo to Luisa, London, 10 August 1660 N.S.

66 Ibid., f. 360^v (966), Melo to Luisa, London, 2 September 1660 N.S.

67 *Thurloe*, VII, p. 590, Maynard to Thurloe, Lisbon, 7/17 January 1658/9.

68 See for example: *S.P.89/12*, f. 136^v, Maynard to Arlington, Lisbon, 21/31 August 1672, where reference is made to 'our' courtiers; *S.P.89/14*, f. 232, Maynard to Jenkins, Lisbon, 8 September 1682 N.S.

69 *S.P.89/14*, f. 142^v, Fanshaw to Jenkins, Lisbon, 10 November 1681.

70 Ibid., f. 143, Maynard to Jenkins, Lisbon, 1/11 November 1681.

71 *S.P.89/15*, ff. 180–180^v, Maynard to Jenkins, Lisbon, 5/15 May 1683.

72 *S.P.89/16*, ff. 371–371^v and 373, Maynard to Shrewsbury, Lisbon, 3/13 December 1689 and 5 December 1689 N.S.; *S.P.89/15*, f. 69, Maynard to Jenkins, Lisbon, 19/29 January 1682/3.

73 *S.P.89/16*, f. 375, Maynard to Shrewsbury, Lisbon, 5/15 December 1689.

74 Ibid., f. 378, Maynard to Shrewsbury, Lisbon, 9/19 January 1689/90.

75 Ibid., ff. 381–381^v, Maynard to Nottingham, Lisbon, 19/29 October 1690.

76 Ibid., f. 383, Maynard to Nottingham, Lisbon, 18/28 February 1691/2.

77 *Add.Ms.* 22908, f. 23^v, Colbatch to Gilbert Burnet, Bishop of Salisbury, Lisbon, 27 October 1696 N.S.

14 *Conclusion*

1 V. M. Shillington and A. B. W. Chapman, *The Commercial Relations of England and Portugal*, p. 294.
2 *Description de la Ville de Lisbonne*, pp. 224, 250–1.
3 S. Sideri, *Trade and Power, Informal Colonialism in Anglo-Portuguese Relations*, p. 82.
4 Ibid., pp. 4–5.
5 J. Lúcio de Azevedo, *História dos Christãos Novos Portugueses*, pp. 244–6.
6 *Add.Ms.* 20951, f. 9, Copy of undated *paracer* from Vieira to John IV.
7 Lúcio de Azevedo, pp. 284–8; *Enciclopedia Universal Ilustrada, Europeo-Americana* lxvii, (1929 edn.) pp. 984–8.
8 Biblioteca National, *Codex* 9228⁶, ff. 262–58; Lúcio de Azevedo, p. 308.
9 Lambeth Palace Library, *Tenison Ms. 782*. For reference to London being 'land of the free', see Lúcio de Azevedo, p. 308, n. 2.
10 Lúcio de Azevedo, pp. 308–9.
11 Ibid., p. 309.
12 *Add.Ms.* 15181, copy of D. Luis da Cunha's advice to D. Marco Antonio de Azevedo Coutinho. The following is a summary of ideas contained on pp. 132, 135, 151–2, 156, 170–3. This work was published as *Instruçoes Ineditas de D. Luis da Cunha a Marco Antonio de Azevedo Coutinho* (Coimbra, 1929).
13 Lúcio de Azevedo, 294–323; A. J. Saraiva, *A Inquisição e os Christãos Novos*, pp. 292–6.
14 *S.P.89/11*, f. 126, Parry to Williamson, Lisbon, 8/18 May 1671.
15 Ibid., ff. 109–109ᵛ, Maynard's memorandum forwarded to Arlington with Ibid., f. 107, Maynard to Arlington, Lisbon, 18/28 April 1661.
16 *S.P.89/11*, f. 140, Maynard to Arlington, Lisbon, 1/11 June 1671.
17 Ibid., f. 150ᵛ, Parry to Williamson, Lisbon, 26 June/6 July 1671.
18 Ibid., f. 202ᵛ, Parry to Arlington, Lisbon, 11/21 September 1671.
19 Ibid., f. 205, Parry to Williamson, Lisbon, 25 September/5 October 1671.
20 Ibid., ff. 209–209ᵛ, Parry to Prince Regent, Lisbon, 2 October 1671 N.S. Article 1 of the 1661 treaty confirmed Article 5 of the 1654 treaty.
21 *S.P.89/12*, f. 218, Maynard to Arlington, Lisbon, 5/15 February 1671/2; Lúcio de Azevedo, p. 293.
22 *S.P.89/15*, f. 200ᵛ, Maynard to Jenkins, Lisbon, 17/27 July 1683, P.S. of 8 August 1683 N.S.
23 Lúcio de Azevedo, p. 337.

24   Ibid., p. 492; Saraíva, *A Inquisição Portuguesa*, p. 86.
25   Saraíva, *A Inquisição e os Christãos Novos*, pp. 202–3. No date given for survey.
26   Torre do Tombo, Inquisiçao de Lisboa, *Livro das Habilitações I*.
27   *Add.Ms.* 15181, ff. 172–3, Da Cunha advice to Azevedo Coutinho.
28   H. E. S. Fisher, 'Anglo-Portuguese Trade 1700–1770', in *The Growth of English Overseas Trade*, ed. W. E. Minchinton, pp. 155–8.

Bibliography

MANUSCRIPT SOURCES
The British Library, London

Additional Manuscripts

4155 Collection of state letters and papers relating to events at home and abroad, chiefly in the time of the Commonwealth.

4157 Collection of state letters and papers relating to events at home and abroad, chiefly in the time of the Commonwealth.

4192 Collection of state papers concerning the relations between the Commonwealth of England and the Kingdom of Portugal.

5540 Letters and Papers of John Cary. Remarks on bullion, coinage, etc., by a seventeenth century Bristol merchant.

15181 Letter or Political Discourse addressed to D. Marco António de Azevedo Coutinho, Secretary of State in Portugal, by D. Luís da Cunha.

19399 Collection of original letters and 'Royal and Noble Auto graphs', 1646–1768.

20722 'Some remarks on Cardinall Mazareene's Negotiation of the Pyrenean Peace in 1659' by Sir Robert Southwell, Secretary of State for Ireland, Kingsweston, October 1698.

20846 'Papeles históricos portugueses e españoles; Phelippe III, IV y João VI.'

20902 Relação das Naos e Armadas da India.

20933 Papeis Históricos de Portugal: João 4°. Copies of papers relating to John IV, Charles II, Conde da Ponte and Queen Catherine.

20951 Decrees, opinions and other papers relative to the powers claimed by the Inquisition over the property of heretics in Portugal during the reigns of John IV and Afonso VI.

20953 Statistical and historical papers on Portuguese affairs under Pedro II and John IV.

22908 Original correspondence of John Colbatch D.D., chaplain to the British Factory at Lisbon, Rector of Orwell and Professor of Moral Theology at Cambridge, 1695–1740.

23726 Account of the kingdom of Portugal by Thomas Cox, c.1701.

25120 Official letters from Henry Coventry, Secretary of State, to Residents in Portugal, 1674–9. Copies of letters.

25277   Political and Miscellaneous papers, XVII, XVIII and XIX centuries.
27344   Carta dos Privilegios concedidos à nasçam Britannica assim pelo foral como pelas capitulações de pazes. Compiled by Abraham Castres.
28721   Miscellaneous papers.
34329–34338   Southwell Papers. Letter Books, despatches and letters to Southwell, 1665–9.
35099–35101   Southwell Papers. Letters from Parry to Southwell and others 1670–80.
36785   An account of the exports from and imports into the City of London for the two years ending at Michaelmas 1663 and 1669.

Stowe Manuscripts

195 (ii)   State documents relating to negotiations with foreign powers.
324   Statistics concerning customs duties and the sugar trade, 1670–1700.
576   Miscellaneous historical and heraldic papers.

Lansdowne Manuscripts

190   'Cartas dos Privilegios da naçam Britannica em Portugal autenticadas pela Chancellaria, colhidas e depositadas na facturia Inglesa'(by order of Lord Tyrawly).
1152 A   'Bridgman's Collections', State Papers.
1152 B   'Bridgman's Collections', Admiralty Papers.

Harley Manuscripts

4547   The Brienne collection of letters and negotiations of M. de Cominges in Portugal.
6446   Samuel Chadwick, 'Military occurrences in Portugall: the spring campagne 1663'.

Sloane Manuscripts

1039   Dr R. Hooke's Papers. Documents concerning Portuguese ships and cargoes sold as prizes in London.

Egerton Manuscripts

1534   80 original letters of Queen Catherine to Pedro II, 1682?–8.
2395   Miscellaneous official papers relating to English settlements in America and the West Indies, chiefly documents of the Council of Trade and Plantations, 1627–99.
2538   Miscellaneous letters.
2051   Register of despatches of Francisco de Melo, Marquês de Sande, Conde da Ponte, Portuguese Ambassador Extraordinary to France, 10 December 1663–26 June 1666.

The Public Record Office, London

Calendar of State Papers, Portugal (S.P.89), vols. iv–xvi, inclusive.
Treaty Papers, Portugal (S.P. 103/57).
1654 Treaty with Portugal (S.P.108/386).
Articles of Peace between Great Britain and Algiers (S.P.108/1).

The Lambeth Palace, Library, London

Tenison Ms. 872.

Ushaw College, Co. Durham

The English College (Lisbon) papers.
The Russell papers.

The Bodleian Library, Oxford

Rawlinson Manuscripts

A.39–67   Thurloe State papers.
A.179   Papers of Samuel Pepys, vol. X.
C.172   Copies of credentials of envoys, letters of compliment, condolence, etc., from Charles II to foreign princes, 1662–80.
D.60   Mss. of the Revd Thomas Turner, Christ Church College, Oxford.

Others

Ms. Fr. C. 28   Copies of memorials from Henry Coventry to Ambassadors relating to shipping and merchants.
Ms. Engl. Lett. C. 28   Francis Parry, letters of foreign negotiations and transactions, 1665–75, and copies of letters to and from private persons, 1665–7.

Biblioteca Nacional, Lisbon

Material of interest for the subject of this thesis was found in the undermentioned codices, which are listed under broad subject headings:

Commerce and the Economy: 29, 206, 234–6, 599, 642, 869, 2282, 4439, 4530, 8759, 9228, 9889, 10563.
Religion: 197–200, 201, 206, 484–5, 557, 656, 668, 717, 730, 859, 1465, 867, 869 1531–2, 1536, 1540, 2675, 4439, 4656, 8759, 9228, 11043.
Diplomacy: 199, 201, 206, 208, 245, 589, 748–869.

As it is impossible to separate religious matters from either the economy or diplomacy in seventeenth century Portugal, codices have been repeated under the different subject headings where necessary. Many of the codices examined contained eighteenth-century copies of documents also to be found in other Lisbon libraries and the British Library.

Arquivo Nacional da Tôrre do Tômbo, Lisbon

Arquivos da Alfândega e da Fazenda, Funchal, Madeira

Codex 146 (Formerly 1233)   'Livro de Entradas, 1650'. A customs register, with details of cargoes, duties, shipping movements and merchant activities.
Codex 396 (Formerly 1232)   'Copiador das Cartas que escreveo a sua Magestade e a seus concelhos, Francisco de Andrada', 1646–60.
Codex 965 A. (Formerly 1146)   'Noticias das alvarás e rezoluções de Sua Magestade'.
Codex 1126   'Livro de Registro de novos direitos, 1649–52'.

Colecção São Vicente

Vol. XIII   Letters of John IV.
Vol. XXI   Papers on Queen Catherine's dowry.

Miscelâneas de Graça

Caixa II, Tomo 2-C   Diplomatic Papers, 1655–67.
Caixa II, Tomo 3-2   Diplomatic and Economic matters, including letters from ambassadors.

Inquisition Records

Evora Inquisition   'Livros da Visita das naus', Faro, 1618–83, 11 vols.
Lisbon Inquisition   Processes Nos. 7522 and 17633.
Lisbon Inquisition   Inventario das Habilitações.

Chancelaria de D. Afonso VI, Livros 23 and 27.
Manuscritos da Livraria, No. 902.

Biblioteca do Palácio Nacional da Ajuda, Lisbon

Codex 44-XIII-32   Cortes e juramentos de principes: Privilegios e Contractos.
Codex 49-IV-20   Memorias para a História da Inquisição.
Codex 49-IV-23   Obras de Padre António Vieira.
Codex 50-V-36   Movimentos do Orbe Luzitano. Vol. II.
Codex 51-V-16   Miscellaneous documents, 1624–1703.
Codex 51-VI-9   Documents on Anglo-Portuguese relations.
Codex 51-VI-11   Papeis juridicos.
Codex 51-VI-16   Miscellaneous documents, including the original alvará of 6 February 1649 concerning the Brazil Company.
Codex 51-IX-2   'Do governo de Portugal' (money transactions).
Codex 51-IX-7   'Do governo de Portugal' (includes opinions by English merchants).
Codex 51-X-17   Anglo-Portuguese negotiations, including original letters concerning the selection and transportation of the Capuchin fathers to England for Queen Catherine's chapel.
Codex 51-XIII-10   Documents on matters of trade, including the Brazil Company.
Codex 54-XI-23   Memorias históricas, politicas e criticas para se terem presentes nas nossas negociações com Inglaterra.

Private Archives of the Condes da Ponte

Arquivos Ponte   Cartas I.

Biblioteca de Vila Viçosa

Livro 1° da Embaixada Letters from Afonso VI to Melo, 1657–60.

As time did not permit me to visit Vila Viçosa, Senhora Castello Branco kindly lent me her notebooks on this volume of manuscripts.

Biblioteca da Broteria, Lisbon

Livro 2° da Embaixada Letters from Afonso VI to Conde da Ponte and Marquês de Sande, 1661–4.

The British Historical Society of Portugal, Lisbon

'Hospital' Committee Book.

PRINTED DOCUMENTS

.cts and Ordinances of the Interregnum, 1642–1660, eds. C. H. Firth and R. S. Rait, 3 vols., London, 1911.

e Agreda, Maria de Jesus, *Cartas de la venerable Madre Sor Maria de Agreda y del Señor Rey Don Felipe IV*, 2 vols., Madrid, 1958.

.rlington, The Rt. Hon. the Earl of, *Letters to Sir W. Temple Bart, from July 1665–1670*, 2 vols., London, 1701.

ernardi, Francesco and Ugi Fiesco, *Oliviero Cromwell dalla battaglia di Worcester alla sua morte-Corrispondenza dei rappresentanti genovesi a Londra*, ed. C. Prayer (Atti della Società Ligure di Storia Patria, XVI), Genoa, 1882.

lake, R., *The Letters of Robert Blake, together with supplementary documents*, ed. J. R. Powell (Navy Records Society, Vol. 76), London, 1927.

alendar of State Papers, Domestic Series (Great Britain):
    1641–49 ed. W. Douglas Hamilton, London, 1882–97
    1650–70 ed. Mary Anne Everett Green, London, 1875–95
    1671–84-5 ed. Daniell Blackburne, London, 1895–1938
    1685–89 eds. F. Bickley et al., London, 1963–71
    1689–92 ed. W. J. Hardy, London, 1895–1900.

Calendar of State Papers in the Archives and Collection of Venice, ed. A. B. Hinds, London, 1927–31.

Calendar of Treasury Books (Great Britain), Vols. 1–9, prepared by W. A. Shaw, London, 1904–31.

Chalmers, George, *A Collection of Treaties between Great Britain and other Powers*, 2 vols., London, 1790.

Clarendon, E. H., Earl of, *Calendar of Clarendon State Papers preserved in the Bodleian Library*, 5 vols.; I eds. O. Ogle and W. H. Bliss, Oxford, 1872; II, III ed. W. D. Macray, Oxford, 1869, 1876; IV, V ed. F. J. Routledge, Oxford, 1932, 1970.

Clarke, William, *The Clarke Papers, selections from the papers of William Clarke, Secretary to the Council of the Army 1647–1649, and to General Monck, and commanding officers, Scotland, 1651–1660*, ed. C. H. Firth, 4 vols. (Royal Historical Society), London, 1891–1901.

Collecção chronologica da legislação Portuguesa, ed. J. Justino de Andrade e Silva, vol. for 1648–56, Lisbon, 1856.

Collecção dos tratados, convenções contratos, e actos públicos celebrados entre a Coroa de Portugal e as mais potencias desde 1640 até ao presente, ed. J. F. Visconde de Borges de Castro, 8 vols., Lisbon, 1856–8.

Cromwell, Oliver, *The Writings and Speeches of Oliver Cromwell, with introduction, notes and sketch of his life*, ed. W. C. Abbott, 4 vols., Cambridge, Mass., 1937–47.

The Deposition Books of Bristol (1650–54), eds. H. E. Nott and E. Ralph, 2 vols. (Bristol Record Society, XIII), Bristol, 1948.

Dumont, M. J., Baron de Carels Croon, *Corps Universel Diplomatique du Droit des Gens: receuil des traitez d'alliance, de paix, de trêve, de neutralité, de commerce, etc.*, Amsterdam and The Hague, 1728.

Elementos para a historia do municipio de Lisboa, ed. E. Freire de Oliveira, vols. V and VI, Lisbon, 1889, 1891.

English Historical Documents, general editor David C. Douglas, 12 vols., London, 1955; 2nd edn, London and New York, 1979.

Evelyn, John, *Diary of John Evelyn*, ed. E. S. de Beer, 6 vols., Oxford, 1955.

Florys, Robert, *The Port Books of Southampton or Anglo-French Accounts of Robert Florys 1427–30*, notes, introduction and glossary by P. Studer (Southampton Record Society Publication no. 15), 1913.

Hatton, *Correspondence of the Family of Hatton*, ed. E. M. Thompson, (Camden Society, I) London, 1878.

Historical Manuscripts Commission Publication:
Fifth Report, London, 1876.
Fifteenth Report, containing Ser.20, Mss. of the Earl of Dartmouth, III Norwich, 1899.
Ser.29, Mss. of the Duke of Portland, 3 vols., London, 1891–4.

Ser.50, Mss. of J. M. Heathcote, Norwich, 1899.
Ser.51, Mss. of F. W. Leyborne-Popham, Norwich, 1899.
Ser.71, Mss. of A. G. Finch Esq., 2 vols., Hereford, 1913–65.
Ser.77, Mss. of Lord de L'Isle and Dudley, 6 vols., St Albans, 1966.
House of Commons, *Journals*, vols. V-VIII, London, 1742
House of Lords, *Journals*, vol. IX, London, 1767
Statutes of the Realm, 10 vols., V (1625–85), VI (1685–94), London, 1819.
John IV, King of Portugal, *Cartas de El-Rei D. João IV para Diversas Autoridades do Reino*, ed. P. M. Laranjo Coelho, Lisbon, 1940.
John IV, King of Portugal, *Cartas de El-Rei D. João IV ao Conde da Vidigueira (Marquês de Niza), Embaixador em França*, ed. P. M. Laranjo Coelho, 2 vols., Lisbon, 1940–42.
Latimer, John, *The Annals of Bristol in the 17th Century*, Bristol, 1900.
Merchants and Merchandise in 18th Century Bristol, ed. P. McGrath, (Bristol Record Society XIX) Bristol, 1955.
The Nicholas Papers, ed. Sir George F. Warner, 4 vols., (Camden Society) London, 1886-1900.
Parry, F., *Letters from the Secretaries of State and other Persons in the Reign of King Charles II to Francis Parry, Esq., English Envoy in Portugal*, London, 1817.
Pepys, Samuel, *Diary of Samuel Pepys*, eds. Robert Latham et al., 11 vols., London, 1970–83.
Prestage, E., *Tres Consultas do Conselho da Fazenda de 1656 a 1657*, (Separata do no. 34 da Revista de Historia) Oporto, 1920.
Quadro Elimentar das relações politicas de Portugal com as diversas potencias do mundo, eds. M. Francisco de Barros, Visconde de Santarem et al., 18 vols., Paris/Lisbon, 1842–76.
Records Relating to the Society of Merchant Venturers of the City of Bristol in the 17th Century, ed. P. McGrath, (Bristol Record Society XVII), Bristol, 1952.
Thurloe, John, *A Collection of the State Papers of John Thurloe, Esq., Secretary First to the Council of State, and Afterwards to the Two Protectors, Oliver and Richard Cromwell*, ed. T. Birch, 7 vols., London, 1742.
Treby, Sir George, *A Collection of Letters and Other Writings Relating to the Horrid Popish Plott*, printed from the originals in the hands of George Treby Esq., Chairman of the Committee of Secrecy of the Hon. House of Commons. Published by order of the House, London, 1681.
Tudor Economic Documents, eds. R. H. Tawney and E. Power, 3 vols., London, 1924; 1965.
Vieira, António, *Cartas do Padre António Vieira*, ed. J. Lúcio de Azevedo, 3 vols., Coimbra, 1925-8.

TRACTS, PAMPHLETS AND NEWSPAPERS

The Case of the British Merchants Trading to Portugal, Tract, London, 1695?

Child, Sir Josiah, *New Discourse of Trade*, 2nd edn, London, 1694.

Clarke, Frances, *A Briefe Reply to the Narration of Don Pantaleon Sá*, London, 1653.

Early English Tracts on Commerce, ed. J. R. McCulloch, Cambridge, 1954.

London – Newspapers
Mercurius Politicus
A Perfect Diurnall
Severall Proceedings in Parliament all covering period Nov/Dec, 1653.

A Merchant, *Discourse of the Duties on Merchandize*, London, 1695.

The Merchants' Humble Petition and Remonstrance to his Late Highness. With an Account of their Losses of their Shipping and Estates since the War with Spain, with a preface by Richard Baker, London, 1659.

Sá e Meneses, Pantaleão de, *A Narration of the Late Accident in the New Exchange*, London, 1653.

Somers Tracts, *Collection of Scarce and Valuable Tracts*, ed. Sir Walter Scott, 13 vols., London, 1809–15.

(Worsley, Benjamin), *The Advocate, or a Narrative of the State and Condition of Things Between the English and Dutch Nations, in Relation to Trade . . . in August 1651*. Reprinted in R. W. K. Hinton, *The Eastland Trade*, Cambridge, 1959.

SECONDARY SOURCES

Abbey, Walter Bulmer T., *Tangier Under British Rule 1661–1684*, Jersey, Channel Islands, 1940.

d'Ablancourt, *Memoires de M. d'Ablancourt, Envoye de sa Majesté très Chretienne Louis XIV en Portugal Depuis le Traité des Pyrenees de 1659 jusqu'à 1668*, Amsterdam, 1701.

Adair, E. R., *The Extra-territoriality of Ambassadors in the 16th and 17th centuries*, London, 1929.

Adamson, J. H. and Folland, H. F., *Sir Harry Vane – His Life and Times, 1613–1662*, Boston, 1973; London, 1974.

Aguedo de Oliveira, Dr. A., *Ministerio das Finanças – Exposição Histórica*, Lisbon, 1952.

Almada, José de, *Para a história da aliança luso-britanica*, Lisbon, 1955.

— *A aliança inglesa: Subsidios para o seu estudo*, 2 vols., Lisbon, 1946–7.

— *Para a historia da aliança luso-britanica*, Lisbon, 1955.

Almeida, Fortunato de, *História da Ingreja em Portugal*, Coimbra, 1912.

Anderson, R. C., 'The Royalists at Sea', *Mariners' Mirror*, IX (1923), 34–46; XIV (1928), 320–38; XVII (1931), 135–68; XXI (1935), 61-90.

Andrews, C. M., *British Committees, Commissions and Councils of Trade and Plantations, 1622–1675*, Baltimore, 1908.

Anonymous – *Noticias Reconditas y posthumas del procedimiento de las Inquisiciones de España y Portugal con sus presos*, reputedly published in London, 1722.

Ashley, M., *Financial and Commercial Policy under the Cromwellian Protectorate*, London, 1934; 1962.

Ashley, Maurice, *General Monck*, London, 1977.

Aungier, G. J., *History and Antiquities of Syon Monastery*, London, 1840.

Aylmer, G. E., *The States Servants. The Civil Service of the English Republic, 1649–1660*, London and Boston, 1973.

— *The Interregnum. The Quest for Settlement, 1646–1660*, London, 1972.

Baião, António, 'El-Rei D. João IV e a Inquisição, *Anais*, VI (1942), 11–70.

— *Episódios Dramaticos da Inquisição Portuguesa*, 3 vols., Lisbon, 1936–53.

Barbour, Violet, *Henry Bennet, Earl of Arlington, Secretary of State to Charles II*, Washington, Oxford, London, 1914.

— *Capitalism in Amsterdam in the Seventeenth Century*, Baltimore, 1950.

— 'Dutch and English Merchant Shipping in the Seventeenth Century', *The Economic History Review*, II (1929–30), 261–90.

— 'Consular Service in the Reign of Charles II', *American Historical Review*, XXXIII (1927–8), 553–78.

Barnes, A. S., 'Charles II and the Reunion with Rome', *Monthly Review*, XIII (1903), 140–55.

Barrett, C. R. B., *The missing 15 years 1625–1640 in the life of Robert Blake*, Extract from the Journal of the Royal United Services Institution, London, 1917.

Beawes, Wyndham, *Lex Mercatoria Rediviva, or the Merchants' Directory*, London, 1761.

Beer, G. L., *Origins of the British Colonial System, 1578–1660*, New York, 1908.

Bindoff, S. T., 'The Greatness of Antwerp', *New Cambridge Modern History* II, pp.50–69, Cambridge, 1968.

Borges de Macedo, J., *Problemas de História da Industria Portuguesa no Século XVIII*, Lisbon, 1963.

Bossy, John, *The English Catholic Community, 1570–1850*, London,

1975.

Bowden, P. J., *The Wool Trade in Tudor and Stuart England*, London, 1962 (1971 edn).

Boxer, C. R., *The Dutch in Brazil, 1624–1654*, Oxford, 1957.

— *The Portuguese Seaborne Empire, 1415–1825*, London, 1969 (1973 edn).

— *The Dutch Seaborne Empire, 1600–1800*, London, 1965.

— *The Golden Age of Brazil*, Berkeley, California, 1962.

— *Salvador de Sá and the Struggle for Brazil and Angola, 1602–1686*, London, 1952.

— *Four Centuries of Portuguese Expansion, 1415–1825: a succinct survey*, Johannesburg, 1961.

— 'M. A. de Ruyter, 1607–1676', *Mariners' Mirror*, XLIV (1958), 3–17.

— 'Blake and the Brazil Fleet in 1650', *Mariners' Mirror*, XXXVI (1950), 212–28.

— 'English Shipping in the Brazil Trade, 1640–1665', *Mariners' Mirror*, XXXVII (1951), 197–230.

— 'M. H. Tromp, 1598–1653', *Mariners' Mirror*, XI (1954), 33–54.

— 'Padre António Vieira, S.J., and the Institution of the Brazil Company in 1649', *Hispanic American Historical Review*, XXIX (1949), 474–97.

— 'Marshal Schomberg in Portugal, 1660–1668', *History Today*, October, 1976, 653–63.

Brazão, E., *Uma Velha Aliança*, Lisbon, 1955.

Brearley, Mary, *Hugo Gurgeny, Prisoner of the Lisbon Inquisition*, London, 1947.

Browne, John, *The Marchants Avizo*, ed. P. McGrath, Cambridge, Mass., 1957.

Brown, L. A., 'Henry Compton (1632–1713), Bishop of London, 1675–1713', *Historical Magazine of the Episcopalian Church*, XXV (1956), 12–68.

Carrel, Armand, *History of the Counter Revolution in England for the Reestablishment of Popery under Charles II and James II*, translated by William Hazlitt, London, 1846.

Castro e Mendonça, Francisco Assis de, *Memória histórica acerca da perfida e traiçoeira amizade ingleza*, Porto, 1840.

Chandaman, C. D., *The English Public Revenue, 1660–1688*, Oxford, 1975.

Chaunu, Huguette and Pierre, *Seville et l'Atlantique (1504–1650)*, 9 vols., Paris, 1955–60.

Childs, J., *The Army of Charles II*, London, 1976.

— 'The English Brigade in Portugal, 1662–1668', *Journal of the Society for Army Historical Research*, LIII (1975), 135–47.

Chrimes, S. B., *Henry VII*, London, 1972.
Church and Society in Catholic Europe of the Eighteenth Century, ed. W. J. Callahan, and D. Higgs, Cambridge, 1979.
Claro, João V., *A aliança inglesa: História e fim dum mito*, Lausanne, 1943.
Colbatch, J., *An Account of the Court of Portugal under the Reign of the present King Dom Pedro II*, London, 1700.
A Collection of the Names of the Merchants Living in and about the City of London, London, 1677. Reprinted as *The Little London Directory of 1677: The Oldest Printed List of the Merchants and Bankers*, London, 1863.
Cooke, C. A., *Corporation Trust and Company*, London, 1950.
Croft, Pauline, *The Spanish Company*, London Record Society, 1973.
— 'Englishmen and the Spanish Inquisition', *English Historical Review*, vol. LXXXVII (1972), 249–68.
Croft, W., *Historical Account of Lisbon College* (with register compiled by Joseph Gillow), London, 1902.
Cunha, Leal, F. P. da, *Portugal e Inglaterra*, La Coruna, 1932.
Davis, R., 'English Foreign Trade 1660–1700', *Economic History Review*, 2nd ser., VI (1954), 150–66.
Davis, Ralph, *The Rise of the English Shipping Industry in the Seventeenth and Eighteenth Centuries*, London, 1962 (1972 edn).
Deerr, Noël, *The History of Sugar*, 2 vols., London, 1949–50.
Demain Saunders, C., 'The early Maynards of Devon and St. Albans', *The Genealogists Magazine*, VI, 1932–4, No. 12, 593–641.
Description de la Ville de Lisbonne, Paris, 1730.
Descriptive List of the State Papers, Portugal, 1661–1780, in the Public Record Office, London, compiled by C. R. Boxer, 2 vols., Lisbon, 1979.
Diffie, B. W., *Prelude to Empire, Portugal Overseas before Henry the Navigator*, Lincoln, Nebraska, 1960.
Dollinger, P., *Le Hanse (XIIᵉ–XVIIᵉ)*, Paris, 1964 and as *The German Hansa*, translated and edited by D. S. Ault, and S. H. Steinberg, London and Basingstoke, 1970.
Elliott, J. H., *Imperial Spain, 1469–1716*, London, 1963.
— *The Old World and the New*, Cambridge, 1970.
— *Richelieu and Olivares*, Cambridge and London, 1984.
Ericeira, Luis de Meneses, Conde de, *História de Portugal Restaurado*, Vol. 1, Lisbon, 1679 and Vol. II Lisbon, 1698. Also in 4 vols., ed. A. A. Doria, Oporto, 1945.
Essays in the Economic and Social History of Tudor and Stuart England in honour of Tawney, R. H., ed. F. J. Fisher, Cambridge, 1961.
Fanshawe, Ann, *Memoirs*, ed. H. C. Fanshawe, London, 1907.
Fisher, Sir Godfrey, 'The Brotherhood of St. George at San Lucar de

Barrameda', *Atlante*, I (1953), 31–40.

Fisher, F. J., 'London's Export Trade in the early Seventeenth Century', *Economic History Review*, 2nd ser., III (1950), 151–61.

Fisher, H. E. S., *The Portugal Trade*, London, 1971.

— 'Anglo-Portuguese Trade 1700–1770', in *The Growth of English Overseas Trade*, ed. W. E. Minchinton, London, 1969, 144–64.

Flecknoe, R., *A True and Faithful Account of What Was Observed in Ten Years Travels*, London, 1665.

Foley, Henry, S. J., *Records of the English Province of the Society of Jesus*, 7 vols., London, 1877.

Fonseca, Quirino da, *Os Portugueses no mar: Memórias históricas e archelógicas das naus de Portugal*, Lisbon, 1926.

Francis, A. D., *The Wine Trade*, London, 1972.

— *The Methuens and Portugal, 1691–1708*, Cambridge, 1966.

Gardiner, S. R., *History of the Commonwealth and Protectorate, 1649–1660*, 3 vols., London, 1894–1901.

Geddes, Michael, *Miscellaneous Tracts*, 3 vols., London, 1714.

— *Several Tracts against Popery*, London, 1715.

Gill, D. M., 'The Treasury, 1660–1714', *English Historical Review*, XLVI (1931), 600–22.

Gillow, J., *A Literary and Biographical History, or Bibliographical Dictionary of the English Catholics from the Breach with Rome in 1534, to the Present Time*, 5 vols., London, 1885–1902.

Grande Enciclopédia Portuguesa e Brasileira.

Grassby, Richard, 'Social Mobility and Business Enterprise in 17th century England', *Puritans and Revolutionaries, Essays in 17th century History, presented to Christopher Hill*, eds. D. Pennington, and K. Thomas, Oxford, 1978, 355–81.

Guedes, Armando Marques, *A Aliança Inglesa: Notas de História diplomatica 1383–1943*, Lisbon, 1938.

Guimarães, Coronel V., 'As Finanças na Guerra da Restauração', separata da *Revista Militar*, Lisbon, 1941.

Guzman Soarez, Vincente de., *Ultimas Acçoes del Rey D. Joao IV Nosso Senhor*, ed. E. Prestage, Lisbon, 1918.

Hakluyt, R., *Principal Navigations, Voyages, Traffiques and Discoveries of the English Nation*, ed. W. Raleigh, XII, Glasgow, 1903–05.

Hall, I. V., *The Whitson Court Sugar House, Bristol, 1665–1824* (Transactions of the Bristol and Gloucestershire Archaeological Society, LXV, 1944).

Hardacre, P. H., 'The English Contingent in Portugal', *Journal of the Society for Army Historical Research*, vol. XXXVIII (1960), 112–15.

— *The Royalists during the Puritan Revolution*, The Hague, 1956.

Harper, L. A., *The English Navigation Laws: A Seventeenth Century Experiment in Social Engineering*, New York, 1939.

Hasclock, John, *A Letter from Lysbone, Directed to Captain Thomas Harrison: Wherein is Contained a Brief Relation of the Several Transactions Between the Parliaments Fleet and Prince Ruperts*, London, 1650.

Hay, M. V., *The Jesuits and the Popish Plot*, London, 1934.

Hill, C., *Reformation to Industrial Revolution, A Social and economic history of Britain, 1530–1780*, London, 1967.

Hinton, R. W. K., *The Eastland Trade and the Common Weal*, Cambridge, 1959.

History of the English Persecution of Catholics, ed. T. A. C. Burrell, (Catholic Record Society Publication, vol. 48).

Holden, J. M., *The History of Negotiable Instruments in English Law*, London, 1955.

Horn, D. B., *Seventeenth Century Diplomacy. The British Diplomatic Service, 1689–1789*, Oxford, 1961.

Hutchinson, M. G., *The English Cemetery at Malaga* (Exeter priv. print. 1964).

Jayne, R. G., 'The Murder of William Colston', *The Historical Association Lisbon Branch* (1946–50), 620–33.

Johnstone, G. F., 'Notes on the Ecclesiastical Registers of the Anglican Chaplaincy, Oporto', *Genealogists' Magazine*, XII (1955–8), 15–19.

Jones, Guernsey, *Beginnings of the Oldest European Alliance: England and Portugal, 1640–1661*, Washington, 1919.

Jordan, W. K., *Men of Substance*, Chicago, 1942.

Kamen, H., 'Confiscations in the economy of the Spanish Inquisition', *Economic History Review*, XVIII (1965), 512–25.

— *The Spanish Inquisition*, London, 1965.

Kennedy, W., *English Taxation, 1640–1799*, London, 1964.

Kenyon, J., *The Popish Plot*, London, 1972.

Korr, C. P., *Cromwell and the New Model Foreign Policy*, Berkeley, California, 1975.

Lachs, Phyllis S., *The Diplomatic Corps under Charles II and James II, New Brunswick*, 1965.

Lane, F. C., 'Venture Accounting in Medieval Business Management', *Business History Review, 1945–1946* (New York, 1962), 164–72.

Lapeyre, Henri, *Une Famille de Marchands, les Ruiz*, Bordeaux, 1955.

The Law and Customs of the Sea, ed. R. G. Marsden, I (1205–1648) (Publications of the Navy Records Society, XLIX, 1915).

Lingelbach, W. E., 'The Merchant Adventurers in Hamburg', *American Historical Review*, IX (1903–04), 265–87.

Lisboa, António de, *Portugal e a sua velha aliada*, Berlin, 1942.

Lists of Men of War, 1650–1700, ed. R. C. Anderson (Society for Nautical Research) Cambridge, 1939.

Livermore, H. V., *A New History of Portugal*, Cambridge 1966 (1969 edn).

— 'The Privileges of an Englishman in the Kingdoms and Dominions of Portugal', *Atlante*, II (1954), 57–77.

Lloyd, C. C., *The British Seamen*, London, 1970.

Lodge, Sir Richard, 'The English Factory at Lisbon', *Transactions of the Royal Historical Society*, vol. XVI (1933), 211–42.

Lodge, Sir Richard, 'The Treaties of 1703', *Chapters in Anglo Portuguese Relations*, ed. E. Prestage, Watford, 1935, 151–70.

Loe, William, *The Merchant's Manuel*, London, 1628.

Lúcio de Azevedo, J., *História de António Vieira*, 2 vols., Lisbon, 1918–20.

— *Épocas de Portugal Económico, Esboços de história*, Lisbon, 1929.

— *História dos Christãos Novos Portugueses*, Lisbon, 1921.

Macaulay, Dame Rose, *They went to Portugal*, Oxford, 1946.

Magalhães Godinho, V., 'Portugal and her Empire', *The New Cambridge Modern History*, Cambridge, 1961, V, 384–97; VI, 509–40.

Manuel de Melo, Francisco, *Taçito portuguez: Vida e morte, dittos e feytos de El-Rei Dom João IV*, ed. A. Peixoto, Rio de Janeiro, 1940.

Mauro, F., *Le Portugal et l'Atlantique au XVIIᵉ Siècle, 1570–1670*, Paris, 1960.

Melo e Torres, Francisco de, Conde da Ponte, Marquês de Sande, *Relaçam da forma com que a magestade del Rey da Grão Bretanha manifestou a seus reynos tinha ajustado seu casamento com a serenissima Infanta de Portugal, a Senhora Dona Catherina*, Lisbon, 1661.

Mercator's Letters on Portugal and its Commerce. A faithful relation of the Disputes which have arisen between our merchants and that Court, London, 1754.

Michelet, J., *Histoire de France*, 19 vols., Paris, 1877.

Miller, J., *Popery and Politics*, Cambridge, 1973.

Mun, Thomas, *England's Treasure by Forraign Trade*, London, 1664.

Mundy, Peter, *The Travels of Peter Mundy in Europe and Asia, 1608–1667*, eds. Sir R. C. Temple, and L. M. Anstey, 5 vols., Cambridge, 1907–36 (Hakluyt Society, Ser. 2, No. 17).

Newton, A. P., 'The Establishment of the Great Farm of the English Customs', *Transactions of the Royal Historical Society*, Ser. 4, I (1918), 129–55.

Norris, A. H., 'Records of the English Factory at Lisbon. A Unique Survival', *The British Historical Society of Portugal*, Third Annual Report and Review, 1976, 34–7.

Ogg, David, *Europe in the Seventeenth Century*, London, 1925; 9th edn, London, 1971.

Oliveira Marques, A. H., de, *History of Portugal*, New York, 1972 (1976 edn).

Overton, J. H., *Life in the English Church, 1660–1714*, London, 1885.

Parry, J. H., *The Age of Reconnaissance*, 3rd edn, New York, 1964.

Paul, Robert, S., *The Lord Protector. Religion and Politics in the Life of Oliver Cromwell*, London, 1955.

Peacock, Mabel, C. W., *Index of Names of Royalists whose estates were Confiscated during the Commonwealth*, London, 1879.

Pearl, V., *London and the Outbreak of the Puritan Revolution: City Government and National Politics, 1625–1643*, London, 1961.

— 'London's Counter Revolution (Presbyterian Movement, 1646–1647), in *The Interregnum. The Quest for Settlement, 1646–1660*, ed. G. E. Aylmer, London, 1972; 1974.

Petersson, R. T., *Sir Kenelm Digby*, London, 1956.

Pollexfen, J., *Of Trade, Also of Coin and Bullion*, London, 1700.

Powell, J. R., *The Navy in the English Civil War*, London, 1962.

Prestage, E., *O Doutor António de Sousa de Macedo, Residente de Portugal em Londres, 1642–1646*, Lisbon, 1916.

— *The Diplomatic Relations of Portugal with France, England and Holland from 1640–1668*, Watford, 1925.

— *A Embaixada de Tristão de Mendonça Furtado a Holanda em 1641*, Coimbra, 1920.

— *Frei Domingos do Rosario, Diplomata e Politico (1595–1662)*, Lisbon, 1926.

— 'O Conselho de Estado. D. João IV e D. Luisa de Gusmão', Booklet extract from *Arquivo Historico Portugues*, XI (1919).

— 'A Catastrophe de Portugal e o tratado da Liga de 1667 com a França', Separata do Vol. IV do *Arquivo Histórico de Portugal*, 1939.

— 'Correspondencia do Conde de Castel Melhor com o Padre Manoel Fernandes e outros (1668–1678)', separata de *O Instituto*, XXIV, Coimbra, 1917.

— 'The Treaties of 1642, 1654 and 1661', *Chapters in Anglo-Portuguese Relations*, ed. E. Prestage, Watford, 1935, 130–51.

— *Memorias Sobre Portugal no Reinado de* D. Pedro II, (separata do *Arquivo Historico de Portugal*), Lisbon, 1935.

Prestage, E. and Mellander, K. F. L., *The Diplomatic and Commercial Relations of Sweden and Portugal, 1641–1670*, Watford, 1930.

Priestly, Margaret, 'London Merchants and Opposition Politics in Charles II's reign', *Bulletin of Historical Research*, XXIX (1956), 205–19.

Previté Orton, C. W., 'The Italian Cities till *c*.1200', *Cambridge Medieval History*, V, 208–41.

Puritans and Revolutionaries, Essays in 17th century History presented to Christopher Hill, eds. D. Pennington and K. Thomas, Oxford, 1978.

Ramsay, G. D., *English Overseas Trade During the Centuries of Emergence*, London, 1957.

Rau, V., *D. Catarina de Bragança, Rainha de Inglaterra*, Coimbra,

1941.
— *A Casa dos Contos*, Coimbra, 1951.
— 'A Embaixada de Tristão de Mendonça Furtado e os Arquivos Notariais Holandeses', *Anais*, 2nd Ser. VIII (1957), 96–118.
— 'Subsidios para o estudo do movimento dos portos de Faro e Lisboa durante o Século XVII, *Anais* 2nd Ser., V (1954), 199–259.
Read, C., 'Queen Elizabeth's seizure of the Duke of Alva's payships', *Journal of Modern History*, V (1933), 443–46.
Remedios, Mendes dos, *Os Judeus em Portugal*, Coimbra, 1895.
Ribeiro de Macedo, Dr. D., *Discurso sobre a Introdução das artes em Portugal* (Obras Ineditas), Lisbon, 1817.
Roberts, Lewis, *The Merchant's Mappe of Commerce, wherein the Universal Manner and Matter of Trade is compendiously handled.* A facsimile of the edition of 1638, Norwood, N.J., 1974.
Roma du Bocage, C., *Subsidios para o estudo das relações exteriores de Portugal em seguida a Restauração (1640–1649)*, Lisbon, 1916.
Roover, Florence Edler de, 'A Prize of War: a painting of 15th century merchants', *Business History Review*, Bulletin of The Business Historical Society, XIX–XX (1945–46), 3–12.
Roover, Raymond, de, 'Scholastic Economics: Survival and Lasting Influence from the 16th Century to Adam Smith', *Quarterly Journal of Economics*, LXIX, May 1955, 161–90.
Rosenthal, E., 'Notes on Catherine of Braganza, Queen Consort of King Charles II of England', *Historical Association, Lisbon Branch*, (1937), 14–17.
Roth, C., *A History of the Jews in England*, Oxford, 1941 (1964 edn).
— *Essays and Portraits in Anglo-Jewish History*, Philadelphia, 1962.
— *A History of the Marranos*, Philadelphia, 1932, (1959 edn).
Rotuli litterarum patentium in Turri Londinensi asservati, ed. T. D. Hardy, London, 1835.
Rowe, Violet, A., *Sir Henry Vane the Younger*, London, 1970.
Ruddock, A. A., *Italian Merchants and Shipping in Southampton, 1270–1600*, Southampton, 1951.
Prince Rupert at Lisbon, ed. Gardiner, S. R. (The Camden Miscellany, x), London, 1902.
Russell, P. E., *The English Intervention in Spain and Portugal in the time of Edward III and Richard II*, Oxford, 1955.
Russell-Wood, A. J. R., *Fidalgos and Philanthropists – the Santa Casa da Misericordia of Bahia, 1550–1755*, Oxford, 1968.
Saraíva, A. J., *A Inquisição e os Christãos Novos*, Oporto, 1969.
— *A Inquisição Portuguesa*, Lisbon, 1956.
Savary des Bruslons, Jaques (the elder), *Universal Dictionary of Trade and Commerce.* A new view of the British Customs; with the computation of the duties, by Postlethwayt, M., 2 vols., London, 1751–

1755.

Scarisbrick, J. J., *Henry VIII*, London, 1968.

Schanz, G., *Englische Handelspolitik*, 2 vols., Leipzig, 1881.

Schedel de Castello Branco, T. M., *Vida do Marquês de Sande*, Lisbon, 1971.

Scott, W. R., *The Constitution and Finance of English, Scottish and Irish Joint Stock Companies to 1720*, 3 vols., Cambridge, 1910–12; New York, 1951.

Select Pleas in the Court of Admiralty, I, ed. R. G. Marsden, London, 1894. (The Publications of the Selsden Society, vol. II, 1892.)

Sellers, C., *Oporto Old and New*, London, 1899.

Sergeant, J., *An Account of the Chapter erected by William, titular Bishop of Chalcedon (and Ordinary of England and Scotland)*, London, 1706; 1853.

Serrao, J. V., *História de Portugal*, 3 vols., III (1495–1580), Lisbon (?), 1978.

Shafaat, Ahmad Khan (ed.), *Anglo-Portuguese Negotiations Relating to Bombay 1660–1667*, Oxford, 1922.

Shaw, L. M. E., 'Consul Maynard – 1656–1689. A Reassessment', *The British Historical Society of Portugal*, XII (1985), 13–33.

— 'The Significance of the Appointment of John Robinson as Consul of the English Nation in Portugal, 1650', *The British Historical Society of Portugal*, XI (1984), 13–19.

Shillington, V. M. and A. B. Wallis Chapman, *The Commercial Relations of England and Portugal*, London, 1907.

Sideri, S., *Trade and Power, Informal Colonialism in Anglo-Portuguese Relations*, Rotterdam, 1970.

Steinberg, S. H., *The 'Thirty Years War' and the Conflict for European Hegemony 1600–1660*, London, 1966.

Supple, B. E., *Commercial Crisis and Change in England, 1600–1642*, Cambridge, 1959.

Sutherland, Lucy S., *A London Merchant, 1695–1774*, Oxford, 1933; 1962.

Taunton, Ethelred L., *History of the Jesuits in England*, London, 1901.

Tawney, R. H., *Business and Politics under James I, Lionel Cranfield as Merchant and Minister*, Cambridge, 1959.

Taylor, A. H., 'Galleon into Ship of the Line', *Mariners' Mirror*, XLIV (1958), 267–85.

Thomas, Gertrude Z., *Richer than Spices: How a Royal Bride's Dowry Introduced Cane, Lacquer, Cottons, Tea and Porcelain to England, and so Revolutionized Taste, Manners, Craftsmanship and History in both England and America*, New York, 1965.

Tovar de Lemos, P., Conde de, *Catalogo dos manuscritos portugueses ou relativos a Portugal existentes no Museu Britanico*, Lisbon, 1932.

Trend, J. B., *Portugal*, London, 1957.

Trimble, W. R., 'The Embassy Chapels question', *Journal of Modern History*, XVII (1946), 97–107.

Unwin, George, *Industrial Organisation in the 16th and 17th centuries*, Oxford, 1904.

The Visitations of the County of Devon, comprising the Heralds visitations of 1631, 1564 and 1620, with additions by Lt. Col. J. L. Vivian, Exeter, 1895.

The Visitation of the County of Devon in the Year 1620, ed. F. T. Colby, (The Harleian Society, VI), London, 1872.

Walford, A. R., *The British Factory in Lisbon*, Lisbon, 1940.

— 'List of British in Lisbon, 1755', *Historical Association, Lisbon Branch*, 1946–50, 639–52.

West, S. George, 'Members of the Lisbon Factory in the late Seventeenth Century', 12th Annual Report and Review of the *Historical Association, Lisbon Branch*, 1954, 704–09.

Whitebrook, J. C., 'Samuel Cradock, cleric and priest (1620–1702) and Matthew Cradock, 1st governor of Massachusetts', *Congregational Historical Society Transactions*, V, No. 3 (1911), 181–91.

Whitebrook, J. C., *Edward and John Bushell, Puritans and Merchants*, London, 1915.

Whitelocke, Bulstrode, *Memorials of English Affairs*, 4 vols., London, 1732.

Willan, T. S., *Studies in Elizabethan Foreign Trade*, Manchester, 1959.

— *The Early History of the Russia Company, 1553–1603*, Manchester, 1956.

Willsford, Thomas, *The Scales of Commerce and Trade*, London, 1660.

Wilson, Charles, *England's apprenticeship, 1603–1763*, London, 1965; 5th edn, 1975.

— *Profit and Power: A Study of England and the Dutch Wars*, London, 1957.

— 'Cloth Production and International Competition in the 17th century', *Economic History Review*, Ser. 2, XIII (1960/1), 209–21.

Wolf, L., 'The Jewry of the Restoration', *Transactions of the Jewish Historical Society of England*, V (1902–05), 5–35.

Wood, Alfred C., *A History of the Levant Company*, London, 1964.

Worden, Blair, *The Rump Parliament, 1648–1653*, London, 1974.

UNPUBLISHED THESES

Cummins, D. C., 'The English Customs Administration under the Stuarts' (University of California, M.A. thesis, 1929).

Duncan, T. Bentley, 'Uneasy Allies, Anglo-Portuguese Commercial, Diplomatic and Maritime Relations, 1642–1662' (Chicago Univ. Ph.D. thesis, 1967).

McFadyen, Alastair, 'Anglo-Spanish Relations, 1630–1660' (Liverpool University Ph.D. thesis, 1967).

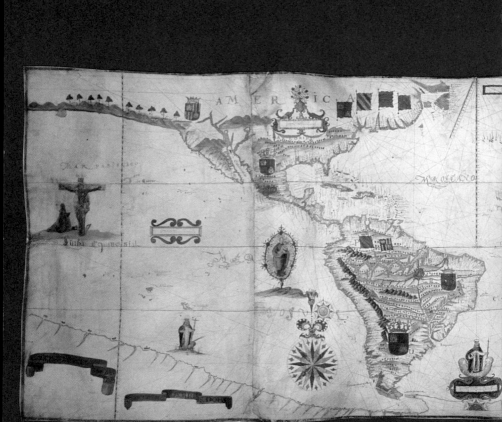